SEEKING
the
SILVER
LINING

Finding Fortune in Your Misfortune

Deanne Persinger

ISBN 979-8-88540-936-0 (paperback)
ISBN 979-8-88540-937-7 (digital)

Christian Faith Publishing
832 Park Avenue
Meadville, PA 16335
www.christianfaithpublishing.com

Scripture quotations marked (NIV) are taken from THE HOLY BIBLE, NEW INTERNATIONAL VERSION®, NIV® Copyright © 1973, 1978, 1984, 2011 by Biblica, Inc.™ Used by permission. All rights reserved worldwide.

Scripture quotations marked (KJV) are taken from the Holy Bible, King James Version, public domain.

Printed in the United States of America

For all who are seeking the silver lining in your own story, may you know God's grace and find the goodness that only God can provide.

For my husband, Charles, who has been part of my story for a long time, I am fortunate to have you by my side on this journey.

For Brandon and Ali, may you always seek the silver lining. You've already traversed some challenges in your young lives, and I pray you will trust that God can turn each of your heartbreaks into hope and goodness.

Contents

The following stories are true recollections of real people's struggles. These brave people shared their stories hoping to encourage others to seek the good in their own lives and recognize that at any time, our neighbors could be facing problems unbeknownst to us. While much of the content can feel dark, know that each story is told through a lens of hope and gratitude. Some names and minor details have been changed to protect the privacy of the individuals involved, but these don't change the heart of the story.

These stories were told to me in person and via video conferences. I've tried my best to keep all information accurate. Still, any errors lie in the hands of the writer, not the storyteller, and my deepest apologies for any unintentional mistakes made.

PREFACE

I am a pessimist by nature. I do not always see the good in a situation as it happens. Who does? While it is difficult to see the positive side of hard times, I try to encourage others as they wade through the darkness. If I am at a loss for words, I seek to comfort, strengthen, or reassure my family and friends by sharing a Bible verse or an inspirational quote.

Every year, I gather with ten of my friends from around the country for a long weekend of scrapbooking. It is a time of catching up as we share humorous stories of our kids and spouses, anecdotes of our jobs and vacations, and all sorts of tales—the bad along with the good. One year, there was far more misfortune than usual in my friends' lives. My friend Jill kept pointing out the blessings in negative situations. She often asked, "What was the blessing in that?" That line of thought resonated with me. As I mulled it over in the weeks and months that followed, I kept thinking about the blessings in my own life that have resulted from my trials.

I pray this book will encourage you, especially if you or someone you know is experiencing a difficult, or even devastating, time. I want you to find the silver lining in your own story. How can there be a blessing in your deepest pain? That's what we are going to explore together through the stories shared in this book.

I am incredibly grateful to those who have been vulnerable and allowed me to share their stories. I hope they will inspire you to always search for the rainbow on the rainiest of days. Perhaps you'll even help others find a reason to smile after their tears have fallen. Above all, I hope this will help you pause and reflect on the good and find fortune in your misfortune.

INTRODUCTION

Life is composed of our collective experiences and stories. Individual stories will be ingrained into your being, but they do not make up your entire being. Your experiences each have varying levels of impact on your life. For example, you can indulge in an amazing dessert, but it will not form a lasting imprint on your being. (Unless, of course, you try my triple-layer brownie cake, which can be life-changing. But I digress.) You can enjoy desserts, fresh mountain air, biking, listening to music, shopping, golfing, walking along a sandy beach, and so forth. Still, those experiences do not necessarily mold and shape you. However, at some point in our lives, we all face poignant experiences that challenge and change us. Some of these redirect our paths, for better or for worse. While some events make massive impacts on our being, others barely make a dent.

Most of us share our struggles with our closest confidantes, while others take to social media with every detail. I, for one, am certainly not going to share my personal business with just anyone on the street. Only those I love and trust are privy to those stories. My friend Cathy and I often text each other, "Can you get together for wine right now?" Code for "Can you talk right now?" We do this after a hard day or week or when we just need to laugh together, with wine in hand, of course.

It is valuable to hear or read a story you can relate to. When we realize someone else has similar thoughts, feelings, and struggles, we feel connected and not alone in our troubles. When we can identify with the circumstances or emotions of the story, a shared bond forms as we realize someone else truly understands our trials. Although our stories may vastly differ, they often have numerous similarities. We are drawn to these relatable stories, but it is equally important to listen to stories outside of our realm of experience. That is how we discover commonality and garner greater empathy for others.

In recent years, I have noticed an increase in the number of people purchasing or building firepits for their backyards. My family has jumped on this bandwagon as well. The smell of a campfire is enticing, the ever-changing flames are entrancing, and roasting marshmallows (not to mention eating them) is delightful. But I believe the true reason people build a firepit is the conversation that often surrounds it. The feelings a campfire evokes are joy, contentment, and community. We long to hang out with family and friends, chatting beneath the stars in the ambiance of a warm, calming fire. How many conversations, both casual and deep, have surrounded a fire? How many stories have been told over the glowing embers? We say we long for the fire, but what we truly long for is the warm connection with those who circle the flames.

We say we long for the fire, but what we truly long for is the warm connection with those who circle the flames.

We enjoy listening to stories that mirror our own lives and reflect our own experiences. When we listen to others, we not only learn about the person speaking, we learn about ourselves. We gain pleasure both from the telling and the hearing of stories. We bring people into our world with our own stories and enter others' worlds listening to theirs. While storytelling is enjoyable and entertaining, the heart of it is the emotional connections that enrich our lives.

If we want others to share their stories with us, we need to be good listeners. As a social services case manager, I have had to work hard over the years to fine-tune my listening skills. It does not come naturally, and it has required significant effort and practice to improve. We are scarcely taught listening skills in school or life, so it is necessary to practice not interrupting or trying to one-up our friends' personal stories. When an experience is shared with us in confidence, the teller is being vulnerable, trusting us with their personal information. They are laying their heart on the table, which takes remarkable courage for them to share. When we cut to "but listen to what happened to me," we unintentionally negate our friend's story and make them feel unheard.

When we cut to "but listen to what happened to me," we unintentionally negate our friend's story and make them feel unheard.

The stories in this book are all about people finding the silver lining in their struggles, the light in their darkness. We all have difficulties in our lives, and often, it is difficult to find the good. We may need to dig deep to identify fortune in our misfortune. It is my greatest hope that these stories will not only uplift you but will guide you to seek the rays of sunlight after the cloudy and stormy days in your life.

I also hope this book will open your eyes to the struggles of those around you. One of the people who generously told me her story posted a brief glimpse into her struggles on social media. She said she was surprised to hear so many people commenting that they had no idea she was dealing with such hardship. Since not everyone wears their emotions on their sleeves as I do, and not everyone bears their emotional scars on their foreheads for all to see, people don't realize the need to be kinder. But what we all need is to garner empathy and understand that others are fighting unknown battles on any given day. We simply need to give others the benefit of the doubt and offer grace, kindness, and compassion, no matter what.

Life Brings Storms

Loss, sorrow, mistakes, struggles, accidents, failures, hardships, burdens, or trauma. We've all weathered our share of storms in life, and we all have a story to tell. There are storms in our life that can be unbelievably destructive. Tornadoes, hurricanes, and flash floods can cause complete devastation. So, too, storms in our own lives can uproot or shift our basic foundations. In the midst of the storm, we hunker down, frightened of the severity of destruction.

Overwhelmed, we wonder how to deal with the results. Once the storm has passed, we must assess the damage. Was there debris left in the wake of the storm? Was the damage minimal or are we looking at a complete overhaul? We wonder if it is safe to move on and rebuild. The storm itself may have been short and unsubstantial, but the effects may be long-lasting. We cannot move on without fixing things. If our home sustained damage in a storm, we would hire a contractor to carry out the repairs. In the storms of life, we may also need to reach out to others, such as a therapist, so we can process what happened and allow others to help us heal.

Finding the Rainbow after the Storm

Here in Indiana, where I live, our land is completely flat, complemented by a large sky, which often allows us to see for miles upon miles. After a storm, as the sun peeks out from the clouds, I often go out in search of a rainbow. Sometimes, I cannot spot one immediately or the one I see is barely visible. Other times, it is glaringly bright and beautiful, shining right before my eyes. On rare occasions, it is a double rainbow, which is a sweet surprise.

Finding the rainbow after our personal storms is precisely the same. Sometimes, we have to search far and wide to find any good that came out of a bad situation in our life. Other times, we see a glimpse of fortune, even though it was not noticeable at first. And then there are times when the silver lining is glaringly obvious, despite the storm that has just passed. Occasionally, I even realize how I was blessed in more ways than one. You must search for the rainbow, even though it's much easier to stay inside and dwell on the storm effects. It is easy to see how the storm brought down limbs from our tree or how the wind knocked over our flowerpots or the rain washed away our garden. Often, we do not see the rainbow shining right in front of us; it is simpler to focus on the damage. But the beauty of seeing the positive side of our storms is worth the effort of searching.

Where Is the Good?

Adversity has affected us all. The question is, what wisdom have we acquired during these trials? What have we learned that can help us later in life or to help others during their difficult days? We don't want trials, tribulations, disasters, or adversity; but if we look within, sometimes deep within, there is insight to be gained. How were we blessed? What good emerged from the bad? What fortune was gleaned from your misfortune?

Even if a difficulty is long over, if we delve into it, we can see how we were blessed by the circumstances, by a person, or by an experience itself. Perhaps we'll see how someone was changed by watching us or hearing our story. Perhaps we will witness God's provision for us. We may even discover a side of our story that we'd never seen before.

We live in a fallen world. I believe that God does not want us to experience pain or tragedies, but He can take the bad in our lives and use it for good. Romans 8:28 (NIV) states, "And we know that for those who love God all things work together for good, for those who are called according to his purpose." And Psalm 34:17–18 (NIV) says, "The righteous cry out and the LORD hears them; he delivers them from all their troubles. The LORD is close to the brokenhearted and saves those who are crushed in spirit."

Are you broken? Do you feel dejected? Are you grieving? Pray. Call out to God and ask to have the bad be used for good in your life. Have faith in the goodness of God that the Almighty Giver of good will take your pain and convert it into something useful, perhaps even beautiful. Unimaginable pain can be tamped down by the unimaginable joy that only God can give.

Unimaginable pain can be tamped down by the unimaginable joy that only God can give.

In my social services position, I work with the elderly and disabled and their caregivers. I see firsthand how even a glimmer of hope can affect a person. It can help someone battling depression. Hope, positive thinking, and gratitude can go a long way to bring someone out of a dark place. I often tell my clients to look for the good in their circumstances. More often than not, they will point out how their situation could be worse, and they are thankful for what they have.

A homeless man with no living family members and multiple health problems pointed out to me how he was blessed. At the time, he could not walk very well and was quite ill. He repeatedly told me that he was extremely grateful for getting the care he needed and felt fortunate for all that he had, which was very little. He did not wallow in his troubles, lack of possessions, major health problems, inability to walk, or absence of family.

I also met a lady who had not just one parent with Alzheimer's, but two. By the time I met her, she had her parents living with her. Both were fairly advanced in the disease process, and I couldn't help but marvel at her outlook. Although saddened that her parents did not always recognize her and that she and her husband had to provide 24-7 care for their health and safety, she still managed to see the good in the situation. She was grateful to have the opportunity to stay home as their caregiver and to give back to them for all they had done for her throughout her life.

It is normal for people experiencing these and other similar circumstances to feel hopeless, especially when the situation seems impossible to manage. Could there be anything more powerful than hope? Knowing God is with us no matter what and that He can use the bad for good—*that* is a source of hope. If I can point out something positive to my clients at work, it may help them with their mental well-being and overall outlook. If we can look at blessings in our lives and appreciate those blessings, we, too, can have a sense of hope.

You must look at the positive in your negative situation if you are to continue living your life without constantly being knee-deep in despair. I do not discount your experience, your sadness, your grief, your anger, or your loss. Yes, you felt all those emotions while going through dark times and you may continue to feel the same well after the trial is over. I'm not advising you to avoid crying or being sad or angry. I don't want you to think that I am saying that you should jump for joy about a bad situation or to be happy if things didn't work out as you'd hoped. Take time to get mad; yell a little, cry an ugly cry, or stomp your feet if you must. It is okay to work through your feelings. However, I'd encourage you to search for the positive once you've worked through your emotions. If you wake up each morning groaning that your day will be terrible, it will be. On the other hand, if you wake up and express gratitude for what you have, your outlook and perspective will be 180 degrees different. I am not suggesting that you completely forget what you have gone through, but if you can look at the good that came out of the bad, you will be rewarded.

In the same light, know that it is okay to begin searching for the good while you are still wrestling with the pain. You can experience both pain and joy simultaneously. You can still grieve the loss of a loved one while delighting in the beautiful memories you have of that person. You can be sad that you lost your job and at the same time be relieved that the stress is gone. You can be angry that a drunk driver totaled your car and be grateful for not being significantly injured. You can be hurt and disappointed that your spouse wants a divorce yet happy that you can remain friends. Emotions are complicated and whatever you are feeling is acceptable. I am giving you permission to feel all the feels.

The following stories were not written to enable you to simply look intimately into the lives of strangers. Rather, they were written to provide an understanding of the scope of the trials our neighbors are facing at any one time while inspiring you to search for the fortunes hidden within your troubles. It is my hope that you will feel less pain and more joy by finding the good in your own story. I also hope that your eyes will be opened to the often-unnoticeable burdens others bear under their smiling facades so that you will be filled with an endless abundance of kindness and compassion. These stories were told to me by courageous souls who were willing to speak about their struggles and heartaches so that you can recognize the possibility of a silver lining after the darkest of days.

Aftermath of "No"

There is no joy in heartbreak,
No happiness in hurt,
No satisfaction in loss,
No serenity in sorrow,
No contentment in failure,
No bliss in misery,
No delight in struggle,
No rejoicing in adversity,
No peace in suffering,
No gladness in anguish,
No comfort in woe,
No jubilation in defeat;
However,
There is hope in possibility,
Strength in determination,
Advantage in intention,
Courage in climbing mountains,
Fortitude in resilience,
Confidence in clearing hurdles,
Fulfillment in diligence,
Gratification in overcoming,
Power in tenacity,
Moxie in conquering,
Grit in dedication,
Achievement in perseverance,
Grace from God,
And blessings to be discovered.

1

God's Timing, Direction, and Provision

Show me your ways, LORD, teach me your paths.
Guide me in your truth and teach me, for you are God
my Savior, and my hope is in you all day long.

—Psalm 25:4–5 (NIV)

I went to a local community college for two years, and I majored in human services with an emphasis in child development. My intention was to be a preschool director or work with abused children, so during my final year of studies, I interned at a local preschool/day care center. As excited as I was about that opportunity, I found it to be a less than positive experience, causing me to second-guess my life path. Now what?

At the same time, a member of our church passed away. His daughter called me and asked if I could stay overnight with her mother, Esther, on an ongoing basis. Esther often needed assistance during the night, and this was not something I thought I would enjoy. I had seen Esther in church, but I knew little about her. Honestly, I did not want to do this. But they were in a bind, so I thought I would stay with her short-term until the family found another solution. I wasn't prepared to grow to love Esther like I did. For the next year, I enjoyed my time with her and realized I actually liked working with the elderly. I only stopped caring for her when I left home to finish my education at Virginia Tech.

After I moved, I got a job at Virginia Tech Adult Day Services, where my love for working with seniors grew. Since graduating, I have worked with the aged and disabled in another adult day care center, an assisted living facility, nursing facilities, and Area Agencies on Aging. My time with Esther took me down a path that I had never considered but led me right where I should be.

> *Isn't it funny how we have something in our mind about who we are, what we love, what we should be doing, and where we will be, but then something happens to change our direction? Sometimes we fight it, but we end up right where we are supposed to be anyway.*

Isn't it funny how we have something in our mind about who we are, what we love, what we should be doing, and where we will be, but then something happens to change our direction? Sometimes we fight it, but we end up right where we are supposed to be anyway. I get chills just thinking about it.

I have learned to watch for windows to open when doors close in front of me. I listen for those subtle nudges directing my path, and I am delighted by God's timing and provision in my life.

Carolyn's Story
Not in My Wildest Dreams

I loved the small, close-knit community I grew up in so much that I remained there as an adult. My husband, Cecil, and I lived in the home my dad built and I grew up in. I imagined this would also be the home where we grew old.

Cecil and I were seasoned teachers who loved our jobs. We were close to retirement when my husband started discussing moving to

Florida to teach there. This wasn't something I wanted to do, nor could I have possibly imagined that Cecil was interested. A coworker had informed him that a county in Florida was so desperate for teachers there was a nationwide search for qualified people. Because of an influx of people to that area, the schools were expanding rapidly, creating an immediate need for teachers. Cecil explained how we could retire from teaching in Indiana and draw our pension while teaching in Florida. I was upset by his persistence in discussing the move. I began to pray constantly, trying to determine if this was God's will for our lives. I asked God to prepare my heart if this was indeed His plan for us. After several days of praying, the heaviness and burden of this potential move were lifted from me.

I told Cecil that if we were indeed going to pursue this possibility, we needed to ask our college-age children for their input. To my surprise, they were fully in favor of the move and agreed we should go for it.

I was conflicted about moving out of the house that held so many memories and leaving the community I loved. I believed my parents, who had passed away, would be disappointed in my decision to abandon the home they built. My concerns were lessened when I had a dream of my mom and dad standing arm in arm, saying it was okay to move. After this initial dream, I continued to have similar visions, which affirmed that this was God's plan, so I felt no regret leaving our home.

We interviewed for jobs over the phone, and I was offered a position in the elementary school and Cecil one in the middle school. Liquidating our multitude of belongings was a monumental task. Although I was overwhelmed at first, one thing after another fell into place. Despite the colossal undertaking of the move, I was filled with peace throughout the process. Many teacher friends told us that they wished they had the same courage to pick up and move. I understood that sometimes we had to be bold and courageous to follow God's direction, especially when it was not in our plans.

We didn't travel to Florida to survey the area before we agreed to our new jobs. Not only did we interview from a distance, but we also bought a home online, which was terrifying. When we arrived, we were relieved that it was a lovely home that suited us perfectly.

Before we started our new jobs, we had to attend classes about teaching, even though Cecil and I had each taught for over forty years. These classes could not have prepared us for what our jobs would truly entail and how different the job would be from how we taught over the last four decades.

Before the students arrived, I was made aware that my entire first-grade class was composed of students who had been held back once, if not twice, and English was their second language. Most of our students didn't even know how to open a book or sit in a chair because they didn't have these things in their homes, so we were given unique methods of teaching these students. I quickly learned that teaching in this school was unlike anywhere else. It was as if we were in a mission field in a developing country.

I worked many hours outside of the classroom researching ways to reach these children. I had to devise techniques to hold their attention while simultaneously teaching them. We were required to teach in English, even though most of the children were the only ones in their families who spoke English. The children would often interpret for their parents. Many of my students were part of families of undocumented immigrants living in homes with fifteen to twenty others. The parents often worked two or three jobs each, and if grandparents lived in the home, they worked as well, in order to stay in America. We would send food in students' backpacks for the weekends and breaks from school. The depths of poverty in such an affluent country were difficult to wrap my head around. My eyes were opened to the destitution right around the corner, not in some faraway land. It was hard to fathom that children in America were living like this. These families needed help getting on their feet. We offered guidance and education but didn't do everything for them. We learned that if we gave them opportunities, they would succeed.

Teaching was tough, but I was never discouraged or despondent. The kids were incredibly kind and loving, wanting to hug me when they would come and go from the classroom. We loved these children unlike any we had ever taught. We were able to experience diversity firsthand, which would never have happened if we had remained in our homogenous community. The relearning we had to do made us better people. Despite the numerous challenges, I never regretted our decision to move and teach there.

Many teachers at the school had recently graduated from college. They often came to me in tears, stating this was not what they imagined teaching to be. Although I was learning too, I became their mentor, providing support, encouragement, and reassurance. I was pleased that God used me in this way.

It was God's will for us to move. I was certainly not in control, as this was not what I originally had in mind for my life. He changed my heart and made this experience a blessing in my life. I knew we were where we needed to be at that time. It was the hardest work we had done in our lives but also the most meaningful. The blessings and teaching that we got from this experience were so much more than we ever gave.

Christina's Story
What Am I Supposed to Do?

Earlier this year, I was in a relationship with a man that I was head over heels in love with, and he felt the same way about me. We were even talking about marriage.

Last fall, I had started praying earnestly for my future because I saw the possibility for drastic changes in the next five years as my parents aged. I had lived my life taking care of people, but what was it that I wanted? Did I want a relationship? If so, what did I want it to look like? Who did I want this person to be? I did much discerning during this time. I also spiritually approached my questioning. I made a list of what I wanted in a future relationship and what kind of person I wanted him to be.

I met this man, and he checked all my boxes. On top of that, he even volunteered by doing music for memory care! I started thinking about the verse "Ask and you shall receive." I felt a kinship to him immediately, and he said he felt the same way. I started habitually writing my prayers in my journal. The one thing I wrote time and time again was "God, if this relationship is not right, shut it down." I wasn't writing "Thank you, God, for sending this man into my life." I kept writing that something was off, but I didn't know what.

As time went on, he told me he loved me and we grew closer, but I still felt that something was amiss. I continued trying to figure out the cause of that nagging feeling. I then remembered the old saying, "If you listen to people long enough, they tell you who they are," so I started listening very closely—and I figured it out.

I realized that he was a narcissist, which meant that everything he told me was a lie. All the emotions I felt were true, but none of his were. When we broke up, I was left with all these paralyzing emotions because I had been in a relationship with a phantom. The relationship did not truly exist except in my mind, a thought that bothered me greatly.

I started doing research and educating myself about narcissism. I wanted to get to the bottom of what was going on.

Narcissistic people love-bomb, which is a type of emotional manipulation where they give you an excessive amount of gifts, attention, flattery, and praise so that they can gain control over you. They say what you want to hear, put you on a pedestal, and then gaslight you. Narcissists manipulate you to rely on them. It is nothing but a big game to them. This is what happened to me, and it is not my style to play games. I am glad I caught on quickly.

I remember him randomly telling me during our time together that his ex-wife thought he was a narcissist, which immediately made me wonder why she would say such a thing. He did all kinds of philanthropic activities, so how could he have been a narcissist? What did he mean, and why did he say that out of the blue?

There was one incident after which I could not ignore the red flags anymore. He was sitting at my dining room table one Sunday morning and, out of the blue, said, "You know, my ex-wife called me a pedophile."

Taken aback, I asked, "What are you talking about?"

He told me that there was a girl who worked at his store whom he called "sugar britches." His wife called him a pedophile because of it. I told him that for her to go from "sugar britches" to "pedophile" was a huge leap. I thought nobody would do that. Then I started remembering stories he had told me throughout our time together. He had told me that his daughter ran away the first night she had to spend the night with him after his divorce. He had also told me that she would not take a bath at his home. At this moment, I knew I had to get out of this relationship.

Before I met this guy, he had been married for twenty-two years to his second wife. After I understood who he truly was, I thought about how that poor woman was stuck with him for way too long. He was a very successful and talented man. He led music in his church. He presented himself to everyone in a positive light, so nobody believed who he really was; however, his mask slipped for me very early on. God gave me eyes to see what was happening, ears to listen carefully to what he was saying, and wisdom to discern what was going on with him.

When I would replay our relationship in my head, I realized that occasionally he would give me the silent treatment. I wondered why I was not more upset by this. Then I vividly remembered that my mom gave me the same silent treatment when I was just a child, begging for her to talk to me and getting no response. It brought up many memories and emotions that I had not realized were there. My mom now has dementia, so I consider that water under the bridge. I reconciled that she did the best that she could with what she had at the time, and I do not believe she did anything intending to hurt me.

Narcissism is on a spectrum like autism, with varying degrees of severity. My mom had narcissistic tendencies, and my dad certainly did. I would also say that my sister could be the same way. Is that why I am drawn to these people? Or are they drawn to me because it is familiar?

This whole situation undoubtedly brought me closer to God because I felt quite lonely during this time. This was not just a breakup. People say to just get over it, but I could not because it had been fake.

I kept questioning why this happened. I truly believed, and still do believe, that everything happens for a reason. There had to be a reason why I was going through this. Why was this happening to me?

7

I began to understand that God saw the big picture that my tiny human mind could not. I started attending counseling. I went through three counselors due to COVID-19. All three of them asked me how I got out of the relationship so quickly. I learned that two of my therapists had been in relationships with narcissists, one of them for thirteen years. They said nobody got out of it that quickly. They said I must have been listening very closely to pick up on it. I thought the only way that happened was through God's help. I was only in the relationship for eight weeks, but it was an intense eight weeks.

It was God shutting the door. When I went back to reread my journals, I noticed the whole time, I was asking God to shut it down, even though I was in the relationship with both feet. I was just having an intuition or feeling (God) stirring in me, telling me this was not what it was supposed to be and something was off.

When I was going to bed one night, I considered the possibility that the only reason I went through this experience was to draw me closer to God. I opened my devotional, and that day's devotion was about what to say to people going through great grief. It had a story about a man who had lost three sons. He didn't want to hear it was God's will or plan for his sons to die. He finally realized that the only good that came of losing his sons was that it drew him closer to God. The timing of that reading was not lost on me.

I am a social worker and work in geriatrics. I recently got new clients, two different couples in which both wives have dementia and both husbands are diagnosed narcissists. Their daughters were talking with me and said they needed help dealing with their parents. They asked if I knew anything about narcissism. I told them that, as a matter of fact, I did and that I had been studying it a lot. I don't think it was a coincidence that we got connected or that I went through what I did—even though I wish I hadn't.

I didn't know anything about narcissism before this relationship. Four years ago, my neighbor told me she had broken up with her fiancé. I asked her why, and she responded, "He was a narcissist." I told her I was sorry, but I didn't think anything more about it. It didn't resonate with me because I didn't truly know what it meant. So when I went through my breakup, and she came over when I was a puddle on the floor, I apologized for not understanding what she had gone through years earlier. It is hard to explain to other people unless you experience it yourself.

When I was in the depths of grief and confusion after the breakup, I kept wondering why there were no support groups for narcissistic abuse recovery. It is something that is often swept under the rug. When I was in the deepest, darkest part of my pain, I was motivated to get out of it. I got books and educated myself. Because of all the work I have put in, the healing part has happened a lot faster than I thought it would. I told my counselor that I wanted to start a support group. I still have that idea and hope to move forward with it after things are better with COVID-19. I felt so alone, walking through the healing process, with almost nobody to speak with about it. I want to make sure others have the support that was not available to me.

I am still learning and growing from my experience, but I don't have to go to counseling anymore. I trust that God sees the bigger picture and that He has divine providence. If I hadn't been so thoughtful about my life and future plans a few months before this, there is a good chance that I would still be in this relationship wondering what was going on and why I felt so horrible.

I think I have come along much further than others I have seen dealing with the same situation because I have a hope and faith that is not of this world. It has made all the difference. As a Christian, I know I am to fix my mind on what is eternal. That can be hard to do in day-to-day life, but keeping that at the forefront saved me from what could have been.

I forgive myself for choosing this relationship. I will be stronger because I walked through it. I will continue being the brave, loving person I am because ultimately, someone will love me just as I am and not take advantage of me.

Because of this unfortunate experience, I have learned a lot about myself and others and grew in my faith. I am far enough removed from it now that I can see the good that has come out of it. I am certain that I will continue to use this new knowledge in my professional life. My relationship with God has never been stronger.

Although I wished I didn't have to go through this painful time, I'm grateful for all that I have learned and for who I have become.

Lynn's Story
Perfect Place at the Perfect Time

My day's plans were set. I was volunteering at my church as a mentor at MOPS (Mothers of Preschoolers), followed by a list of rather urgent errands. My phone vibrated during the meeting, but I ignored it, even though I saw it was a call from my doctor's office.

After the meeting was over, I went out to my car and drove to the back of the parking lot as I listened to the voicemail message. A feeling of dread bubbled up inside me. I returned the call.

"I'm sorry to inform you that you have cancer," the nurse said.

"Okay." I didn't know what else to say. Just "Okay."

"Do you know who to call to schedule your next appointment?"

I told her I would call the breast surgeon I'd seen many years before for an unrelated issue.

Suddenly, my list of urgent errands didn't seem quite so urgent after all. I sat in the car, staring out the window. Then I called my family to tell them the news.

"Now what?" I wondered. I didn't have the name and number of the surgeon with me, so I had to place the next step on hold. I didn't feel quite ready to make the call anyway. Starting the car, I headed toward home.

As I passed the front of the church, I felt drawn to go inside and tell someone there about my diagnosis. This was my church family, and I needed their support. I parked my car and went inside.

I sought out Suzanna, our associate pastor, feeling as though I would be more comfortable speaking about this with another woman. Unfortunately, her office was dark. The lead pastor's office was also dark. Finally, I walked to another office where Ross, our young new associate pastor, was sitting at his desk.

"Hey, Lynn, how ya doin'?" he asked.

"Well, I'm not very good."

Ross pushed back his office chair. "What's up?"

Bursting into tears, I told him about my cancer diagnosis. As I bawled, I sputtered, "I'll probably be the first funeral you ever do."

His eyes were gentle. "First of all, I've already done a funeral. And secondly, will you sit down?" He took my hands in his and asked, "Can we just pray about it?"

I put it all, the whole situation, in his hands...and His hands. That was what I needed. After we finished praying, I felt a wave of comfort wash over me. It really was that simple.

That was the last time I bawled about my situation. Yes, I cried from time to time because cancer and the treatment you go through give you plenty of reasons to cry. That kind of news merits some tears. But the tears were few because I knew my situation was in God's hands.

God used chemo and radiation to heal me and now I am cancer-free! How would have I responded had I not been at church when I'd heard the news? I don't know. I only know that Ross helped me turn over my concerns to God and go from there. It was that prayer and the ongoing prayers of many that brought me to where I am today—cancer-free!

Mai Xia's Story
From Laos to America

I was born in Laos; the fourth child of six and the first daughter. When I was two years old, my family fled Laos because of the Vietnam War. While there, we lived in the boonies in the mountains. My parents were poor, uneducated farmers. My dad finished fourth grade, but my mom never went to school. Only rich girls from that country in that era attended school. As was the norm in our culture, my parents married when they were ages sixteen and eighteen.

The Americans came over to Laos during the Vietnam War and recruited Hmong (mountain) people to lead them through the jungles of Laos. My dad was recruited and had six months of training before becoming an army medic. He searched for downed pilots and passengers via helicopter and saved their lives. At the age of eighteen and with only six months of training, my father was performing amputations on American soldiers. He never talked about the countless horrible things he saw, so I didn't learn about any of this until after he died. When the Americans pulled out of Laos in 1975, the Vietnamese communists began coming after our people, so we had to leave. The people with higher ranks in the military escaped first. The American military sent huge cargo planes to fill with people. Unfortunately, since we were mountain people without high rank, we were not included in these military evacuations. We had to escape by ourselves.

My parents packed up, and we traveled through the jungles, hiding for days in abandoned homes by the Mekong River, which forms the border between Laos and Thailand. My parents had heard of refugee housing in Thailand and were eager to get there. They dug into their life savings to pay men to take us across the river on their boats in the middle of the night. Shots rang out in the darkness, and we didn't know where they came from or if we were the target. My parents were told that if one of their children cries during this crossing, they would have to kill that child in order to keep the rest of them safe. Forced to remain quiet, we all made it to Thailand safely.

Eventually, we settled into a refugee camp and stayed there for about four years. I still remember that place. Surrounded by barbed wire, it was a complex of around forty long communal buildings with tin roofs, which were annoyingly loud when we had hail storms. Initially, we slept on plastic sheets on the dirt floor. Every family had a set amount of space allocated to them, with material to separate bedrooms. The kitchen was a thatched hut with a dirt floor. Between the kitchen and the long building was an open sewer.

People couldn't leave without special permission. Fathers were the usual ones to leave, as they went into town to work for the day, bringing money back to the camp each evening. Armed guards patrolled the gates of the two or three entrances into the complex. There was a school and a hospital at the camp. People learned to adapt. My parents were given a plot of land and began growing a large garden to supplement our food supply. Once a week, the United Nations would do a supply drop, delivering food to the post office. The quantity of food given was based on the number of people in the family. With these rations, we each received a dividend of rice, a can of condensed milk, a dried fish, and a small individual loaf of bread. This was all our food for the entire week. For water, we would place our large cooking pots outside when it rained to collect rainwater. There was only one spigot in the entire camp, and at the end of every day, my seven-year-old brother and I would wait in line with our buckets at the specific time they turned the spigot.

We left this refugee camp when I was almost seven. I never learned the following story until after my mom died. Apparently, while in Laos and Thailand, my dad was addicted to smoking opium. It wasn't unusual for people to do so, especially with all my dad saw and experienced in Laos. Because of this, it was my mother who got us into the United States because my father could not pass his drug test. My cousin told her to take the test for my father or they were never getting to America. So my mom hid behind the tent and passed the urine test to my dad as his sample. This faked test worked, and we were cleared to go.

After filling out vast amounts of paperwork, my parents waited for a sponsor in the United States. By this time, my oldest brother and grandparents were already there. They had searched the country for a church to sponsor us. One day, they spoke with the pastor at a church in Indianapolis. The church agreed to sponsor us, which meant they had to prove they could house and feed us for six months. My parents were notified by refugee camp workers that they had received a sponsor and could travel to the US. We boarded a bus in Bangkok, a new experience for us, and we stayed there for two weeks to receive shots and prepare for the trip. There we boarded a plane and traveled through Hong Kong to Seattle to Chicago. We arrived in America in 1979.

The trip was not without problems. Since we weren't used to transportation of any kind, we experienced motion sickness. We did not enjoy the food on the plane. We were all thirsty on the plane, so Dad went to a machine he thought had water but returned with black coffee. We refused to eat the hot dogs served on one flight because we thought it was actual dog meat. There was much we needed to learn.

The last leg of the trip was supposed to be from Chicago to Indianapolis, but due to icy conditions, we had to take a charter bus to the Indianapolis airport. We came from the tropics and arrived right after the blizzard of 1978 wearing flip-flops, skirts, and other warm-weather clothing. Fortunately, we were given coats, shoes, and other weather-appropriate clothing in Seattle. The pastor and his wife, along with my oldest brother, and an aunt and uncle, all greeted us at the airport and brought us to our new home.

The church owned this duplex. It was a ranch with an unfinished basement. My oldest brother moved in with us, so two adults and five children lived in a one-bedroom half of the duplex. We had to sleep in the living room and dining room, but to us, the house was great. After all, there were no dirt floors! We were thrilled to have flushing toilets, which my oldest brother had to teach us how to use. He also had to teach my mom that the toilet wasn't there for washing rice! He had to show us how to use a shower too. We all adjusted well, despite the four feet of snow outside.

Different families from the church were responsible for helping us adjust to life in Indianapolis. One family made sure that we children got all of our vaccinations so we could attend school. Another was responsible for furnishing our home. A third helped teach my parents how to drive. A fourth family took my parents to adult education classes so they could learn English. Yet another family taught my mom to grocery shop, use coupons, and manage money. Many people in the church helped us transition to life in America. They became like family to us.

After living in that house for five years, my family searched for another home. My sister was born after we moved to the US. Having six kids and two adults crowded in this house was difficult, and my parents determined that they couldn't afford a bigger house. In the spring of 1979, my dad started working third shift on an envelope folding machine, making minimum wage—$3 an hour—but even that was much better than what we had before moving. We were unbelievably grateful. He maintained that job for the next thirty-two years.

After five years, the church gave us the other half of the house. We had two kitchens and three bedrooms. We installed a door between the two sides of the home and closed off the other living room and dining room, which became bedrooms for the boys. We lived in this home for sixteen years, eventually paying $130 a month for rent, which never increased the entire time we lived there. By the time three of us kids were out of college, my mom was working in a suburb many miles away from our home. My parents decided to get a bigger house closer to her job, and we gave the house back to the church. In turn, the church surprised us with all of the money my parents had paid in rent for sixteen years. The church never intended on keeping that money. They simply wanted to teach my parents how to pay bills. We were amazed! It totaled approximately $30,000 and was what my parents used as a down payment on our new home.

I am incredibly grateful that my family was able to get out of Laos safely and move to America, finding a church that became an extension of our family. It is an amazing church that was wonderful to us. We can now see exactly how fortunate we were. Not only did we make it to the US, but we experienced more success than we could ever have imagined.

Shauntae's Story
Following God and My Heart

I met my husband when I was sixteen. We were friends at first and then started dating. We were always bickering, so many people asked us why we were together if we did not get along. After nine months, we finally called it quits.

I didn't speak to him for years, but after 9/11, he gave me a call to discuss that horrific day. That conversation sparked us talking again, and we got back together. After a while, he suggested we get married. I entertained the idea, but in the back of my mind, which I now believe was God, I didn't think I should marry him. I never wanted to get married, but at that point, I didn't know how to say no. I didn't want people to think I was the bad guy. "No" was not something I said much.

We got married two weeks after my twenty-first birthday. Two months later, I found out I was pregnant. We had a hard time dealing with my pregnancy because we were young, and he felt the attention wasn't on him anymore. We moved from his home state of Indiana to my home state, California.

As soon as we arrived, he was different. The lifestyle in California can change people, and it changed him. He left me home on weekends. He wanted to experience California, so he was often not present for my son and me. We were young parents, and I was trying to grow our future, but he was stuck in a mentality that I couldn't understand. I started to feel invisible and wasn't dealing well with my emotions. It was hard because even though I could handle things on my own, now I had a son I had to consider. My son was young, but I knew he was feeding off my sad emotions. I didn't want to get a divorce, so I tried to stay positive and decided to stay in the relationship.

Our relationship hit another rough patch when my husband left me four days before Christmas. He said he needed to get away. After some time apart, we ended up reconciling. I wanted our marriage to work, especially because of my son.

One day, my husband was disrespectful to me in front of my son, who was just two at the time. Even though I knew my son didn't know what was being said, I thought it was awful that my husband would be so vulgar in front of my child. I went into my room and cried and prayed. I told God that I couldn't be married to him any longer. We were divorced by the end of the year.

After the divorce, I was bitter and felt like a failure, especially because my ex had moved on with a new wife, who was pregnant. I cried and asked God, "Why is his life better than mine?" I felt like I was being obedient to God and following His Word and yet I wasn't getting any of my desires and dreams. I also felt alone as I continued to care for my son.

I found Joyce Meyer on television and my faith ignited. I began reading her books and my faith grew exponentially. Around this time, at my church we did a corporate fast, which is not eating (or with the Daniel Fast, only eating plant-based foods) for a length of time while praying for God's will for your life. I was afraid to do it at first because I didn't understand fasting, but I decided to give it a try and fasted for twenty-one days. (Please consult your physician before beginning a fast.) I felt that God spoke to me the entire three weeks, which led me to write to my ex-husband. I sent an email apologizing for the divorce and stated that our relationship falling apart was not entirely his fault and I did forgive him for everything. He didn't write back, but I know he received the message, so a weight was lifted off my shoulders. God was telling me to close that door and release the bitterness from the divorce, which was keeping me stagnant. I had so much peace being obedient to God.

Ever since that time, God has led me to many wonderful things. For years, my biggest passion has been to be an actor. I often told God that if this wasn't His will for my life to take this dream away from me. One Sunday in church, the pastor said in his sermon to stop thinking that God is going to fulfill our dreams without us having to do anything on our end. We must step out on faith and pursue our dreams. This was an "aha" moment for me. Before that day, I thought God would just orchestrate my meeting with an agent, but this pastor was telling me that I needed to meet God halfway. Faith without works is dead. I walked out of that church in tears because I felt I had wasted so many years of my life thinking God was supposed to do it for me. Mustering my faith, I started acting classes.

If I had stayed married, I wouldn't have found the gift that God has given me because my ex-husband was holding me back in my faith. My relationship with God was not as strong when I was married to him. However, I feel like God still wants my ex-husband in my life. When I met him at sixteen, he was coming from a broken home. His father was not present, and his mother was very derogatory toward him. I think my ex thought there was something special about me and that is why he latched on to me. I was his ticket out of Indiana, and he knew it. He liked to be around people but didn't know how to have a proper relationship with them. He continually took things personally because his mother rejected him for so many years. It was a long time before I realized this. Even though we were no longer married, he would still call me because he had no other family members to talk to. We got to a better place in our relationship to raise our son as best as we could. I felt God wanted me to be a light for him in his life. While married, I was more of a mom, friend, and sister to him than a wife.

Since I stepped out in faith, God has orchestrated the last eight years. I continue to fast every January. One year during the fast I found out that I could not keep my condo. I heard God reveal that I was leaving in a year and that this was where things would shift for me.

The house was finally sold in an auction a year later. During my fast the following year, I felt God calling me to quit my job. I had already started that process but had not fully resigned. Then I felt God calling me to Burbank. I knew nothing of this city, except that it was near Los Angeles. I was initially unsure but was willing to go if God was calling me there. I had many people question whether I had heard wrong or concerned that as a single mom I would have trouble caring for my son in a new place. However, I kept hearing God telling me to go.

In July that year, we packed up our car and left with no idea where we would land. I had been in contact with a hotel that had extended-stay rooms, and when we arrived, we were told that they were no longer renting long-term. We went to another hotel, filled out an application, and by the next day, had an agreement for a long-term stay. I thanked God for giving us a roof over our heads.

I had a job by the end of the month and an apartment two months later. It was affordable, and I was grateful that the apartment manager allowed me to lease it without confirming my income with check stubs because she was familiar with my employer. I also needed help caring for my son. I went on Craigslist and found a lady looking for a child to care for. We communicated a bit, and then she asked us to come to dinner. I was leery at first but agreed to go. During dinner, after she heard my story, she said that she didn't have the heart to charge me for caring for my son. She said would pick up my son every day after school and keep him until I got off work. On the days I worked, she watched him from 3:00 p.m. until sometimes midnight, and I never paid for anything. God kept bringing people into my life during this time to help me out until my son was old enough to be home alone.

God kept opening doors with my acting, but I took a detour to my previous job with the state while acting gnawed at me. People told me I should go per diem and have one foot remaining in my job while still having time for auditions. When I was sitting in my cubicle one day, I heard God tell me to quit my job. He said that I was not fully trusting Him by continuing to work this job. I was sorry for not trusting His path for me, so I walked into my manager's office and quit.

The next month, I started doing some food delivery and Uber driving so I would have some money coming in. At this time, I found an agency for actors doing background work on set, and I began to book some gigs. People I knew explained how to get a SAG (Screen Actors Guild) card but warned that it would take me a while to get it, so I decided I was not going to pursue it right then. Within a year, I got a speaking part while on set, so I became eligible for SAG. I felt like God orchestrated that as well. I got some jobs that I didn't think I would get. Unfortunately, not long after that, COVID-19 hit, and TV and movie production came to a screeching halt.

During this time, God put writing on my heart. I wrote a children's book, which got published, and I proceeded to write five more books in seven months. I'm not sure if God is shutting the door on acting and opening the door on writing, but I am okay with it if that is the case. I still have the desire to act but feel I can be more choosy about what productions I will be a part of to ensure the jobs align with my morals.

I know 2020 was hard on many people, but it was good for me. Not only did I publish a book, I got chosen to be a contestant on *Wheel of Fortune*. I had been asking God to bless me to get my car paid off. I thought this was how He was going to take care of me financially. I won $1,000, which was not enough to pay off my car, but I was not disappointed. I decided to trust in His path for me.

One day as I delivered food with the company car, I saw police officers and a tow truck on my street. As I got closer, I noticed it was my car on the tow truck. I went up to a police officer, and he explained that my car had been hit by a drunk driver. I cried over the loss of that car, but then I laughed because I had been praying for God to pay off my car and it was now going to be paid off by the insurance company. My prayer was answered, not in the way I would have imagined, but now I am debt-free and I still have my work car. In fact, not only was my car paid off, I had enough money left over to buy my son a car as well.

Being a divorced, single mom is not where I imagined my life, but I feel God can use me where I am. I now know not to be passive in my faith but to work toward where I am called. I have no idea what God has in store for me for my acting career or writing, but I am leaning on Him and listening.

Cheryl's Story
Not as I'd Planned, but Better

Juggling schedules when you're a wife and mother isn't always easy, especially when you're a full-time nurse with unpredictable shifts. As a cardiac nurse, I found it nearly impossible to coordinate my work schedule, the kids' after-school schedules, spending time with my husband, and sleeping. Enough was enough. Something had to give.

I discovered there were three openings for a school nurse position in our district. One was in the same school as my children. Perfect! That was my top choice, although I applied to all three just to be safe. It was hard to disguise my disappointment when my prayer for the job wasn't answered in the way *I* wanted. I didn't get my first or second choice. I was pleased to receive an offer for the third available position. Although grateful to have a job with a steady daytime shift, I wasn't sure how this new position would work with my children being in a different school and having a slightly different schedule.

Surprisingly, however, I quickly fell in love with my new job. I loved the school, the staff, and the students. My days were full of fun, and I told everyone I knew how much I loved working there. In the midst of my joy, I discovered that the two nurses at the other schools were miserable in their new jobs. I had to wonder if I'd feel the same way as they did if I'd gotten the job I'd prayed for. Apparently, God knew which job was right for me. He knew where I would be happiest. He knew exactly how to bypass my specific prayer and answer it His way, the best way. Sometimes what we think we want and what is best for us are two different things. The best surprises come as gifts we didn't even know we wanted.

Ashley's Story
God's Direction, Not Mine

After three years of marriage, my husband informed me he'd accepted a job in North Carolina. I didn't want to go. West Virginia had always been my home, and I wanted to keep it that way. It's where I grew up, went to college, and got married. As newlyweds, we settled there. Our families were there. Move? Really?

Our realtor in North Carolina took us to see several homes before our move. None of them seemed right. Mike and I drove around the area and stumbled upon a "For Sale" sign. It was a house our realtor had not shown us and the one we decided to buy.

When we purchased the home, we couldn't have imagined that our new neighbors would become not only lifelong friends, but a second family as well. Their kids were like our kids; our kids like theirs. Despite having been petrified of moving away from our home and starting a family in a new state, I believe God led us exactly where we were meant to be.

After moving to North Carolina, I began unsuccessfully searching for a job as a math teacher. My husband mentioned my search to a coworker who just happened to know a local school principal. The coworker gave him a call, only to discover the school was fully staffed with one exception—a math teacher. I was the only new teacher hired that year.

I stayed home for twelve months after having my first child, returning to my teaching job the following year. The childcare I had lined up ended up falling through, so my mom came down to help take care of the baby until I found suitable childcare. While she was helping us, she attended a small church with a congregation of only twenty people. In that tiny assembly, my mom met Celia, the woman who ended up becoming my daughter's babysitter. I have no doubt

21

that God led my mom to visit that church that Sunday. It brought us to Celia.

I gradually realized that being a teacher, mom, and wife simultaneously was not good for me. I didn't believe that I was able to give 100 percent to any of these roles. My desire was to quit working and stay at home with my daughter. However, I had been given a repayable college scholarship that required I work for at least eight years after graduation as a teacher or pay back the scholarship money. I had only worked five years to this point. Mike and I discussed it and decided that if I had to pay back this loan, we would be willing to do so to allow me to stay at home with our child. I called to explain my situation to the organization that had given me the scholarship. The person I spoke with asked where and what I taught. When I told her, she said that this was an area that they have a hard time staffing, and thus, if I had taught at least four years total, I did not have to pay back the scholarship. God paved the way so I could be a stay-at-home mom.

I was concerned about informing my principal that I wasn't returning the following semester. But I was equally concerned about telling Celia that I wouldn't need her to care for my daughter because I knew she needed the money. After speaking with the principal, the teacher across the hall approached me and asked if I knew anyone who could care for her children. She simply wasn't happy with the day care center they attended. The timing of this conversation was nothing short of remarkable! Celia ended up babysitting that teacher's children and several other teachers' kids after that.

When my three children were in fifth grade, second grade, and preschool, Mike got a job in Tennessee. I did not want to move again. We had great friends in North Carolina. I was comfortable there. It was now home. I knew God had provided before and put my trust in Him, but I still did not want to go.

After six months in Tennessee, my husband was asked, yet again, to pull up stakes and move to Missouri for his job. I wasn't about to uproot my kids again after being in our new home for such a short time. Besides, Mike's parents had decided to move to our town to be closer to us. With Mike working out of town, I often needed to be in two places at once with my three children, so my in-laws were able to step in to assist with the kids. Mike ended up living in Missouri for ten months, and following that, he worked in Arkansas for four months. It was difficult being a single mom while Mike worked in other states, but having his parents there to help me with the kids was an incredible blessing.

As much as I did not want to move to Tennessee, this is where I found my passion in life. Until this time, I had heard about mission trips that ministered in various locations around the world, but I never had the desire to be a part of them. I preferred staying in the comfort of a Hampton Inn. I didn't want to go work in a part of the world that took me out of my comfort zone. When we moved to Tennessee, we immediately found a church that we loved. During the services, they kept discussing Justice and Mercy International, the nonprofit organization they'd started. The two areas they served were Moldova and the Amazon. Going to the Amazon, with its abundance of spiders and snakes, didn't appeal to me whatsoever. While I knew nothing about Moldova, including its location, it already started to pull at my heartstrings.

We moved to Tennessee in October, and our church started having meetings about mission trips in February. I felt the Holy Spirit's nudge—"You are going to Moldova." I told Mike I wanted to go and so I attended the meeting. I learned Moldova is the smallest and most impoverished country of the former Soviet Union, and I ended up signing up to go there the following June. During that trip, I fell in love with the people, the place, and the mission of Justice and Mercy International.

Traveling to Moldova has been a yearly trip for me ever since. I am passionate about the kids there and the work that Justice and Mercy is doing. I'm in awe of what God is doing in that place. Currently, I lead the mission teams from our church to Moldova. My daughter and husband have each gone on three trips with me and our family sponsors children there, relationships we treasure. If I'd refused to move to Tennessee, I never would have discovered this passion in my life.

Looking back, I can see God's hand in so many situations along the way and can recognize His perfect timing over and over again. He placed people on my path right when and where I needed them. His timing and provision are now abundantly evident. When I said things such as "I do not want to move" or "I do not want to go on mission trips," I know God was saying, "I have better plans for you than you can even imagine." He did and still does.

Jocelynn's Story
Saving a Life

My son was born in 2006. After his birth, cancerous cells were found in my ovaries, which led to surgery. Within a year and a half, I had six laparoscopic surgeries in an attempt to avoid a hysterectomy. At the time, I was a divorced mom of two, and I wasn't sure if I'd want more kids in the future, so I didn't want to have the surgery that would end my childbearing days. Despite the chemo medication, the cancer was persistent and the pain meds I was given following each surgery were addictive. In 2009, after I tired of the frequent surgeries, I opted for a full hysterectomy. By the time, there was no longer a need for pain meds, it was too late; I was dependent on them and couldn't function without them. I couldn't do routine daily tasks like laundry without them. I couldn't gather the strength to get my kids to school on time without the medications in my system.

My addiction accelerated, and in 2011, I became an IV drug user. Desperate for my next fix, I did anything I could for the money, including frequent break-ins and theft. During this period, I was arrested sixteen times and lost everything: my license, car, house, job, self-respect, and self-worth. Understandably, most people actively avoided me. I was a horrible, miserable, broken human being.

In 2012, my kids and I were staying at my ex-husband's house because I had lost our home. On November 5, my picture appeared on the TV screen, announcing I was the county's most wanted individual. Hearing the newscaster ask for information on my whereabouts made me realize just how weary I was. I resigned and called the sheriff. I explained that I was sick of living this life and asked what I could do to resolve the situation. Acting on his advice, I turned myself in. After being in jail for six months, I spent the next eight months in rehab.

While in rehab, I surrendered to Christ. I started doing things God's way since my ways were obviously not working. Within weeks, I saw a massive transformation in my life. The minute I was saved, I walked out of the room, and my thoughts about others instantly changed. When I first arrived at rehab, I mentally made fun of one girl. But that day, I saw her in a radically different light. I know God does not always change people immediately, but He transformed me rapidly.

I resolved to help others suffering from addiction as soon as I left treatment. I wanted to lead others to Christ, to be the disciple and guide that I wish I had during my addiction. When I was an addict, people mocked me and gossiped about me in person and on social media. I wanted to be the support for others that I never had.

Since I had no home, car, driver's license, or job, my mother graciously let me live with her when I got out of rehab. While she was quite supportive, my family didn't understand how to deal with the addiction. My mom simply tried to love me. For a year, I sat at home, doing little but dive into God's word and form a relationship with Him. I couldn't drive, and He kept me still for that year so I could learn His word and discover ways to reach out to people. I prayed, asking God to show me how I could reach anyone in a meaningful way. I wasn't into social media; however, I saw a woman I barely knew post a cry for help with her addiction, begging for treatment. I reached out to her.

From there, I started using Facebook as a platform to share what God had done in my life. I didn't have to go anywhere physically to find people who needed my assistance. God placed people in front of me. They started calling me five to six times a day for help, a pattern that has continued. I now have an entire board established for a non-profit. I am convinced that God placed me on this Earth to help people and to lead others to Christ. My heart is dedicated to the broken and addicted, and I work multiple jobs to help pay for other women's treatment. People think I am crazy for what I do, but I am proud.

Late one night in November 2019, I arrived at home, exhausted. All I wanted to do was lie down. While in bed scrolling through

Facebook, I read a post about Terrell, a local police officer who had arrested me several times. I vaguely knew his daughter, April, through my ministry work, and she posted that her father needed a kidney.

The Holy Spirit told me right then and there that I had the kidney that man needed. I responded with excuses: I was already far too busy with my jobs and ministry work to donate a kidney and was in constant communication with seventy-six people who needed my help. I shut down Facebook and went to sleep, dismissing the idea.

At 4:00 a.m., I woke up and started praying. If it had been up to me, I wouldn't give anyone a kidney. I was kind and sweet, but that was a bit out of my comfort zone. Still, I fasted and prayed for three days while discerning if God was telling me to give away my kidney. I was hoping He would give me some sort of sign. By the end of those three days, all I had heard was "Love thy neighbor." Nothing fancy, loud, or clear. But in my heart, I knew I was to give Terrell my kidney. Early that morning, I sent a message to April. "I just wanted to let you know that I have your daddy's kidney. What do I need to do next?"

April was happy but told me I would need to be tested. I followed a link she sent, and I received a call a couple of hours later saying that they were going to mail me the testing kit. I called my nurse practitioner and told her that I didn't want anybody to know about this. I explained that the blood work I needed was to be done under the radar.

Two days later, I arrived at the doctor's office. The nurse practitioner had set up the appointment so that no one saw me come in with the kit. She was familiar with my story and aware of everything I had overcome. However, the woman who drew my blood was a stranger. I sat in the chair in the lab while the lab tech read the labels. The kit clearly said it was a donor package, so she knew what I was hoping to do. My track marks were exposed when I pulled up my sleeves, and I immediately grew defensive. I looked up to see that the woman was crying. I asked venomously, "Why are you crying?" She softly replied, "My friend recently donated a kidney to a stranger." This selflessness was heartwarming for her. Then she asked me why I was crying. "Because I have the devil on my shoulder, telling me I shouldn't donate because I have track marks on my arms."

She told me I had to keep the paperwork myself, but I didn't want my kids to come across it so she agreed to keep the papers on her desk, where I could retrieve them when needed. I knew I had this man's kidney, and I didn't doubt that I would donate it, but I still needed time to prepare my kids. I wanted the right words to express what I was doing and the reason why.

My son and I were headed to a Christmas parade when I got the phone call from Vanderbilt. I fruitlessly tried to switch the call from my Bluetooth to my phone, but the woman's voice began coming through the car speakers. Luckily, I switched it before she told me that I was a perfect match for my daddy. I explained that the man I was donating to was not my daddy, which genuinely surprised her.

When we got home from the parade that evening, I prayed for the right words and timing to explain my choice to my kids. I asked my son if he would watch a Christmas movie with me, which he rarely did. He agreed and chose a Hallmark movie that was playing. To my surprise, the film was about a kidney donation. The movie was on at the perfect time to help prepare my son for what I was about to do. Still, I didn't say anything directly about my plans.

Later that month, we visited with my mama and watched another movie, which also happened to be about organ donation—another of God's plans. My mama bawled during the film, with no idea what I was planning. Not only did she not know, nobody did. I hadn't told a soul what I was going to do. Mama knew that I had a twenty-four-hour urine test, but she did not question me. In February, I took her with me to Vanderbilt. I planned for her to be my caretaker after the transplant surgery since my boyfriend worked long hours far from home, but she still didn't know about it. On the way to Vanderbilt, she asked if everything was okay with me. I told her that it was recommended I use Vanderbilt for the testing. I couldn't outright lie to her because lying was part of the life I left behind.

We arrived at the psychologist's office at Vanderbilt, where I was asked if my mother was going to be my caretaker. My mom asked, "Caretaker for what?" It was then that I finally told her I was donating my kidney and wanted her to take care of me afterwards. She was

27

shocked and started crying. The psychologist was surprised that I hadn't even spoken with my mother about this, and I explained that I hadn't told anybody.

Then COVID-19 hit, and the surgery was postponed. In May, we scheduled it for July 21. In June, I finally sat my children down and explained that I was donating my kidney to Terrell. My daughter was good friends with Terrell's grandson, whom he had been raising since his daughter had passed away. My children didn't have much of a response to my news. My daughter was not surprised, and my son said, "You are going to mess around and die one day."

Later on, I learned my daughter had questions and concerns. I asked her if this was her grandfather who had raised her and was dying, wouldn't she want someone to give them a kidney? Explaining that I had two kidneys, I told her I could live a functional life with just one. She asked what would happen if she or her brother needed a kidney someday, and I assured her that God would provide. No matter what, I was determined to give Terrell my kidney.

The surgery was a success. The doctors would have never known that I once suffered from addiction had they not seen the track marks or my medical record. God had restored my body, and I was in perfect health. All my lab numbers were excellent; they could not believe I was ever an IV drug user.

Even though Terrell had arrested me on several occasions, two of them for felonies, God still chose me to give him the kidney he needed. Now there is an indescribable bond between the two of us. It is humbling that God used a piece of me to save another man's life. The fact that God used someone with my history for such good shows that anyone can be a part of His story. I want to give God the credit for the transplant, as this is His work, not mine. I often tell others that if they're not dead, they still have a purpose. I certainly have one. God can use you for good no matter what. If He could do this with my life, imagine what He could do with yours. I didn't have to do what God asked, but I chose to be obedient. Learning that I had Terrell's kidney was not only terrifying, but inconvenient as well.

There is often nothing convenient about being a disciple. At the time, I was a single mom. I had to take off work for two months and prepare myself financially for that time. Things started to turn south for a while, but God still provided for us. Terrell remains healthy. Even though recovery from surgery was a struggle for me, I am now completely healthy, thanks to God's providence. I am remarried, and my husband was a huge support for me during the transplant and recuperation.

Once, I was broken, but God restored me. And for that, I am eternally grateful.

Terrell's Story
I Got a Kidney and a "Daughter"

I started having kidney problems in 2019 and my kidneys' ability to function was continually declining. Five years earlier, I had cancer, which is where I believe my kidney problem began. Most kidneys are so efficient that problems only start to become evident at around 25 percent. At one checkup, that is what my kidney functioning was. Every time I returned for an appointment, the functioning level decreased, eventually dropping to 12 percent. At that point, the doctor told me I either needed to spend the rest of my life on dialysis or get a transplant.

Feeling so ill, I was unable to do much of anything. I was already retired and felt that I was not really living. I was simply surviving.

My wife and I began to talk and pray about our options. God reminded me that if I trusted in Him and remained faithful, He would take care of me. He told me He would supply a kidney, and I trusted that He would follow through on His word. I had no second thoughts. My next prayer was for God to supply me with the right kidney, one that would not only match but be the kidney He wanted me to have.

I was approved for a transplant at Vanderbilt. My daughter, April, wrote a post on Facebook that I needed a kidney, and over eight hundred people from all over the southeastern United States shared my need. It was incredible how many people directly contacted me to offer a kidney, but God knew exactly which kidney I needed.

April called me and said, "Dad, I've got you a kidney." She told me a young woman I knew, named Jocelynn, was a perfect match. I remembered Jocelynn as a former schoolmate of one of my daughters. She had gotten into quite a bit of trouble during a dark time in her life. To support her drug habit, she shoplifted, committed credit card fraud, and other various illegal things. Her bad reputation extended beyond our small community to the entire county. During my career as a police officer, I even arrested her a couple of times.

With the current unfavorable climate for police officers, I found it remarkable that someone whom I put in jail would step forward to donate a kidney to me. Jocelynn had seen the Facebook post and went to Vanderbilt to be tested. Since we weren't kin by any stretch, only God would design us to be the perfect match. I didn't have anything against her personally since I was simply doing my job when I'd arrested her. The question was, did she hold a grudge against me? God had told me that He would give me a kidney, and I would never turn down a gift of His.

Jocelynn and I quickly opened communications. Sometimes she came over to my house to chat since she lived only two miles away. We discussed the transplant, and I asked her to pray about it. She told me she'd already been praying and that the Holy Spirit led her on this journey.

The transplant took place, and all went well. Jocelynn and I keep up with each other by talking or texting nearly every day. She's become like another daughter. One of my two daughters passed away, and now Jocelynn is a wonderful addition to the family. There is an indescribable bond between us. To know a part of someone else's body is within me and has extended my life is an amazing feeling. I am beyond grateful that Jocelynn followed God's leading. I believe it all came together because of obedience: I was obedient in asking God for the right kidney and she was obedient in heeding that call.

It has been several years since Jocelynn has straightened out her life. God restored her and used her for good, a story that provides hope. I wish others could see that the world is full of good people doing great deeds, despite the troubles that afflict us. We cannot afford to throw people away for making mistakes. I am so thankful that God restored her health and life, and in so doing, allowed her to follow His will and do good.

As her life improved, so did her reputation. I started hearing good things about her from others. She was known to be someone who reached out to help other people. Eventually, she even started a nonprofit agency, A Place of Grace, to help people get back on the right track from addiction.

Currently, I am doing wonderfully. Life is going as well as could be expected. All my health statistics are good, and my kidney is functioning. At first, I had weekly follow-ups at Vanderbilt, and now I am going every two weeks. My strength is returning, and I am starting to do some things I was unable to do before the transplant. I will be on anti-rejection medication for the rest of my life, but I am doing so well, they've already cut back the dosage. However, since my immune system is weaker, I must be extra cautious to avoid any germs and viruses. However, I should be back to near normal in eight or nine months.

I hope our story gives hope and encouragement to others. I want God to receive the glory for the wonderful acts He has done in our lives. God is still performing miracles, touching lives, and healing people. He could have healed my kidneys so I wouldn't need a transplant, but He chose to involve Jocelynn. Now others can hear our inspiring story, and God gets the credit He deserves. This journey of trust and healing has shown me that if I am obedient to God's will, He will take care of me. I am so thankful and blessed to have been given a new kidney, a "daughter," and a firmer faith.

Sheila's Story
Holes in the Wall

Suffering for a long time with Lambert-Eaton myasthenic syndrome, there were times my mom couldn't walk and was in intense pain. Even her skin hurt. In the final week of her life, she was done with the pain and didn't want to deal with the condition anymore. She understood she wouldn't recover.

She resided in a nursing facility while her health declined and eventually wanted nothing other than to curl up and nap. My sisters knew she was done fighting, so they took her home from the facility to spend her last days in her own bed.

I called my childhood friend Kara and I told her my mom was dying. Kara was out of town at the time and was genuinely sorry that she couldn't be there with us. She loved my mom and had gone through a similar experience with her sister, so she shared some insight on what I could do to keep Mom comfortable.

My mom crawled into her bed at home on Friday, and she passed away the following Tuesday with her four adult children surrounding her, just as she'd wanted. Her passing was full of peaceful beauty. In addition to the heavy sadness, we also felt relief by the calmness of the experience.

Cleaning out her house was hard. First, there was a mountain of clutter. Second, nobody wanted to clean it because the task was both physically and emotionally draining. The undertaking itself was sporadic, with random breaks for hours or days. On some days, we would piddle around, not making any progress. We giggled, laughed, and cried throughout the process. It was as if we didn't want it to end because once the cleaning was complete, the house and a piece of her memory would be gone.

To this day, we still talk about mom's decorating skills. She had many "dustables," as we liked to call them. A true collector, she had a comical number of shells in the bathroom, a wreath for every season on a wall in one of the bedrooms, and many other things that made the house quite quirky. It was a house that nobody could love, yet we all did because it was Mom.

The house couldn't be put up for sale as long as it still held her possessions. My older sister, the executor of the estate, issued instructions to work on purging and organizing or to lay off. By the time we finally had the house ready for sale, it was empty. Little did we know, our procrastination was all a part of God's timing.

When I had spoken with my friend Kara as my mom was dying, she hadn't said anything about her own life. Unbeknownst to me, she was going through a separation and was looking for a house. She had put bids on two homes in my mom's neighborhood but didn't get them. The neighborhood was in such high demand that Kara's realtor called her as soon as a home showed up on the market. When we finally listed my parents' house, the offers came in quickly. My sister sorted through them and chose the best one. It just happened to be Kara's. She did not know whose house this was because the seller was listed as "executor." She had only visited with us in our childhood home, which my parents sold when we grew up. My sister didn't recognize the name of the buyer and it was only after accepting the offer that my sister found out it was my friend Kara.

It is now Kara's house. I still have a key for it on my keyring. Kara never changed the locks since she knows and trusts my family, and we visit on occasion. Even though it is her house now, she admits to feeling the love in it from my parents and family. It radiates a peaceful atmosphere my parents cultivated, which Kara and I both sense.

Here is an edited piece that my daughter Joanna wrote about my mom's house, and Kara's response:

> I heard someone say after they lost someone close to them, "The last act of love we can show a person is to grieve for them," and I just can't get over how sad it is that they believe that love ends in grief. I lost my grandma a few months back, and I have already seen the millions of ways to love her beyond grief.
>
> But the thing that caught me off guard was the holes that the picture frames left in the walls.
>
> See, I went back to school and I missed the part of cleaning where everything came off the walls. I walked into the house that was filled with memories and the white walls looked too white, and I stared at them and then saw the tiny black dots littering the paint—there was the front wall that all of her children's wedding photos had been, three girls diagonally placed under a light. There was the front bedroom where all those dang holiday wreaths were hung too high…and the nails were still there but the wreaths that had to be

changed out for every holiday and every season were gone, the nails left behind scattering without pattern under the apex of the ceiling. And then there was the hallway. The hallway had nine holes in the wall of one side, where nine children had been displayed for as long as I remember—the first of her grandchildren, who had been her pride and joy. The tenth baby was shown on the other wall in five photos. See, the nine of us came within eight years of each other, but then came the baby, over twelve years later. So there were all these holes in the hallways that no one would ever know used to hold up the memories of the mess she made.

And I think that's why the holes got to me... No one would see the blemishes for what they were—holding laces of precious memories out of thousands that she wanted everyone to see.

I will drive by the blue house later on, and maybe it won't even be blue anymore, and the people inside will have covered the walls with their own children or grandchildren or parents or maybe nothing at all, and to them, it will be their house where they don't hang wreaths in the front bedroom or duct tape cords behind the desk. To them, it will be a completely different world, but as I looked at the holes in the walls and saw in my head every picture that had been there, I knew that the house that would one day be someone else's would always be the bearer of my memories there. And when the holes are patched and sanded and painted over, no one will know what used to lie there but us, and it's those memories that can't be explained or understood.

There are holes in the walls of my grandma's house, and I love each and every one. And I love her for each one. And I will miss her for each one, even when they are patched up like time patches up the holes that grief rips through the soul.

I love her past the grief, to the holes in the walls and the love that once filled them.

Kara's reply is the following:

Dearest Joanna, I am the new owner of your house of holes. Those holes will always be there. They may be hidden by paint or other memories, but they will be there to remind me of the wonderful woman who lived here before me. See, I have known your mother since I was six. Buying a house for me has been an emotional roller coaster. A "should I, can I, do I, and if so, where?" I looked high and low. Made offers on two other houses that didn't quite "feel" right. As I walked into the little blue house, I felt peace. I love everything about it and how it made me feel. It was the next day I got a text from your mother stating "Ummmm…did you just buy a house?" To which I said, "What the heck…yes?!"

She then said that your aunt read to her the name of the buyer, which was me. Your mom and I talked and cried, and I said my prayers had been answered.

That little blue house will have different loved ones on the walls, but I will always remember your words explaining the meaning of what had hung before. Those holes are there. They are the foundation of love and peace. For that, Joanna, I thank you for allowing me to love your grandma's house. It means the world to me that I can carry the torch in their name and keep the memories that hung in those tiny holes before."

2

Accidents

After being told by a teacher that he was too dumb to learn, my husband's grandfather, Charles, dropped out of high school in 1923. Unfortunately, he believed his teacher, so instead of completing his education, he started working in road construction.

On the night of November 10, 1927, he went raccoon hunting with others and his right (dominant) hand was torn to pieces by a blast from a twenty-gauge shotgun. Charles never discussed the details of the story, but there were some accusations that this was intentional. His hand had to be amputated, making him ponder what he was going to do since he no longer would be able to work road construction. When his aunt came to see him in the hospital, she asked what his next steps were and how she could help. He said that there was no way he could work a job that required physical labor such as road construction or farming, so he might have to go back to school. He said he would have to learn to use his left hand to write, so his aunt gave him a pencil and paper.

At one point, he contemplated suicide because he could not figure out what he was going to do with his life. He was nineteen at the time of the accident. He did eventually acknowledge that he had to have hope, so his next steps included finishing high school and going to college. He had already decided marriage was not something he could look forward to because nobody would want to marry a one-handed man, yet he knew he had to have a partner who could do the things he could not. In those days, raising food was the only way people knew how to survive and Charles could not imagine he had the physical ability to garden or farm.

By the summer after the accident, he said he wanted to build up his muscles. He learned to chop wood and do other farming activities using only his left hand. Even though he could not do them well, he gained strength and did things as best as he was able. He also realized that he could not continue to live with his parents; he had to rely on himself.

He routinely went to church and met a lovely young lady there named Mary. One day, he asked Mary if he could walk home with her, and a year later, they married. He had already begun college at that point. Charles found a good partner in Mary because she did not mind assisting with the chores where he struggled. She was the gardener. She also helped him with tasks most people take for granted, such as tying shoes and cutting up meat. They made a great team.

Once he had some college credits under his belt, he was allowed to teach grade school. At that time, he did not need to finish his degree to begin teaching. He taught during the school year and then worked on his degree during the summer. In the years that followed, he not only went four years to college, but three years to graduate school. He taught in one-room schoolhouses, then larger schools, and later became principal. He eventually worked his way up to superintendent of the school system.

He often told his children that losing his arm was one of the best things that ever happened to him. If that had not occurred, his direction in life would have been unclear. All of the jobs he had thought about before his accident required two hands, so his adaptation to using one arm was life-changing in the most positive way.

My husband's grandpa's story has touched and influenced all in our family and all who knew him. When life gave him this impairment, he could have given up and almost did. We are so grateful that instead, he focused on his abilities and became an educator at work and life.

Car, work, and home accidents can cause physical and mental trauma, just like this hunting accident did for Charles. These mishaps may change your life path, or at the very least, will often change your perspective.

Cody's Story
Lucky to Be Alive

One spring night at around one in the morning, I, along with three of my friends, was out truck riding on rural dirt roads. This was common for many college students in the area since there was little to do in this small Southern town. My friends and I would go riding nearly every night. This particular night, I was in the back seat on the right side.

We came upon a tight turn in the road that went ninety degrees to the left. We missed the turn, hurtling straight off the road and over a ditch, hitting a large oak tree, the only substantial one in the area. All the other trees there were small pine trees that we could have safely plowed through. If we had gone a little to the left, we would have ended up in a peanut field and not hit any trees. Unfortunately, we hit the oak tree head-on at about 50 miles per hour. None of us were wearing seat belts, and alcohol was involved. I am also fairly certain the driver was on the phone.

After the impact, the first thing I remember was someone touching me, telling me to wake up. I came to, assuring everyone that I was fine. I got out of the truck and started walking into the woods. My friends turned me around, leading me back to the road. I repeatedly told them not to worry, that I was not hurt, but they explained that I was bleeding substantially from my face. I asked them to take a picture so I could see what I looked like. When I saw myself, I felt the full pain for the first time, quickly collapsing on the road. None of my friends had cell service, but someone nearby had heard the crash and alerted the police.

I remember little after the picture other than flashlights from the paramedics while they told me to stay calm. I told them that everything was fine; I wanted to go back to school. I have been told that I tried to fight with the first responders because I refused to go to the hospital. I didn't realize how badly I was injured. The paramedics had to sedate me to make me cooperate. They took me by ambulance to a helicopter that was waiting to fly me to a hospital better equipped than the nearest one to deal with my head injury.

I woke up with absolutely no idea where I was. At first, I thought I was watching a hospital scene on a television show. It took me a few minutes to realize that I was the one in the bed. One of my friends was sitting beside me crying. I wasn't in any pain at that point because of the medications I had been given. I still didn't understand that I was injured.

My neck began to hurt so badly that I thought it was broken. I then noticed there was a neck brace on me. I told the doctor how much pain I felt in my neck. From scans that had been done earlier, the doctor knew it was not broken, so he took off the brace, which lessened the pain.

The nurse asked for my mom's phone number. Since I was over eighteen, the hospital was not obligated to call her. I refused to give them her number at first; I didn't want her to know and worry. My phone was not with me at the hospital because I did not have the wherewithal after the accident to retrieve it from the truck. When it was returned to me, I saw a text from my mom checking in because her motherly instincts told her something was wrong. She had sent that text before she found out about the accident. I decided at that point to give the nurse permission to call her.

I fell back asleep and didn't wake again until after my parents had arrived at the hospital from their home seven hours away. When I opened my eyes, the doctor was showing my mom the x-rays. Once again, I did not know where I was and thought I was watching a TV show. When I saw the x-ray, I understood that someone had a severe head injury. Then I realized whose head it was.

My skull was fractured into thirteen pieces. I had a collapsed sinus, and my eye socket was cracked. When we crashed, my head had hit the handle on the door, breaking off a metal bar with the force of my face. My whole body had flown forward into the seat in front of me, but my head stopped on the handle, creating a crater in my head. It was so large that if they had put a golf ball in the indentation, it would have been flush with my forehead. I was in the hospital for fourteen days, and every time I awoke, I was confused and disoriented. It took me a few minutes to get my bearings and realize that I was still in the hospital.

They could not operate on me for seven days because the swelling first had to subside. After the surgery, the surgeon explained that putting my skull back together was like doing a jigsaw puzzle. The whole structure had to be rebuilt because it was in so many pieces. I had ten metal plates and several screws inserted in my head. When I woke up from the surgery, the pain was overwhelming, significantly worse than before. I woke up but didn't open my eyes because there was so much pressure in my head. I knew if I opened my eyes and saw light, the pain would be even worse. I quickly asked for pain meds, but the nurse said that I had all they could give me already in my system. Nothing curbed the excruciating pain for days.

I stayed in the hospital for a total of two weeks, which I hated. I was used to spending my time outdoors and staying physically active, so being confined to a bed for that time was torture.

I was told it would take eight to twelve months for my skull to heal to full strength. I was given some restrictions when discharged from the hospital, including not to ride motorcycles or horses, or to do any other activity where I might fall and re-break my skull.

My parents took me back to their home in North Carolina to recuperate. I was in bed for an additional two to three weeks there because I experienced so much pain. I had many follow-up appointments where I argued with the doctors because I wanted to go to work and finally do things again with my friends, which they, of course, refused to allow.

Because of the extent of my head injury, I was likely to have seizures, so I was put on preventive medications. In addition to that potential, I had three brain bleeds and a concussion, so I wasn't allowed to drive, which I missed more than anything. I never did have a seizure, so I was later tested to see if I was truly at risk for them. The tests concluded that I had no chance of seizures, so I was weaned off those medications and cleared to drive.

That accident happened the night before finals in the spring semester of my junior year. All but one of my professors allowed me to be exempted from finals and settle with the grade I had prior to finals. The doctors warned me that I likely wouldn't be able to return to school in the fall, but I proved them wrong. By the end of June, I was able to resume my internship. I was supposed to work outdoors with hogs, but because of my recent surgery, I had to work in the office. I wasn't permitted to do any physical labor. When I got back to school that August, I procrastinated taking the one final exam from the previous semester that I wasn't exempt from. When I finally went to the professor to take it, he pulled out a contract for me to sign, which said that I would take the grade that I had before finals. He said that by showing up, I demonstrated the necessary effort, so he let me pass the class without taking the final. I was incredibly pleased, as I was unsure of how well I would do after so many months without having been in class.

The fact that nobody died in this wreck is remarkable. Besides my injuries, one friend had a sprained ankle, and my other two friends weren't injured. I was told that I threw my arm across the girl next to me, preventing her from flying forward. The friend who was driving that night fully understood the danger of driving intoxicated. He would have gone to jail for at least fifteen years had I passed away. The accident was a massive reality check for him. He was still arrested that night, and his license was suspended, but that was the extent of the punishment. He told the police officer that he didn't care if he went to jail, he just wanted to be sure his friend was all right. He was worried about me and constantly asked for updates on my condition. We are still good friends and talk every day.

Every doctor that has since seen my x-rays marvels that I am alive. From an outside perspective, it is hard to imagine that some-one would survive their skull being shattered and pushed into their brain. There was a large chance that I would have a permanent brain injury. I was unbelievably lucky that I returned to good health and my brain functions normally. My only lingering issue from this acci-dent is minor neck pain at the end of workdays and headaches when the weather changes. No doctor understands how I survived those injuries, yet here I am, feeling as healthy as if nothing ever happened.

The gravity of my situation didn't fully sink in until long after the accident, when I finally reflected on what happened. The expe-rience has made me slow down and think about the possible conse-quences of my actions in any situation. I appreciate life much more, now that I feel I have been given a second chance. I am convinced that God was looking out for me that night and that it's only by His grace that I'm still here today.

Mary's Story
Forever Changed

When I was ten years old, I moved to a rural town in Ohio. My family built a home on the property where my grandparents lived. My grandparents set me up to be playmates with a girl named Michelle when she came into town to visit her grandparents. We quickly became friends. She lived in Michigan, and we were also pen pals when we were apart. Our parents were also friends, as were our grandparents—three generations of friendship.

Michelle was horse-crazy and loved riding. She took lessons and became quite a good rider. She was the one who initially got me into riding. I also took lessons and enjoyed riding. My grandfather was supportive of my riding, but my parents saw the hobby as dangerous. My dad knew how to ride and would sometimes go with me on the weekends.

There was a family down the road from my house who owned three horses. I arranged that I would take care of the one belonging to their daughter, who gave me informal riding lessons. During the summer, I would take out the horse, Robin, and feed her. The other two horses belonged to their sons, who were skillful riders. One of the boys, Troy, was a couple of years older than me and we would occasionally ride together.

Also down the road from us lived an older man, a doctor who owned a beautifully grand and powerful horse named Apollo. He was a seasoned rider, but he didn't allow many people to ride Apollo. However, since he trusted Michelle's riding ability, he allowed her to ride his horse. When she would come to visit, that was the horse that she would ride.

By this time, I had been riding Robin, who was a smaller quarter horse. Because of all the time spent taking care of her and riding her, I became fond of her, even though she could be a little ornery.

One late October day in 1981, when I was fifteen, Michelle and I made plans to go riding together. I was to ride Robin and she was to ride Apollo. It was a gloomy, windy, and cool fall day. We rode to many places, including to my house to visit my mom. Afterward, we went down the road and into a field that was about a quarter of a mile away from my home.

Michelle was riding ahead of me in the field when all of a sudden, Robin was spooked by something and threw me off. Michelle swung around on Apollo and came back to me as Robin ran off. My neck was aching, but I was more stunned than hurt. Michelle said that she was going to go after Robin. We figured she had run toward home, but there was a road between the field and home that we were concerned about her crossing. Michelle said that she would go so she could keep Robin in sight. I remember feeling a bit annoyed that I was going to have to walk back. I headed in the general direction Michelle had gone. When I came into a clearing, I saw Apollo way down the road—without Michelle—and then I spotted her lying in the road about 30 feet from me. She was not moving. Knowing something was wrong, I ran to her side and called her name. Her beautiful brown eyes were open, but she was not conscious or registering any of my words. I knew this was serious, but I knew I couldn't go for help since she was lying in the middle of the country road. I had to be there to stop a car if it was coming toward her. Fortunately, it didn't take too long for a car to come by, and I flagged down the driver. This was before cellphones, so I could not simply reach into my pocket to call for help. The couple in the car asked me if I knew the girl and if I knew what had happened. For whatever reason, I did not cry. I may have been in shock. The couple decided that they would stay with Michelle while I ran to get help.

I knocked on the door of the first house I came to. I told the homeowners that there had been an accident and that I needed to call for help. They would not let me in, saying that they didn't want to get involved. I got upset, but I still did not cry.

As I went on trying to find help, Troy, the boy I used to ride with, happened to come by. We went to the house of the doctor, the one who owned Apollo, and called Michelle's mom. I explained to her what had happened and where Michelle was. She said that she would be there right away. I also called my mom and told her the situation. Both Michelle's mom, Debbie, and my mom got to Michelle before the ambulance came. Michelle was still unconscious. By this time, some other people had gathered around, asking what had happened. When the ambulance finally arrived, and they were loading Michelle in, Debbie looked at me and asked if I was all right. I had always admired and loved her before then, but for her to have the presence of mind to do that as her daughter was being taken to the hospital was impactful on my life.

I went back home while Debbie went to the hospital to be with Michelle. When I entered my house, my mom and dad were in the kitchen. My dad said to me, "Well, her riding days are over, and by the way, so are yours."

Michelle's stepdad came over to our house that evening to relay an update on Michelle. She had a fractured skull from ear to ear. They assumed that when Apollo had reached the road, he must have skidded, and Michelle went over the top of the horse. She hadn't been wearing a helmet. She remained unconscious.

On the night of the accident, we had a Greek play at our school with mandatory attendance. My parents made me go. They were trying to keep everything as normal as possible for me. I sat in the audience telling my friend, Jackie, about what had happened instead of watching the play. She was a great listener, and talking about what happened was helpful. Since Michelle didn't go to our school, nobody else seemed to know about what had happened.

For days, Michelle didn't regain consciousness. Everyone was preparing me for her not to be okay; they thought she was going to die. It was touch-and-go for a while.

That next week at school, there was a homecoming dance and a friend of mine had asked me to go. I went, partly for the distraction. Half of my thoughts that week had been on the accident and Michelle. Since she was from Michigan and nobody knew her at school, this was not the news story or gossip of the students. It felt very lonely for me to be dealing with this alone.

When I got home from the dance, there was a card waiting for me. It was from Debbie. I have that card to this day. Debbie wrote how Michelle was doing: She had a feeding tube, and her heart rate was becoming more stable. Debbie said that she had high hopes that Michelle would be okay. I pinned my hopes on that message since everyone else was bluntly saying that she was not going to make it. Even though my family was praying for her, they wanted me to be prepared for the worst. I clung to this card and read it over and over. I focused on how Debbie was handling this. Her optimism was what I held onto.

I had a wise teacher, who was also my adviser, and I asked her how to deal with this situation. She knew I was really into writing, so she told me to write about my feelings. She helped me with this piece of writing for weeks. It helped me process the experience. I struggled with survivor's guilt. Why didn't this happen to me? I had to understand that it was not my fault that Michelle chose to go after Robin. I had to recognize that it was just something that happened that was beyond my control, but I did have control over what that meant to me. It helped me understand my own story.

While Michelle was in the hospital for three weeks, I went to see her once. She was still unconscious but was starting to respond to stimuli. They didn't accurately know the extent of her brain injury since her brain was so traumatized. The family decided to airlift her back to Michigan to be closer to home. They were still unsure how her brain was going to heal or function.

I called Debbie a couple of weeks later to check on Michelle and to tell her that she was the only one who believed Michelle was going to be all right. I asked how she was able to do that. She replied, "Because I have to. That is how I am getting through this, by believing that she will be okay." I hung my hopes on Debbie saying that Michelle would recover—and she did!

She had some initial delays with her speech, but for the most part, she made a full recovery. She is now a single mom with two daughters and is doing well.

Michelle's injury was a pivotal moment in my life. I think of my life in two chunks: before the accident and after. I learned the power of optimism. I now always try to look at the bright side of things. When I have the choice of hope or despair, I choose hope because time and time again, hope significantly changes how we experience life.

Jessica's Story
Broken and Blessing Others

Six years ago, I moved to Indianapolis from Ohio, something I was not thrilled about. Five hours from my family, we were farther than I would have liked, but I was glad to be within driving distance. My husband and I began "church shopping" to try to find and join a church family. We felt we had not been doing a good job of teaching our three kids about the Lord. We both grew up in church, but even though I attended church as a child, I would not say that it was particularly important to us. I had always prayed, believed in God, and leaned on Him during hard times, but I don't feel that I had a personal relationship with Him.

We had been in Indianapolis for about a year when I received a devastating message. I was up early that day when I got a text from my dad. I noticed it come through but decided that I would look at it later. However, I felt a nudge to read the text, so I picked up my phone. The message said to pray; my dad had been in an accident, hit a runner, and she had died. First of all, my dad was one of the most amazing human beings: compassionate, caring, loving, thoughtful, and generous. He was one of those people that everyone loved. I was in shock when I read that text and could not imagine that this was happening to him.

I am someone who feels deeply for others. I wrestled with the thought that a family had lost someone they loved. My dad told me that he didn't know how old the runner was, but he was praying that she didn't have little children. We later learned that she was forty, her kids already grown and out of the house. To think that someone found out that their mother, wife, or daughter had died from that kind of injury overwhelmed me. I struggled with the idea of losing a piece of my dad, who I knew would never quite be the same. I recognized deep within my soul that Jesus was the only way through this.

I locked myself in a room while I cried. I eventually pulled myself together, got my kids situated, packed up, and drove home to Ohio. On the way, I turned on a Christian radio station, which I had never really listened to before that day. The first song that came on was "Just Be Held" by Casting Crowns. There were many lyrics in that song that felt incredibly fitting for the situation, one along the lines of turning ashes into beauty. Hearing those lyrics made me believe that my dad would use this situation for good in some way. I do believe that we get little "Godwinks" where God uses people, songs, or other small nudges in our lives at specific moments to speak to us. At one point earlier in my life, I wanted to hear God's voice, but I would get frustrated because that wasn't what happened. I slowly began to realize that I can hear God through other mediums. I would encounter little snippets of goodness, such as this specific song being played at this particular time, the unlikely coincidences that seem best credited as God's way of speaking.

I had five hours in the car to pray and mentally process everything. I have always been an optimistic person and knew I had to find the blessings on that day, thanking God for them. I came up with a few quickly. My dad was not texting while driving. Also, he worked in the Amish community and had many Amish friends who were strong in their faith and incredibly loyal. For him to have that support group surrounding him was immeasurably valuable. Additionally, my dad's boss was well versed in Scripture, and his coworkers prayed over him and were supportive of him. Lastly, as much as I did not want to be in Indiana, I was grateful that I was only five hours away.

When I walked into my dad's house, he wouldn't look me in the eye or speak. He was too ashamed. I could not imagine what complex mixture of emotions he was feeling. I never once heard him ask, "Why me?" The night I was there, I remember holding him, sitting still, and praying. He told me he knew that God was using him as a tool in some way to help others. I remember him saying that he did not know how anyone could get through this without God.

Immediately, people told him to go see a lawyer. He didn't understand why he needed one. He knew that he did indeed hit the woman, and he was willing to go to jail if that was asked of him. He knew he had no choice but to live with this every day for the rest of his life.

We called one of my husband's friends, an attorney who explained everything to us. He said that my dad would be prosecuted, that twenty years ago this accident would not have had any legal consequences, but a deadly accident by today's standards usually meant a case. He told us to expect stages of grief from the family. My dad's situation was unique because many of my dad's friends in the small Amish community knew the victim and her family personally. They kept telling my dad that the family was praying for him, that they were strong Christians, and that they were looking at this simply as an accident. However, our lawyer kept telling us not to bank on that because he had never before seen a case where the victim's family had been forgiving. He prepared us for the worst-case scenario, in which the family would scream in the courtroom that their lives had been ruined. He told us to be ready for this forgiving attitude to quickly fade away.

We had to wait a month before the hearing. In the time leading up to this, my dad's niece, Carrie Ann, died from a rare genetic disorder. She was like my dad's third child; he called her every single day. She was in and out of the hospital throughout her life. He learned that she had died peacefully in her sleep, which was not what we expected, considering her condition. She was often getting infections and going to the hospital, so we figured she would die from pneumonia. God meant everything to her. She was someone who could have easily wallowed in self-pity, but she did not. Before she passed away, she would sometimes reach out to my dad to let him know that she was praying for the family and him. My dad had her support for the first three weeks after the accident. She was nothing but a wonderfully bright light in the world.

After the accident, my dad would not leave the house because of his shame. He didn't want to see people or talk about what happened. He felt like the world viewed him only in a negative light, especially since the local newspaper published the story the day after the accident. The one blessing of my cousin's death was that it forced my dad to leave the house and go to the funeral home. Everyone who cared about him was there, voicing their support, a turning point when he finally understood that people still loved him.

The day before the hearing, the lawyer called me, wanting me to know that he had asked my dad to speak at the hearing. He said that he had never asked a client to do that but felt the court needed to hear the story from him. Nobody would be able to convey my dad's feelings better than he. At the time, I hated for the attorney to ask this of him. I didn't understand how my father was supposed to stand in front of someone whose family had lost a member by his vehicle, look them in the eye and recall the cause of their pain. Jail time was projected to be 160 days, and my dad expressed that he would do the jail time if it would ease their hurt. He never attempted to weasel out of punishment; he wanted to be given what he deserved.

On the day of the hearing, my brother and I were quite emotional, but the lawyer still wanted us both present. My dad stood up to speak and looked directly at the victim's husband and mother, meeting their anguished eyes. I didn't know until the hearing that he had stayed with the woman the entire time after the accident, held her hand, and prayed with her. He wanted the family to know that she did not die alone. He promised that he would dedicate his life to doing good and being a light in others' lives. He received his sentence: one year of probation and a fine. He didn't get jail time, and I believe the family of the woman had something to do with that.

When we were walking out of the courtroom, our lawyer told us that the family wanted words with my dad. I looked down the hall where the family was standing with their arms wide open. They entered a room and prayed with my dad, letting him know that they forgave him. They felt it truly was an accident, and God was ready for her. To see such powerful forgiveness was life-changing. It changed how I treated situations in my own life where forgiveness was an issue. If this man and woman could embrace and pray with the man responsible for their loved one's death, how could I ever withhold forgiveness from someone for anything less? I had always known that God was good, and I knew God would use my dad's unique situation for good, but to be given the blessing of a family who completely forgave him was life-changing. Forgiveness was difficult and being forgiven lifted a weight off him.

Now, whenever my dad reads an article about someone else in a similar accident, he reaches out to them by sending them a letter or Facebook message citing 2 Corinthians 1:4 (NIV), "[God] comforts us in all of our troubles, so that we can comfort those in any trouble with the comfort we ourselves receive from God." My dad has since been able to offer many people comfort because of his own experience. Just because we are Christians doesn't mean we aren't going to experience hardships or struggles; however, if we can use those to help others and further God's glory, then we are doing our part.

Because of the life-changing forgiveness that was shown, I joined a Bible study, got baptized, and now have a relationship with God. If the accident had not happened, I doubt any of those things would have happened. I am way better at giving forgiveness. There truly have been some amazing things that came from this, not that I would ever wish it on anyone else.

From the very beginning, my dad wanted to do something meaningful for the victim's family. My dad had always loved going to the lake and boating. He referred to it as his happy place. He called my brother and me two years after the accident and told us that he was selling his pontoon boat to get a bigger boat, one that could fit all of the grandkids. He listed his old pontoon boat on Craigslist. My dad's name was not listed on the ad, just his phone number. The first person to text him was the husband of the woman he had hit. The man did not know it was my dad, but my dad had his name and number saved in his phone from when they had conversed several months after the accident. He said that he was answering the Craigslist ad and wondered if he could come to look at the boat. My dad told him who he was and said that he could come check it out. The man lived an hour away, and he and his son came to see the boat. They hugged and talked about the boat. My dad asked what he thought, and the husband replied that he had no idea why he answered this ad, as the boat was way too much for him to afford. My dad asked him what he wanted to do with it. He said he just wanted to spend time at the lake with his grandkids. Seeing this opportunity to do something for the family, my dad handed him the keys. My dad said that he had just one stipulation: to send a picture on the first day they used it.

I happened to be out on the lake one day with my dad when his phone pinged. He looked at the text, a tear sliding down his face. He handed me the phone, and I saw a picture of the husband and his family out on the boat. It was so comforting to my dad to see that the family was still living life, spending time, and making memories with each other, despite their loss. That moment was certainly a product of God, that otherwise would never have happened.

The example this family has set and the grace they gave to my dad was life-changing for everybody. The blessings of that experience were the kickstart for my faith. I hated feeling that way because it came at such an expense. However, God can do great things with great pain, "beauty from ashes," as the song said, and that use of a tragic accident to bring good into the community and closeness to Himself is just one example.

Aliyah's Story
Funny, But Not

I was in my final year at university (uni) in the United Kingdom when we went into lockdown due to COVID-19. I was having to study at home, and it was extremely difficult because I was in a full house, videoconferencing was not working well since it was so new, and I was struggling in my final-year courses without in-person teaching. I enjoyed working out at home because it gave me an outlet for the stress I had with my tough classes.

One day, I was trying to get some exercise while cleaning up. I was wearing headphones and dancing vigorously around my kitchen, and with a slight misstep, I dislocated my knee. When I told my friends how I had injured myself, they all laughed at what they imagined I must have looked like dancing as I cleaned. I must admit it was quite funny and I would have found it funnier if I had not had horrible pain. From that moment, I couldn't walk without limping, nor do any of the physical activities I was used to doing. This was a huge change for me because I am the type of person who has always been physically active. I was not one to be idle. I had to be moving around all day long. I also exercised to reduce anxiety and to promote good sleep, and now I couldn't do any of it.

I had several phone consultations and telehealth appointments since I couldn't see a doctor in person because of COVID-19. It was the worst possible time to hurt my knee. I was given some exercises to do to increase mobility, but for about five months, I spent most of the time sitting in one position because it hurt incredibly, and I could not walk well. I needed to heal.

I remained stagnant at my desk the majority of my days, studying for my classes while eating a lot of food because there was nothing I could do because of my injury and the lockdown. I was distraught by the pressure of school, my lack of mobility, and the pandemic. I began eating constantly, and I wasn't only eating an abundance of food but a lot of unhealthy food. I gained a lot of weight and my self-esteem plummeted.

I nearly quit school because it was so taxing, but something inside me told me to just go one day at a time and finish. I ended up passing my classes. I had never experienced the tough grind as I had during those few months. I had to find it deep within myself to push toward achieving that goal.

Because of the lockdown, I couldn't initially get the rehab I needed for my knee. After finishing uni, I could not bend my knee as the knee pain persisted, causing trouble with walking. I was frustrated with my limited mobility, so I borrowed some crutches from a friend. I thought if I pretended the injury didn't exist and kept moving, then it would be fine. Eventually, comprehending the extent of my injury, I got scared and somewhat depressed that my knee might be like this forever.

Once I could finally get in-person rehab, it was still difficult. I focused on getting healthy and thought more about what food I was putting in my body. I learned that I shouldn't give up and that I had to be patient with myself. I understood that I couldn't magically fix my knee, that it was going to take some time.

This little accident took half a second to happen and my life was drastically altered, but after a while, I realized that besides my knee, everything else with my body was healthy. I decided to be mindful of the good things in my life, even if that was just the basics. That mindset was so important for overcoming the physical and mental pain I was enduring. My knee has now healed, and I know it is such a blessing to be healthy and I will not take it for granted anymore.

Ashton's Story
Battered and Broken

When I was nineteen, I moved back in with my parents because I was switching to a college close to home. One evening, my friend Tonya, my cousin Connor, and his friend Steve picked me up to go riding, an activity that many of my family and friends did regularly. I told my mom I would be home by ten because I was to babysit my four-year-old brother the next morning.

On our ride, we went to a local ridge to do hill climbs. Tonya and I were in a side-by-side utility terrain vehicle (UTV) together; neither one of us was wearing a seat belt or helmet. We went up the hill climb, and when we were on our way back down, we slid into a muddy ditch, kicking the UTV sideways. I had enough time to yell, "Hold on!" as I realized we were going to wreck. We rolled down the hill, turning over and over about twenty times. Midway through the accident, Tonya landed on top of me. I was then thrown out of the vehicle, and the UTV briefly landed on top of me but continued to roll. I ran a couple of feet down the hill yelling for Tonya, who was still in the UTV, trying to determine if she was injured. I didn't initially feel any pain, but once I did, I immediately fell to the ground. Since I couldn't get to her, I screamed for her.

Fortunately, Tonya only had a slight shoulder injury. Connor and Steve ran to help me. I cried while my friends panicked because we had no cell service and no idea how to get me out of there. I was lying in a ditch in the middle of nowhere, a place virtually inaccessible for a regular vehicle. My cousin ended up riding his dirt bike to the closest house to call 911 and my mom. I told Connor to simply tell my mom that I had broken my leg so she wouldn't worry as much and to ask my dad to come to meet me. I was in that ditch for two hours waiting for the ambulance to get there, the pain inconceivable. My stomach began to swell, so I assumed I had internal bleeding, but at that point, I could not move anything from my hips down.

When the EMTs finally got to me, I was put on a stretcher and slid down the hill. They moved me into an ambulance, as it was too foggy to life-flight me out of that area. I was continually going in and out of consciousness, so they tried to keep me awake as we traveled to the nearest hospital, where my dad was waiting for me. An MRI confirmed my pelvis was shattered and that I had internal bleeding. I was to be transferred to a larger hospital in Pittsburgh. I cried out in pain as a wrap that resembled a rubber band was placed around my hips and pulled tight to keep everything in place and to stop the internal bleeding. My dad asked me to remain calm while I called my mom before I was transferred to the new hospital. It was difficult to hold it together while I spoke with her, especially because I felt guilty for getting injured and not being able to babysit for her. I was remorseful for making my parents go through this. The conversation with my mom was the last I remember until I woke up in the hospital in Pittsburgh. I had blacked out from the pain and the medications.

When I awoke, my dad was in a chair beside me and I was being prepped for surgery. I blacked out again and didn't wake again until after surgery, and when I did, I had a halo, a metal ring that encircled my hips affixed with two large pins, to stabilize my pelvis. When the doctor came to check on me after surgery, he told me that my pelvis had shattered into fifteen pieces; I was lucky to be alive. One of the major veins in my leg had been nicked and caused internal bleeding. It was centimeters away from the artery, and had that been severed, I would have died long before getting to the hospital. He also explained that I had a very long road to recovery ahead of me. I was concerned that I was going to be paralyzed, but he said that I would eventually walk again. The news that recovery was to begin with being bedridden for three to four months wrecked me.

While in the hospital, I started physical therapy, which didn't go well because the pain was overwhelming. I had to lie on my back in bed with the halo on, and I could not move my legs at the time. Since I couldn't get up to go to the bathroom, I had a catheter that remained during my entire recovery. The entire situation was miserable.

An ambulance had to bring me home since I couldn't sit in a car. My family and friends had put encouraging signs for me along the route home that I could see out of the back of the ambulance. When I arrived, all my friends and family were at my house, welcoming me home. My parents had a hospital bed in my room, and they had decorated, making the room warm and cheerful. My family had previously been experiencing some friction, but my accident brought everyone together again and made them realize what was most important in life.

It was difficult for me to remain in bed all the time and to rely on others to do everything for me. When I was at my lowest mentally, four of my friends showed up one night with movies, popcorn, candy, and drinks. They hung out with me for several hours, and I appreciated the laughter and how it made me feel normal again. Not only had I missed hanging out with my friends, but I had also been lonely in my misery.

My days were filled with taking medication (twenty-three pills each day), participating in physical therapy, and not being able to do much else. With the therapy, I was eventually able to sit up, but still could not move my legs or leave bed. My mom took care of me for the entire three months. It was a long three months, but my mom was a blessing, and I was incredibly grateful for her care.

About six weeks after my surgery, I was repeatedly getting sick, and the doctors could not figure out why. I went to the emergency room and learned that my medications, along with dehydration, were making me feel miserable. I got new medication and felt better soon thereafter. I had a second surgery two months after the first to remove the halo. When I returned home, I began to get sick again and my mom was up all night with me, but she was not feeling well either, so she went to wake my dad to come be with me. On the way, she passed out in the hallway and had a seizure. An ambulance took her to the hospital, and it was soon determined that stress was doing damage to her heart, but she was medically stable. That same day, an ambulance took me to the hospital because I continued to be sick. I was in kidney failure, again due to all of the medication I was taking. I stayed in the hospital for a week until my kidneys resumed their normal functioning.

At my next follow-up appointment with the surgeon, three months postsurgery, I was cleared to begin therapy to assist with trying to walk again. I came home, got out of my wheelchair, and refused to sit back down in it. I didn't want to ever again be confined as I had been the previous three months. I wanted to do whatever I could for myself and no longer rely on others. I did aqua therapy for two months at the local hospital until my insurance ran out. Then I learned to do things on my own.

I slowly started to live my life again. I fell in love and got married. We tried to get pregnant for years without success. I went to the doctor to see why, and it was because my left fallopian tube was injured during my accident and no longer worked. I was told that I only had a 0.1 percent chance of having a baby because of the fallopian tube and scar tissue from my accident. After trying for three and a half years, I scheduled an appointment to get oral infertility medication. A few weeks before that appointment, I found out I was pregnant. I was shocked, yet grateful, that it happened naturally. My miracle daughter was born later that year. Then I had a second daughter, another miracle, just eighteen months later.

Even though accidents happen every day, I never would have imagined this would happen to me, that my life would be changed in the blink of an eye. I am thankful to my surgeon for repairing my body. Without him and a successful hip repair, my life might have looked quite different in regard to walking, marriage, and children. I am thankful for the nurses, EMTs, and hospital staff, who were a big blessing to me in my journey to healing. I am not only thankful to be alive, but thankful to be living the full life I had always dreamed. I wake up every single day and thank God for allowing me to make it through the accident, for being able to physically get up and put one foot in front of the other, for being a mother, and for my happy, healthy life. I have often wondered why this happened to me and why I was given a second chance, but I know it brought my family back together, and when my children are old enough, I hope it will teach them the importance of patience, strength, and resilience when overcoming trials. This taught me to love fiercely and never walk out of the door angry. Life is a blessing, and I no longer take even one second for granted.

3

Illnesses and Conditions

My daughter recently got her braces off. When the orthodontist was looking at her final x-ray, she noticed something askew. We were shown the images and my stomach dropped when I saw that her lower left jaw had a piece missing. It looked as if someone had taken a small bite out of the bone. The orthodontist said she had never seen anything like it and was not going to speculate what it was, but it was abnormal. We needed to see an oral surgeon to better understand what was going on. The news was terrifying.

The orthodontist was able to speak to an oral surgeon, and we were squeezed in for an appointment the next day. We spent the next twenty-four hours in a state of fear. Was it cancer? Was it a cyst? Was it life-threatening? We worried. We fretted. We cried. And cried some more. We prayed. And prayed some more. We were beyond grateful to see the oral surgeon the next day to try to get some answers as quickly as possible because the unknown was nearly unbearable.

The surgeon completed a thorough physical examination and verbal medical history. She palpitated the area and felt bone, although it did not readily appear on the x-ray; however, upon looking closer at the 3D x-ray, she saw a thin layer of bone was faintly visible. While we were at the appointment, the surgeon received the x-rays from the previous few years and found that the spot had been there for at least three years (although nobody had noticed it previously), but it had grown. The surgeon asked many questions, trying to pinpoint a possible cause, and speculated that it could have been trauma, perhaps from my daughter hitting her face on a diving board years prior. After the examination, the surgeon told us that she was not worried about it but understood why we would be. She said she would need to do a biopsy to be completely sure she was correct in her assessment. As we were getting ready to leave the appointment, she assured us we did not need to worry because she was not worried, and that she would tell us if there were reasons to worry, but she saw none.

The biopsy surgery took place four weeks later. Then it took another two weeks to get the results. It was an agonizing time, even though we tried to remain hopeful since the surgeon was optimistic. I spent a lot of time in prayer and gained a sense of peace during the wait. Even though I remained calm and positive, it was a *long* six weeks!

The results of the biopsy were exactly as the surgeon suspected: bone cavity due to trauma. How can it be fixed? The surgeon had performed the technique to heal the area during the biopsy. Nothing more needed to be done at this time. Tears of joy!

I feel a little guilty because I know that we had it much easier than those who are diagnosed with chronic or terminal illnesses; however, it did not make it any less terrifying in the short term for my family when we were dealing with the unknown. Physical illnesses can bring emotional torment, especially in regard to the what-ifs. We are so grateful that my daughter's condition was treatable, and she is healthy at this time.

Every illness is different, and no story will be the same, even with similar diagnoses. The silver lining in your story may not be in healing like it was for my girl, but I am certain you will find some good if you wish to find it.

Tony's Story
Perfect Timing

My dad had an inherited liver disorder called alpha-1 antitrypsin deficiency, increasing his risk of lung and liver disease. Because of this, in the fall of 1997, when I was a junior in college, he needed a liver transplant. The first liver, unfortunately, was not viable. His situation was dire. The doctors were hoping to get another liver within twenty-four hours and thankfully, they did find one. He had two transplants within three days. Afterward, he continued to experience major complications and remained in the hospital for three months. It was a very difficult recovery for him. He never did return to work after this operation, nor return to perfect health.

Since my dad's liver disorder was genetic, there was a chance that my brother and I would have it as well, so I was tested not long after my dad's transplant. I was told that I didn't have the gene for the disease and thus, I assumed that I didn't have to worry about this being a possibility.

One evening in the fall of 2017, I walked into my garage and felt a pop in my foot. It hurt a great deal. The next morning it was not any better, so I went to see an orthopedic doctor. I was told that I had torn the plantar fasciitis ligament in my foot and needed to be in a boot for six weeks. While the orthopedic doctor was examining me, she noticed that my legs were extremely swollen. She asked if I had heart problems and I told her that I did not. The edema was so bad in my legs that she urged me to see my family doctor right away. I had never noticed the swelling. My family doctor was not concerned and thought the edema was probably due to being on my feet all day but decided to go ahead with blood work to be sure. The results showed that my platelet levels were dangerously low. This was a huge red flag to me because that was the exact marker that had showed up in my dad's blood work when he became ill.

I was referred to an oncologist and underwent a bone marrow biopsy, which came back normal. Then, because of my family history, they performed a liver biopsy. That is when I got my diagnosis: stage 4 liver cirrhosis. I was then referred to a gastroenterologist. He explained that this diagnosis did not necessarily mean that my life would be altered. Many people with this diagnosis can live their entire life in stage 4 cirrhosis. But if my liver stopped working, a liver transplant would be needed since there is no cure for this disease. After further testing, it was determined that I indeed had the same genetic disease as my dad: alpha-1 antitrypsin deficiency.

Fast forward to January 2019. I was feeling pretty good and had not been experiencing any symptoms. In hindsight, I can remember being a bit fatigued, but I chalked it up to being a parent with young children. In retrospect, it probably had to do with my liver not working as well as it should have.

I can remember the moment things changed. It was right after the New Year. I stood up from the couch and had a very strange sensation. It was like a release from my lungs, and I nearly passed out. I had to sit down after losing my breath and becoming dizzy. It scared me to the point that I went to the ER. They did not find anything wrong, and I was embarrassed that I had gone to the hospital. The doctor thought I was just lightheaded upon standing, so I came home.

That next week, I had trouble breathing. I thought I might have had bronchitis because I had always been susceptible to it. Looking back, I can deduce it was because my lungs were not functioning properly, another effect of alpha-1 antitrypsin deficiency. I am a professional singer, so my lungs are used a great deal. This probably helped me stay healthy as long as I did. I decided to go to urgent care because my right lung was hurting so badly. I did a breathing treatment and it didn't help, even though it normally helped me in the past when I have had bronchitis. I also had an x-ray done. Results showed my entire right lung was surrounded by fluid, but there was no fluid inside my lungs. This fluid around the lung is called a pleural effusion. I was told to go to the hospital immediately. In that ER visit, I had more chest x-rays done. Nobody was connecting the dots at this time that this was liver-related. I was told I needed to have a thoracentesis, a procedure to drain the fluid. I was not put to sleep, but they numbed my back and used a needle to get the fluid out of my body. It was extremely painful even though they had numbed the area. When it was over, I remember thinking that I hoped to never have that done again.

For the next week or so, I felt great. I followed up with my liver doctor, but still, nobody made the connection between what had just happened to me and the liver disease. The liver doctor said that he hoped the thoracentesis did the trick. One week later, I felt the same sensation on my right side with lung pain and trouble breathing. I knew it had to be the exact same thing. I called my doctor and they scheduled me for another thoracentesis. These two procedures drained about two liters of fluid each time. Then the fluid buildup started happening more frequently. It started out happening every ten to twelve days and then it became every seven days, and eventually, I was going three times a week to get the fluid drained. At that point, they were getting four to six liters of fluid out of me each time.

It progressed to the point that it became evident that my liver was not working. The liver is on the right side of the body and is supposed to be the body's filter. When it cannot function or filter correctly, the fluid goes elsewhere. For most people, it goes to the abdomen, and their belly swells. But for others, like myself, the fluid goes up through the diaphragm, which is porous, and it continues straight up the right side of the body and around the lung.

Around mid-March, my GI doctor determined that these pleural effusions were indeed happening because of my liver, so he referred me to the transplant team at the University of Cincinnati, which is not only close to my home, but also one of the top hospitals in the country for liver transplants.

At this point, I was having a thoracentesis so often that it was taking its toll on me. I was turning very yellow and becoming jaundiced. I had no energy and was incredibly sick.

Around April 1, I started the process to get listed for a liver transplant. I had to go through all kinds of testing to be approved by the hospital and UNOS, the United Network for Organ Sharing, to be on the national list. It can take quite a bit of time to complete all of the necessary steps to be placed on this list. It took about a month for the testing and approval. We also had to have a living will to be placed on the list. We knew the risks: one in twenty, or 5 percent, do not survive a liver transplant. We also planned my funeral, down to the songs that were to be sung, because I did not want my wife, Joy, to have to deal with that if I didn't make it.

By May 1, I was on the liver transplant list. The process for an organ transplant is based on a MELD score (Model for End-stage Liver Disease), on a scale of 0 to 40. This number determines your place in line for a liver. Zero is someone with no liver issues, and 40 is someone on death's door. They will do a transplant for anyone with a MELD score of 13 or above, and my score was fairly high, in the midtwenties, so I was placed in line for a liver. What liver you get and when you get a liver is based on the MELD score along with blood type, quality of life, and body size.

At this point, I was still getting a thoracentesis every Monday, Wednesday, and Friday because it was completely uncomfortable to breathe. I would have this procedure done in the morning and would feel better for about half of a day, and then I could feel the fluid filling up around my lung again. These procedures became more painful. They were hard on my lung because when they were draining the fluid out, my lung would often collapse. There was concern that my lung would never recover from the trauma of having this done so many times. I ended up having a total of fifty-three thoracentesis procedures.

Because this was so frequent, it bumped me up on the transplant list. In addition to the MELD score, doctors can request bonus points to move a patient up on the list based on quality of life. The doctors were concerned about other risks I faced: I might get infections, my lungs might not recover, and my quality of life was rapidly declining.

When I got on the list on May 1, I was told by my team at the hospital that I would probably get a liver quickly. The team included a coordinator who is my point person for communication and the one who would call if a liver became available.

During this time, there was a situation that created a lot of angst for my family. My wife, who is a professor, had agreed to teach a study abroad program in Austria in the summer of 2019. She was supposed to leave on May 25 and return on June 25. We had to decide if she would continue with this commitment that she had made over a year earlier. We knew I could get the call for a transplant while she was away. Months earlier we had decided that she would take our daughter with her, and I was excited for this opportunity for both of them. We discussed this with our surgeons, and the best piece of advice we got from them is that we cannot stop living our lives. There is no guarantee when this would happen. If we would get the call, Joy and my daughter were just a plane flight away. After receiving this advice, we decided that Joy would fulfill this commitment. I was sick, but I could still drive and take care of my son. Even though I couldn't work and I spent most of my time in a horizontal position on the couch, I was well enough to still care for myself and my son.

I would never have said no to a call saying they had a liver available for me, although a person can reject a call when it comes. I was praying that I wouldn't get the call while my wife and daughter were gone; however, four days before they were to come home, I did receive my first call. We were warned in the process that we could get multiple calls, meaning something might not work out after initially getting the call; thus, it could be a roller-coaster ride of emotions along the way.

When I got this call from my coordinator, the first thing she asked me was if Joy was back from her time away. I told her that she was not home yet but was scheduled to fly back in four days. She said that they might have a liver for me that day. My heart was racing. Another thing that was simultaneously happening was my son was away at summer camp that week and I was to drive and pick him up that day. As my mind was trying to figure out a way to get him from camp, my coordinator explained that the liver might match with me, but I was second in line for it. There was another person ahead of me, but that person had liver cancer. If they went into surgery and found cancer had spread to other organs, they would not transplant the liver to him and I would get the liver. The coordinator told me she would let me know in a couple of hours. I was thankful for the potential opportunity but was also thinking that it could not have come on a worse day. I also had a thoracentesis scheduled that day and the coordinator told me to go ahead and proceed with that, but to make arrangements for someone else to pick up my son at camp.

I texted Joy and told her not to do anything yet, but we would be in touch. I am glad that she did not jump on the next flight out because it did not work out for me to get a liver that day, and thankfully, for the other man, he was able to get his liver. I was able to go pick up my son at camp. Four days later, my wife and daughter returned home from Austria.

My second call came in mid-July. We were at a baseball game on a Friday night. I was feeling so lousy during the game that I went out to our van and lay down in the back. My phone rang, and my coordinator said they had a liver for me and asked if I could get to the hospital in the next two hours. It is strange because I was expecting and hopeful that a call would come, but when it happened, I was shocked. I texted my wife, and we left the game and dropped my kids off with their grandparents. I had a bag packed (I was told to always have one packed), so we raced home to get the bag. On the way, I got another call from the coordinator stating that something may have come up, and they may not need me after all. We continued to make preparations, but when the coordinator called back, she said that someone that was sicker than me had jumped ahead of me in line for the liver, so it was not going to work out that night for me to get the transplant. It was quite a letdown after getting so hyped up.

Life went on, and I continued to have thoracentesis every other day. Every time my phone rang, my heart would skip a beat because I never knew when a call might come.

One week later, on the morning of July 24, my coordinator called to let me know they had a liver for me. She said it was not a huge hurry for me to get to the hospital, but to get there around 4:00 p.m. We got ready, dropped the kids off with Joy's parents. When we got to the hospital, they were waiting for me, and I went straight to my room. I got a chest x-ray and a couple of other tests. We were told the surgery was planned for the next morning between 5:00 and 6:00 a.m. When the surgeon was not there by six, we talked with the nurse. She said that as far as she knew, the transplant was still happening. We knew the liver was being flown in and once it got to the hospital, it had to be biopsied to ensure it was viable. Just after 6:00 a.m. the surgeon came in and said he was very sorry, but the transplant was canceled. They had received the liver, but after testing, it was determined that it did not meet their standards. This was incredibly heart-wrenching. After getting the call and staying overnight in the hospital, we thought it was going to happen. We were devastated.

I was discouraged, questioning why we must go through all of this, but we believe that often God works in ways we cannot see.

We went home and thought that the transplant will happen when it happens, regardless of how much we wanted it. I had an endoscopy scheduled on August 1 to band varices on my esophagus related to my liver disease. We had checked in for that procedure and my coordinator called. She said they had a liver for me. They told me not to get the endoscopy done because they did not want me to go under anesthesia since they would have to put me under again for the transplant. We went from one hospital to another and settled into the room and had the chest x-ray and a few tests again. The surgeon came in and said, "I think this is going to happen, but I may have called you in a little too soon because we have a donor but there may be more organs that we can use from this donor so it may take a little longer." Donors generally have had some sort of accident and are brain dead but kept alive on a machine for as long as possible so that the organs remain viable. They needed time to find recipients for each organ and get them to the hospital. The staff was also working with the family who was deciding to take their loved one off of life support. There is an incredible amount of logistics, combined with the grief of a family, involved in the process of organ donation.

The surgeon told us that since we were local, we could go home, but he preferred that we stay. I decided we would stay. By midday of August 2, I was told that surgery would probably be around 1:00 a.m. on August 3, and that is indeed what happened. It took approximately nine hours to perform the transplant. The liver I received was from a woman who was exactly my age, in perfect health, and the surgeons deemed it a perfect liver. Out of all of the surgeons at the hospital that are part of the liver transplant team, we got the one who is world-renowned. I feel I got the best of the best: the best liver and the best surgeon. It reminded me that when I am disappointed and discouraged, God has the best intentions. He sees the big picture. When I thought my first, second, and third calls were the ones and then was disappointed, I now know it was God saying, "Wait, I've got something better in store for you."

Even though my wife and I are private with our personal lives, we did make my condition public on social media because we believe in the power of prayer. People can't pray for what they don't know about. All through this process, I felt this sense of peace. I was never afraid, even though I had seen what my dad went through. My biggest concern in this whole process was the fact that I would have to be on a ventilator. The doctors had prepared me by letting me know that most people after surgery are on a vent for a couple of days. The thought of waking up and having that was my biggest dread, but God was so gracious and my surgery went so well that they were able to remove the vent while I was in the operating room before I even woke up. That was an extra blessing in this entire experience.

The surgery went splendidly and afterward, I was released to go home after only five days in the hospital. I was told that some people are there for ninety days after the same surgery. I was on a lot of medication when I was sent home and have been weaned off of most of it, except for the anti-rejection and immune suppression medications, which I will remain on for the rest of my life. Recovery has been great. I am coming up on my one-year "liver-versary," and I feel the best I have felt in years.

There is an organization in town that works with transplant hospitals and organ donation organizations to coordinate organ distribution. It also coordinates donor families and recipients. They are a middleman. For instance, if a donor family wants to meet a recipient family, they must go through this center. There is a substantial process involved and both parties must agree on the level of communication wanted or not wanted. Nobody is obligated in any way to participate. Usually, if any communication is involved, it takes several months, but I was surprised to receive a letter just three weeks after my surgery. It stated that my donor family wanted to communicate with me. I gladly gave my permission. A week later, I received two letters in the mail from two young girls. We do not know their names, but based on their handwriting, we are guessing one was around fourth grade and one in middle school. Their letters explained that my liver had come from their mommy. They talked about how their mom always loved to help people. They knew that even though she was gone, she was still helping others. It was unbelievably emotional. I have such a sense of gratitude to be given another chance at life, but it is a strange feeling that someone had to die so that I could live, which is quite the parallel to the Gospel. It brings mixed emotions, but a definite sense of gratefulness. It was not that this lady's life ended because of me, but my chance of living came at a cost. I am also left with a sense of responsibility to take care of myself physically more than I ever did because I want to protect this organ and not waste my life in any manner—not that I did before—but I was given a rare opportunity.

Looking back at everything, I appreciate God's hand in *all* of this, from the torn ligament in my foot to getting the perfect liver with the ultimate surgeon. Although at times I thought my world was falling apart, I realize now that God knows the bigger picture, and as Scripture says, He works all things for the good of those that love him.

Jackie's Story
Not Again!

I am Jackie, and I hold many titles: wife, mother of four, daughter, sister, friend, godmother, and preschool director. The other title that has shaped who I am is two-time cancer survivor.

When I was fifteen, I was diagnosed with thyroid cancer. I was a sophomore in high school, lying in bed one night, when I felt a lump on my neck. My mom felt it, but she simply assumed my lymph nodes were slightly swollen, so we thought nothing more about it. A few weeks later, we were out to dinner, and my mom noticed the lump on my neck from across the table. It appeared more prominent than weeks prior. She took me to the doctor the next day and a biopsy was done.

By the time I got examined, the lump was large and cancer had spread to lymph nodes. I had no other symptoms besides the noticeable lump. Even though they told me this cancer was easily curable, and I should not worry, it was terrifying. I was a young girl who was overwhelmed by this diagnosis and the unknown of what

I was about to walk through. I spent the next three years having surgeries, treatments, and countless scans. I had three major surgeries, including having my entire thyroid and the lymph nodes on the right side of my neck removed. In the third surgery, my sternum was cracked open and the lymph nodes in that area were removed. I also had radioactive iodine treatments, not chemotherapy, which didn't have any side effects, but it wasn't easy to deal with as a teenager. I got through this challenging time with three powerful Ps: positivity, prayer, and people (my support system).

Even though I could say I beat cancer after those three years, I followed up at the Mayo Clinic for the next twenty years, getting scans and tests done every visit. They were not finding cancer, and I wasn't receiving any further treatments, but there wasn't enough evidence to say the cancer was eradicated. I was being monitored to ensure nothing was changing. Finally, in May 2018, I got the all-clear; I didn't have to return for scans nor have to worry about this for the rest of my life.

The following month, my four children were having a playdate with seven friends at our home. At the end of the fun day, when parents started to pick up the children, I began having severe abdominal pain. I thought it was either gas pain or a stomachache from the sweet treats I had indulged in with the children, but it kept getting worse. When my husband got home from work, I was in a cold sweat and could not stand up because the pain was so intense. To not worry my kids or the three additional children left at the playdate, my husband stayed home while my mom took me to the emergency room.

The doctor speculated that I had a gallbladder attack. I had never had this happen before, but the pain was worse than labor pains. I couldn't take a deep breath and I was highly uncomfortable. After several hours, some pain medication, and a few scans, the emergency room physician told me that I had a gallbladder attack, but I also had renal cell carcinoma. Even though I am not a medical professional, I knew carcinoma was merely a fancy word for cancer. I could not believe I had kidney cancer and was confused, angry, and sad. How could I have cancer again when I was just declared cancer-free the month prior?

Unfortunately, all of the scans done at Mayo Clinic ended right above my kidneys. We may have found it sooner had they been scanning more than just my chest, but I couldn't fret about what could have been. I had to focus on fighting this new cancer.

All of those same feelings of fear and uncertainty that I had at fifteen came rushing back. The difference now was I was concerned about my husband and four kids, not just myself. My mind immediately wandered to all the potential scenarios. Still, I decided I needed to stay positive, believe it would be okay, and know that my family could make it through this.

The surgery to remove my kidney took place three long months after my diagnosis. The waiting was hard for all of us and I noticed my daughter, who was in third grade, started to experience anxiety. As much as I had tried to stay positive and sugarcoat my diagnosis, so it didn't seem as bad as it was, it was still frightening. I tried to teach my kids by example how to have a positive mindset, even when things were scary and not going our way. I tried to exude faith over fear.

My gallbladder and right kidney were finally removed, in the same surgery. I had the support of many family and friends during this time, including many people praying for me. Once again, I got through this cancer battle with the three Ps: positive attitude, prayer, and people. Family and friends were my hands and feet, taking care of my family and me when I was unable. They lifted us and helped where needed. I found my strength and inspiration in them.

After recovering from surgery, I didn't have to have any further treatments. I endured this ordeal by accepting what I was dealing with while I kept moving forward with a bright outlook. I continued to have scans regularly but remained healthy and cancer-free.

As a full-time mom with a full-time job, I used to get bogged down in the hustle and bustle of the day-to-day, but now, as cliche as it sounds, I want to be sure I am living every day to its fullest. When I lay my head on my pillow at night, I take the time to look for the good in that day and find the blessings in life. I would have preferred not to have cancer *twice*, but the way I live my life now is because I have survived cancer *twice*. I am very grateful for that perspective, which is one not many people get. I make sure I instill these important lessons in my children. They do not have to have cancer to have a hard life, but I hope they will remember that the three powerful Ps will sustain them through whatever trials they face.

Gerri's Story
From Healthy to Hurting

I have enjoyed good health for much of my life. I have done aerobics, worked out at the gym, and eaten reasonably healthily along the way. Around ten years ago, I began having medical issues.

One day, I started experiencing a terrible headache. It was so painful that I even emailed a friend and explained how I couldn't get rid of it. After typing the email, I went downstairs, where my husband sat reading with his back to me. I went to give him a hug when my head felt like it was hit with a baseball bat. I don't remember much after that. I later found out that I had a cerebral hemorrhage and an aneurysm. I needed to undergo two brain surgeries. Whether or not I would live was dicey. I was in intensive care for several days and in the hospital for over three weeks.

I am convinced that if events had not aligned as they did that day that I would not be alive right now. My husband was usually not home at that time of day, but he happened to be there. Also, if I had been upstairs when it struck, who knows how long it would have taken my husband to find me. In addition, the ambulance came quickly, and we happened to live close to the hospital.

After my surgeries, I didn't have many repercussions aside from infrequent headaches the first few years, along with minor hearing loss. I do have some lingering word retrieval problems, especially when tired. Occupational therapy taught me a few memory tricks so that these problems do not hinder me as much. It took six months to recover, but overall, my recuperation went well. The worst part for me was that this happened the day before school started, and I was a kindergarten teacher. It was essential for continuity for the teacher to be there all year, and I didn't get to meet my students at first. I did end up going back part-time for a bit and eventually full-time that year as I recovered. I feel blessed that I came out of this life-threatening condition primarily unharmed.

Five years ago this spring, I was at the dermatologist getting a regular checkup, and I happened to mention that my breast was itching all the time, even though there wasn't anything on it. She immediately sent me for a mammogram, even though I wasn't due for one. After I had it done, they called me back for additional testing, which they normally do because of my dense breast tissue. Unfortunately, this time I was diagnosed with breast cancer. I had surgery to remove the lump then had an additional operation because the margins weren't clear after the first surgery, meaning there were still cancer cells at the outer edge of the tissue removed. I now tell my dermatologist that she saved my life. My breast cancer was caught early, so I did not need chemo, only radiation. I had a short, high-intensity round of radiation that lasted about three weeks, and I was later cleared of cancer.

Then, a couple of years later, I was cooking dinner and started to notice some indigestion. Suddenly, I started throwing up. Hurrying to the bathroom, I undressed because I was overheating, covered in sweat. My husband, home again when he usually would not have been, came running. I explained that I was having severe pain that I thought might have been indigestion, but I soon began projectile vomiting. He drove me to the emergency room, which I later learned was a terrible idea. The chest pain grew worse on the way there, and I told him I was having a heart attack. When I got to the window in the emergency room, I told the staff that I was having chest pain that felt like indigestion. I was whisked away for an EKG. The hospital was out of wheelchairs, so they strapped me to an office chair and wheeled me down the hallway. I felt the stares of confused staff and patients as I rolled by, almost as if in a parade. I wanted to wave to the onlookers, but the pain overpowered that urge.

The staff was fantastic, and the ER was a well-oiled machine that quickly got me the help I needed. The nurse told my husband and me to say our goodbyes; they took me to the cardiac cath lab. Because of the way she phrased it to us, I asked if I was going to die. She clarified, "No, no, no. You are just going to the lab." The pain was getting worse at this point. I was awake as they put the stent in. When they finished the procedure, the doctor said the pain should be alleviating, but I told him it wasn't, so I once again asked if I would die. He started on an in-depth explanation of what was happening, but I just wanted him to tell me that I would be okay. After the stent placement, I continued to have issues with fatigue and shortness of breath, so they decided to insert another stent. I was only hospitalized for three days. I did get to the hospital early in the attack, so there was minor permanent damage to my heart.

I have been healthy ever since. My husband was wonderful and supportive through all of my issues. I was also blessed to have two wonderful dogs. I feel like I would not have gotten through all of this without the joy they brought me. People should never underestimate the comfort of pets.

Two wonderful things came from these health problems. I am part of a program for breast cancer survivors that allows me to chat with other women in the same situation. After my heart attack, I also participated in cardiac rehab. I met three other women with whom I became very close, and we call ourselves "the cardiac girls." We get together every few weeks for lunch and to walk together, and the presence and support of these women has been abundantly beneficial to my mental well-being.

On account of all of my health issues, I don't like asking God for things; instead, I tell Him thanks each morning when I wake, something I never did previously. I now harbor more gratitude and feel incredibly blessed. I've had a bit of a medical adventure, but I am thankful to be healthy at last.

Christie's Story
Grateful for Each Day

When I married Jason in 2008, I already had two daughters, Leslee and Lauren, from a previous relationship. Jason was a firefighter but took a new, less time-consuming job to be home more often. Unfortunately, he was almost immediately moved to a job site two hours away from home. He would leave on Sundays, be gone all week, and arrive home on Friday evening. The girls and I would go visit him when we could.

In 2011, Jason was back working at the local fire department, and we were relieved that he no longer had to travel constantly. He had hurt his back, so his primary care physician sent him to have an MRI done. That evening, his doctor called to give us the results. She said nothing was wrong with his back that physical therapy could not fix, but the radiologist accidentally scanned too high and found something in his brain. This had to have been more than a simple accident, and I believe that the nurse finding this was the touch of God in our lives.

We got the news on Thursday and didn't sleep much that night. The brain scans were done first thing on Friday morning, and that afternoon his doctor called to tell us the results, instead of waiting the whole weekend. She didn't know what exactly was there, but it was something. I cried my eyes out after hearing this news.

On the following Monday afternoon, we received a call from a neurosurgeon. He scheduled to see us the next day, telling us that we should not worry: He saw patients with this disease all the time. I was not satisfied with the diagnosis he gave or the information I received. Jason's daddy suffered from cluster headaches and had a world-re-nowned neurologist. Jason's mom called that doctor to explain what was going on and to ask if they could squeeze him in their schedule. That neurologist instructed us to bring him the next day, which was highly unusual and concerning. She was a busy doctor, and appointments were typically scheduled *months* in advance. We were beyond grateful for her agreeing to see Jason so promptly. He had more scans done. She told Jason his diagnosis was a tumor, a combination of glioblastoma and astrocytoma. It was rare to have two in one. We asked if the tumor needed to be removed; she said that it did not. Most of the time, these were benign. She planned to watch it closely and not take any action unless it grew, so he continued to have scans regularly.

In 2014, Jason was offered a job with a railroad company. We thought this would be a lifelong job. Immediately, he was on the road again, only home on the weekends; however, we could go out and visit him when he was away.

In March 2015, Jason had the scans done again. The doctor called the next day, instructing us to see her the following day, a Saturday. It was not unheard of to have an appointment with her on the weekend since she generally worked seven days a week. When we arrived, we learned that Jason's tumor had quadrupled in size. It was now the size of a Rubik's cube, while it had started the size of a silver dollar. She explained that it had to be removed as soon as possible. He was put on steroids and scheduled for surgery at the end of April.

After the procedure, the surgeon informed me that Jason had done well and was in recovery. However, he warned us that Jason might not recognize the girls or me, and he might not remember where he was or what had happened. Later, when I got a call from the recovery room nurse for an update, Jason snatched the phone from the nurse and asked, "Hey, doll, how are you?" I was able to see him about four hours later. I didn't recognize him with all of the bandages on his head, but he did remember me and was doing well.

He was supposed to stay in the hospital for about a week, but we were home in three days. We had his follow-up appointment a few weeks later. It was confirmed that it was cancer, glioblastoma. We learned that this was most likely what was going to take his life.

The same week that we got the diagnosis, the railroad told him that he could not come back. Thankfully, they did agree to pay us for insurance, which was helpful since Jason started chemo in June.

I never got a college degree; I have always been a farm girl. I learned how to raise cows and horses, but not chickens, due to an allergy. Before Jason went to work on the railroad, he looked to get some chicken houses as a potential for income. That was the biggest fight that I ever had with him. I explained how my eyes would swell, and I could not breathe when I was around chickens. He finally stopped talking about it around the time he went to work for the railroad. After he lost that job and started chemo, I was the one who brought up the idea of getting chicken houses.

I made a phone call to an agricultural realtor who said he had a piece of property he wanted to show us an hour and a half away from us. I was concerned about the location because my family and Jason's doctors were conveniently close to us. We visited the property, and I instantly fell in love with it and its owners. We decided to buy it, but we learned that you cannot rush an agricultural loan, which could take a year. We started the process of purchasing the property in July and I signed for it in October. Everything was falling into place.

My daddy came over from Georgia to help with the move since Jason still couldn't do much while on chemo. We bought our first batch of chickens in December. Within the first week, I asked Jason, "What have we done?" We had made some upgrades to the farm prior to getting the chickens, but the new systems clashed with the old ones, and alarms kept going off to indicate low pressure or temperature. We ended up staying in our camper next to the chicken houses that week because even the short drive from our home to the chicken houses was too much for me to handle alone. Jason couldn't do much work because he was still feeling bad from the chemotherapy. I often cried for our situation and worried that we would have to sell this place so soon after buying it. I doubted that we could handle all that needed to be done.

After much consideration, I called our banker and explained that we needed to do more upgrades, requesting another loan. We were able to get the upgrades, and finally, the farm was working smoothly. I could handle working with the chickens now that the systems were operating correctly and my allergy medicine was working.

In spring 2018, my daddy was visiting, checking out the farm. By that time, we owned five chicken houses and were discussing building a sixth. We started clearing the land, and the bids were made. My daddy talked his wife, Linda, into moving close to us to help when needed. In August 2018, the newest chicken house was completed, and in September, we obtained our latest batch of birds. Daddy and Linda were helping, and everything was proceeding smoothly.

In June 2019, Jason's scans revealed new growth. The plan was to do thirty-five radiation treatments. We saw a specialist who could do the treatments locally instead of driving two hours each way. On the day of Jason's thirtieth treatment, his head hurt. He had been driving himself to his treatments up to that point, but that day, I asked if he wanted Lauren to drive him. He agreed, even though she only recently had gotten her license. When he came home from the treatment, he lay down to rest, which was unlike him.

The following morning when he got up, he did not recognize me or the house, and I immediately panicked. It took an hour to convince him to get into the truck with me. I took him straight to the radiation doctor, and they sent us to the local hospital. The chickens at home needed to be cared for, and thankfully daddy was able to help while we were away. The doctors quickly started the scans. Later, the doctor asked to speak with me in the hallway. He said that Jason had a brain tumor and that I needed to get our affairs in order. I told him that he needed to read Jason's chart, as we had been dealing with the tumor since 2011, but I needed him to figure out what was going on now because his confusion and memory loss were new. We didn't see that doctor again. The next doctor we saw thought Jason had some swelling from the radiation, so he put Jason on a steroid and sent us home.

When we got home, our pastor and Jason's best friend both came by. Jason didn't recognize either of them. We needed to wait until the steroids kicked in before we would see any changes. The next morning, Jason's sister tried to get him to eat ice cream, which Jason thought was an attempt to poison him. I knew we needed to get further medical clarification, so we drove him two hours away to a bigger hospital. The following day, Jason's mom and I were with him when he had a seizure and coded. He had never had a seizure, which made this experience all the more terrifying. Jason was a big man, 6 feet tall and 280 pounds, so it took fourteen nurses and five security guards to hold Jason down on the bed. He coded again, and the staff took him down the hall. I had no idea if he was dead or alive. They instructed us to go to the ICU and wait. While there, I started making phone calls to Lauren, Leslee and Leslee's boyfriend, Austin. Within a couple of hours, my whole family was at the hospital with me. When I finally got an update, we were told that Jason was on a ventilator, and they wanted to put in a PICC line, to which I consented. He stayed on that vent for seven awful days. On day eight, when they were weaning him off the vent, he was awake but still tubed and unable to speak. His best friend John Albert and I were there, and I asked if he knew who I was. He shook his head no. I lay my head on his chest and began to cry. I heard John Albert say to Jason, "I am going to kill you." I raised my head to see Jason smiling and winking at his friend. I was flooded with relief that he recognized us.

They put Jason in a regular room on day nine, and he came home on day 27. Before leaving the hospital, he was put on new medicine that put him in a catatonic state for two weeks. He only got up when we helped him to use the bathroom and shower. He started getting blood clots, so we ended up back in the ICU for a week. He went from taking no medicine to needing several pills both morning and night.

Jason's tumor was still there, and he remained weak. I needed help at home, so I moved Austin into an upstairs bedroom to assist. Not long after that Austin came to Jason and me, asking if he could marry Leslee. Jason told him that he could marry her on two conditions: Love her as he himself did and never hurt her.

Jason helped Austin plan the proposal. Jason still couldn't drive, so one day when I was taking him to a store, he told me to pull over, seemingly at random. It was a bridal store. He entered and said to them that he needed the most beautiful cathedral veil that they had in stock. He had always heard Leslee say that was the kind of veil she wanted. The salesclerk brought one out, and it was indeed beautiful, so Jason bought it.

Jason had always been a little rough around the edges, but after his experience with the tumor, he softened up. On Christmas, Jason propped up a large mirror in the living room, and Austin had his grandmother's ring in hand. We blindfolded Leslee and put the veil on her. When she opened her eyes, Austin was under the veil, down on his knee with the ring. Jason said the sweetest words to them: "God kept me around here for lots of reasons, but one of them is to see my girls get married."

Jason was still not allowed to drive, so I drove us to a venue nearby that we had always heard Leslee say was where she wanted to get married. He asked the manager what he needed to book the place, which was simply a deposit. Jason opened his wallet, got a check, and told me to write it out for the deposit. I didn't know what date they wanted to get married. According to the manager, it did not matter because she had all of June open, which I knew to be the month Leslee preferred.

We didn't tell Austin and Leslee what we had done. We took them to the venue that evening and hung out at the gazebo. Leslee sat there, googly-eyed, and said that she would love to have her wedding there someday. Jason responded, "Well, you are." Many happy tears were shed that evening.

Jason said that God had him here so that he could walk his daughter down the aisle in June. He also said that God had been one step ahead of us the whole way. Every time we thought we had reached the end, God had other plans. I often cried about Jason's diagnosis, but I now know that Jason lives on borrowed time, so we see the time we have together as the best time ever. This tragedy has turned into a massive blessing, bringing our family closer than ever. It brought my daddy back to me, after I had not seen him much since my parents divorced. Thanks to Linda, he again became a part of our lives.

The diagnosis gave Jason a new outlook. We learned how precious life is. We don't know what tomorrow holds, but we try not to worry; rather, we thank God for the joy we experience each day. We still have scans every eight to twelve weeks because Jason's cancer remains aggressive. Treatment continues every two weeks. However, Jason is alive, and we spend all of our days together, which I would not give up for the world.

I see life differently now. I know I have plenty to be sad about but am not. I could curl up and cry some days, but I see Jason and am reminded of my gratitude that he is here because I know he won't be one day. Cancer has taken much from me, and it will in the future; however, the experience has given me more: a reason and an opportunity to rejoice in every day I spend with my family.

Jeanne's Story
Praying for Healing

Three years ago, I was diagnosed with triple-negative breast cancer at the age of seventy-eight. I have always understood the importance of getting mammograms and thus have been diligent about getting them done. I found the lump in my breast one month before my scheduled mammogram. When I got the diagnosis, I thought triple-negative sounded like a good kind of cancer to have, but I was wrong. The origins of this cancer are unknown and it is fast-growing.

Upon learning about my diagnosis, many people prayed for me. I quickly went into treatment. One lady at our church, who I am pretty sure is an angel, brought me a journal with "Live Life Inspired" on the front cover. She told me that this book was meant to be used to write down my blessings. I secretly wondered if she was crazy. I was in the hospital with breast cancer, and she wanted me to write about blessings?

When she left, I pondered her suggestion and eventually decided to start writing. I wrote in the journal throughout my treatment, and in doing so, I realized that I was blessed far more than I was hurting. It was helpful to be cognizant of the good happening to me along the way.

The first blessing I wrote about was that I never had a problem getting appointments. It seemed the road was paved so I could navigate it easily.

To get my diagnosis, I underwent an MRI and needle biopsy. I had to lie flat on my stomach with my breasts down through little canisters while my arms were straight over my head. I couldn't move at all while the machine was working. They had to put dye in me and use a needle to get what they needed for the biopsy. I was nervous about going through this. I remember lying there on the table, praying, "Lord, you are just going to have to hold my hand through this." When I was in the correct position on the table, the nurses left the room because they could not be there during the MRI. After they left, someone came up to me, held my hand, and said, "Your nails look so pretty!" I thought, *God, You didn't have to physically take my hand*, but I took this as a sign of His presence with me during this procedure. I still have no idea who took my hand, but I must believe they were heaven-sent because of how much I needed that small reassurance.

A lady from my church was a surgical nurse and she offered to be my nurse during surgery, which I greatly appreciated. She was able to recommend an anesthesiologist whom she had seen pray over patients. I thought that sounded wonderful. I also knew another lady from church who was a semi-retired nurse navigator, who offered to be my personal navigator. It was nice to have ladies I knew be a part of my treatment.

After telling people about my diagnosis, I often heard that I was their reminder to get their annual mammograms. I hoped that some good could come from my disease and was glad to see that some had.

My son and daughter-in-law came into town for my first chemo treatment and spent five hours with me. They even canceled their fall trip so that they could be with me. My daughter-in-law was also a recent breast cancer survivor. She was a blessing to me for the duration of my struggle. I am also thankful that my daughter, who doesn't live far from me, would drive to almost every appointment with me. It was incredibly uplifting to have family caring for me.

My friends from college wore pink bracelets to support me. They were all praying for me, along with numerous others. I felt their prayers every time I went in for treatment. Perhaps I should have been nervous about undergoing all the treatments, but I never was. I felt peace from all the love, support, and prayers. There is no way that I could have done this on my own.

My neighbors raked leaves in my yard and retrieved my mail for me. It was little things like this that I genuinely appreciated. People were incredibly kind to me.

A friend of mine I used to teach with has worn a wig for years because she has alopecia. I knew that I was going to lose my hair, and she recommended a particular wig shop. I went there and those women were incredible, helping me pick out the perfect wig.

When I started losing my hair, it was an itchy mess. The hair went everywhere, and I looked ugly. I was glad to get it shaved off. The lady that shaved it for me generously didn't make me pay. After this, some friends brought me caps to wear so my head would not get cold.

I learned that there were perks of losing my hair and wearing a wig. I did not have to keep shampoo, conditioner, or hairspray on hand, nor need a comb or brush. It was no longer required to shave my legs. I didn't have to pay to get my hair cut and styled, so that all saved money. My "hair" always looked great and it acted like a hat in the winter, keeping my head warm.

After a couple of treatments, I felt sick, so my son, daughter-in-law, and two grandchildren stayed with me on the weekends to help care for me. They would fix whatever food I felt like eating. I would tell them what sounded good, but I often couldn't eat it when I put it in my mouth. I felt terrible about that since they went to all of the work of making meals for me. Even though I didn't have much appetite, it was nice to have them there to help when I felt miserable.

In December of that year, I realized that I had partially lost my vision. I didn't know that chemotherapy could have that effect. After each treatment, I was experiencing different side effects. I began laughing about it and would sarcastically say that I could hardly wait to see what would happen after the next treatment. I am incredibly grateful that I was never nauseous during all the treatments.

The following May, after I had been cleared from cancer, I had the privilege of serving as a speaker at the Great Banquet, which is a weekend designed to strengthen the faith of Christians. I was able to share my story about healing. I loved sharing all that God was doing in my life.

Two months later, an abnormal growth was found. I underwent two more chemo treatments, which doubled the size of the growth, so I had to have my breast surgically removed. Altogether, I have had six chemotherapy treatments, fifty-five radiation treatments, and ten surgeries in the past three years. People cannot believe how well I have been able to bounce back at my age.

At one point, I was having a pity party for myself, considering all that cancer had taken from me: my hair, part of my hearing and eyesight, my stamina, and ultimately, my breast. Immediately I felt God speak to me, reminding me of all He has given me: healing, love, family, friends, support, hope, and ultimately, salvation.

I had a recent PET scan, and my body remains clear from cancer. I have now had a year of clear PET scans. Although I would not have wished to have this disease, I feel like all the time that I have spent with family during the process has been precious. I have felt God's presence with me each step of this journey. Even though I initially rejected the idea of writing down blessings in the journal I was given, it was an incredible gift to be able to look for the good throughout my difficult treatments. I thank God for everyday blessings and especially for the miracle of healing.

David's Story
Lingering Effects of Vietnam

I volunteered to enter the US Army during the draft in 1964. I assumed I was going to be drafted anyway, so I sped up the process by volunteering. While I was in Vietnam, we received incoming small arms fire nearly nightly, sometimes brief periods of gunfire, but other times more substantial. The experience was terrifying. There were times that I thought I might be killed, including some uncomfortably close calls, but I am so grateful that I survived my year at war because I knew many others who weren't so lucky.

Looking back, being shot at was not the only danger we encountered. Agent Orange, a liquid used on rubber tree plantations and other tropical plants to kill the foliage that provided enemy cover, was a more significant hazard than we could have imagined. At one point, my fellow soldiers and I were accidentally sprayed with it. While in Vietnam, we went weeks without showering, and thus, I am sure I had Agent Orange on me for a long while. At the time, we didn't know it was bad. We frequently marched through areas that had been recently defoliated.

Since that time, I have done much research on the effects of Agent Orange. One thing people may not understand about it is that the consequence of exposure can come many years down the road. It is now known that there are many long-term health issues from Agent Orange, such as diabetes, Parkinson's disease, ischemic heart disease, and numerous varieties of cancer. It is suspected—and I truly believe—that the medical conditions I have had over the past several years result from my contact with Agent Orange.

Upon returning from Vietnam, I was healthy for many years. My first health crisis wasn't until the age of sixty-five, when I had an emergency aortic dissection. My descending aorta split and part of the blood went where it belonged, but part of it went to my left foot. I was sent to the hospital and I had surgery that night. Since that time, I have gone to many doctors and I often hear them say there has to be a reason why I am still here because this was not something that many people survived. I did pull through the aortic dissection and had a year of recovery following that surgery.

I had chest pain about three years later, so my wife took me to the heart hospital. I was having a severe heart attack, commonly known as a widow-maker. I had to have surgery again. I knew it would be difficult since they had to cut through scar tissue from my previous heart surgery for the aortic dissection. I survived that heart attack and the surgery, enduring another year of recovery after that.

A couple of years later, I kept losing my voice. I went to an ENT (ear, nose, and throat specialist) who found a growth beside my vocal cords. I had the growth removed and biopsied. I was diagnosed with laryngeal cancer. I couldn't have radiation treatments on it; instead, I had to have it monitored with monthly checkups. Unfortunately, cancer started growing back. The ENT said she could remove it again, but that was all she could do. I got a second opinion from another ENT in our area, who used a laser to remove the growth, which is less invasive. I have to go back every few months to get it checked. Upon my last checkup, everything looked perfect. The ENT commented that perhaps the cancer drugs I am taking now are also helping with recurrent laryngeal cancer.

Currently, I have non-Hodgkin's lymphoma. The medications I am on for this are strong and quickly wear me out. I feel fine in the mornings, but by the afternoon, I'm exhausted. It is yet another medical battle I am fighting.

All of my health problems have changed what I can do and how my family functions. I can no longer do yard work or shovel snow. My wife and other family members have to do those tasks for me. One thing that has helped my wife through this, besides that she has always been self-sufficient, is that she remains optimistic. She has always believed I was going to pull through each illness I have experienced. Her mindset has been great for me because it helped me maintain a positive outlook throughout my health issues.

Looking back, I feel like I have been blessed so many times. I survived every firefight in Vietnam. I lived through aortic dissection, which doesn't have a high rate of survival. I endured the widow-maker, which gets its name because it can cause immediate death. I have had recurrent laryngeal cancer and pulled through that as well. Now, I'm battling non-Hodgkin's lymphoma, and even though I am worn out, I am doing well. I can see all the good despite all I have been through with these health problems. It makes me emotional to think that people in the medical field appear stumped that I am still here after all I have been through, but I know that God has blessed my life and continues to do so. I am here for a reason.

Candi's Story
Courage with Cancer

In January 2020, I was diagnosed with breast cancer. After receiving that devastating call, I first asked God for three things: (1) To show me the good. I did not want to sit in anger or depression and I didn't want it to affect my daughter's view on life or her view of God. (2) Not to let me ask why. I knew there was no answer to that question, so I asked that God help me lean into Him and strengthen my faith. (3) I told Him that if this has to be a part of my story, I wanted Him to help me use it somehow.

I am not entirely confident how I am supposed to use my story, but as uncomfortable as I am sharing it, here I am doing just that. I hope it is helpful, even for just one person who needs to see this. My plea to all women is *not* to skip your yearly mammogram. I never once felt either of my tumors before this journey started. I also want to be clear that this is *my* story and it's the only story I can tell. I don't take for granted how fortunate I am. There are as many types of cancer, reactions to treatment, stages, outcomes, and emotions as there are people with cancer.

Right away after my initial prayer, I started to see the good with my medical team. Even my primary care physician called me to ask how I was coping with the news. Throughout this process, I have never felt like just a patient. My nurse navigator cried with me when chemo was more challenging than expected. In every step of my treatment, my opinion mattered and the doctors always made sure I understood the plan and why they thought it was right for me. My friends and family stepped in immediately. I never once felt alone. Until COVID-19 hit, I had someone with me at every appointment and every chemo treatment. Once the world shut down with COVID-19, I had to go alone to my appointments but still felt the support of my loved ones. The plans that I had in place to keep the house in order, so the effects of my illness didn't affect my daughter, had to be thrown out the window. I was worried that what was being placed on my daughter, in addition to no school, not being allowed to see her friends, or even going to her dad's house due to my low immune system, would hurt our relationship. A year has passed, and I can honestly say that this journey has made us closer. In addition, I had the privilege of watching her grow closer in her relationship with Jesus.

Just because there were so many good things doesn't mean what I went through wasn't hard. 2020 sucked for all. COVID-19 sucks. Cancer sucks. Chemo sucks. For me, chemo included an allergic reaction to one of my targeted chemos that I needed. That meant we tried for five sessions to convince my body to accept it and five sessions where my body said no. It also should be noted that I have experienced many side effects of chemo, some of which can last up to two years. I was whiny at times. I cried some days. I did not always feel hopeful. Every so often I wanted to throw a tantrum and tell anyone who would listen that it was not fair!

I just completed my last targeted chemo. I have one more surgery coming up. I also have been transitioned to survivorship treatment. It is exciting and scary all at the same time. My oncologist and nurse practitioner both came to see me during my last treatment. I will still see someone on my medical team every three months for two to three years. After being so closely monitored for a year, three months sounds like a lifetime. I cried when they congratulated me and they told me that it is normal to feel scared and anxious. Yes, my body is cancer-free and I am so, so thankful! However, cancer does not just go away. My oncologist told me that I need to discover my new normal. Cancer changed my body and my mentality. Just because the IV treatments are done doesn't mean the journey is over. I will continue to take medication for the next ten years to reduce my risk of recurrence for my particular type of cancer. I have to pay attention to my body to make sure I know symptoms of medication side effects or recurrence. Learning to do all of that while simultaneously loving life and not living in fear can be challenging. I can say most days I am pretty successful. I have come to understand this is not something I can do alone. It requires me to lean into my faith and the support of my amazing friends and family. I am thankful for the group effort.

Despite the challenges of 2020, I can say that it was also a good year. My faith has never been stronger, and I would never have fully realized how many amazing people love me. I am more content with myself and like myself more despite the weight loss, weight gain, weight shifting, and losing parts of myself. The chemo worked and there are no traces of cancer left. God has taught me to appreciate the little things. I never had a day when I did not have a reason to smile about something. I appreciate every day. God has kindly and generously answered the prayers I said on the day of my diagnosis. I have so much to be grateful for in my life.

Braden's Story
Benefits of a Brain Tumor

The summer before seventh grade, I started having some strange sensations that are difficult to describe. I had feelings of deja vu and vision anomalies. It happened off and on for a couple of months and then happened more frequently, including at school. I often had to go to the school nurse during these episodes.

One day, I was in science class doing a lab when suddenly I could not feel my feet. I told my teacher and he walked me to the nurse's office. The nurse called my mom and suggested she take me to see a doctor. A week later, I went to my pediatrician. My mom had documented that I had four similar episodes over the previous week. The pediatrician said that I should see a neurologist and get an MRI. The dad of one of my best friends worked in neurology and got me in to see a neurologist quickly. I got diagnosed with seizures at that time. That was what was happening when I couldn't feel my feet in class and when my vision would go awry.

I was then scheduled for an MRI and a twenty-four-hour EEG the same day. I feared getting an MRI because I am a bit claustrophobic, but it went well. Afterward, I got all set up for the EEG, with electrodes attached to my head to monitor for seizures. I had family visit me and bring me cookies to help brighten my day. The doctor came by and called my mom out into the hallway. When my mom came back in, she let me know they found a mass in my brain. I didn't know how to take the news. I didn't understand what that meant for me, but I couldn't sleep that night and just watched movies to pass the time.

My uncle was also in the room when I got the news. He had connections to an anesthesiologist at a local children's hospital. My uncle requested that my images be sent there, home to one of the best pediatric neurosurgeons in the Midwest. By the next morning, my mom had spoken with that neurosurgeon and was told it was one of the most ideal tumors to have. It wasn't great, but it would be reasonably easy to remove and treat, and all of my symptoms would be alleviated. The tumor was slow-growing, but it was in a location in my brain that was fragile enough to make the symptoms severe and intruded into the part of my brain causing seizures.

For the next couple of months, as I went about everyday life waiting for the surgery to occur, it was strange to think that I had a tumor in my brain. I did continue to have seizures during this time. The seizures weren't convulsions and they all presented a little differently, but in general, my vision would zoom out, my nose would feel bizarre, and when I tried to talk, I could say words, but I didn't feel like I could control what I was saying. It was all quite peculiar. I got on medication to prevent the seizures. It not only made me tired, but

I ended up having an allergic reaction to it. We did find a med that worked to stop the seizures and the side effects were not as severe, although it did make me tired like the first med.

Before I went in for the surgery, it was necessary to have my head shaved. That morning I had an MRI, which measured my tumor at 2.5 centimeters by 3 centimeters in my right temporal lobe. Several members of my extended family were with me, along with my pastor supporting me and praying for me before I went into surgery. It was an eleven-hour procedure. The tumor was successfully removed and it was deemed benign.

My mom's biggest concern was that I would not be the same boy coming out of surgery as I was going in. When I was able to see my family, I was aware enough to pull a little prank. I called my sister by the wrong name. My mom got scared, but I quickly retracted and told them I was kidding. After the initial scare, I think it reassured her that the surgery had not changed her prankster son.

During recovery in the hospital, I was not sleeping or eating well. I remained in the hospital for a week and I couldn't walk out of the hospital. When I got home, I was sensitive to light, so I had blackout curtains in my room and I couldn't look at a phone screen for more than a couple of seconds. I was sleeping around twenty hours each day for the first week I was home while healing. I would wake up after sleeping for many hours and still be tired. I wasn't walking much or doing hardly anything during this time. I wondered if this level of exhaustion would ever go away. I had to learn to walk again, and to walk up and down stairs was a chore. I was physically capable of bearing my weight and moving my legs, but it was just hard to tell my legs to move. Tasks like walking or even texting were tiring because I had to put so much focus into it.

I started back to school after two weeks. Because I was still so tired, I alternated going in the morning one day and afternoon the next, to get a balance of my classes for the two weeks before returning to school full time. I felt that I went from diagnosis to surgery to recovery quickly because of our connections and for quick healing, for which I am grateful. I feel fortunate. Even though two weeks of recovery at home seemed like a long time while I was going through it, it really wasn't long in the grand scheme of things.

The type of tumor I had is generally one that should not grow back, but I still had to have imaging done for the first two months to ensure it wasn't. Then I had to go back once a year for five years and then every two years for four years, and then I will only need to have scans done every ten years. I am already four years postsurgery and have had no issues since that time. I had been diagnosed with epilepsy when I had the tumor and remained on seizure medication for a year and a half after surgery. The summer after I was weaned off that seizure med, I felt fully alive again. I was not as tired and could focus better.

Now that my body is healed, I can say that there were benefits to having a brain tumor. It is easier to put things in the big picture now. When I have a bad day, I realize that it could be a lot worse. I also understand that my brain tumor could have been more severe. It is this perspective that makes life easier. Even though I had one challenging year, the brain tumor showed me how I shouldn't sweat the small stuff and what is truly important in life.

4

Infertility, Adoption, and Parenthood

Many of us dream of becoming parents. Conceiving is supposed to be "natural" but can end up being difficult and, perhaps, unattainable. Thankfully, there are other ways to become a parent if "natural" does not work. I have family and friends who have had trouble conceiving and have used medication, in vitro fertilization, or adoption as methods to have children. Even though these methods have become more common, resulting in the child that you dreamed of, the path to parenthood is often fraught with feelings of frustration, anxiety, loss, sadness, disappointment, heartache, inadequacy, and jealousy.

Then, once you have that cute bundle of joy in your arms, the love you feel is overwhelming and powerful and you would do anything for that little person. That love will guide and sustain you through the hard days and periods that you will undoubtedly go through because the days and years of raising a child will not be entirely filled with rainbows and butterflies. Your child may walk through some of the same trials an adult would face, but now you walk through it with them, feeling the pain even more intensely than if it were your pain alone. Your child may deal with a physical or mental condition or illness, social struggles, heartbreak, loss, or trauma. Some of what they will navigate will be minor and some will be life-changing for you and them.

A couple of years ago, my heart broke for my daughter. If any of you have children who participate in travel sports, you will understand our pain. It may seem minor to those who haven't walked in these shoes, but it is an emotionally charged time filled with worry, anxiety, hope, dread, excitement, and uncertainty. I have often said that soccer tryouts are the worst time of the year, and that year was particularly torturous for us. My son got an offer for the same team he had the previous year on the first day of tryouts. He was happy and thus, we were happy. However, my daughter's story was not so delightful. She did not get an offer on the first night. Not getting an offer for a travel team on the first night makes for an anxious twenty-four hours leading up to the second day of tryouts and waiting for an offer. I was nauseous; I barely slept. I tried my best not to let my nerves show and add to her anxiety. We encouraged her to do her best on day two and told her we were proud of her, no matter what. When the offer finally came, it was not with her current teammates and friends. She also was aware from the team text string that everyone else had received offers to remain on the same team, and she was the only one left off of that team. So incredibly hard!

Here is what I wrote to my girl after the devastating news: "My dearest daughter, life does not feel fair sometimes. Please stop the negative talk. You are good enough. You are not horrible or stupid. Don't doubt yourself. You are more than a soccer team. You are enough. Use this time for you to figure out if this is going to make you work harder in soccer to obtain your goal of getting back on your old team or if you are going to be content with where you are and focus on another sport or even decide to go another direction. I know this hurts. I know you will miss your friends. I know you are extremely upset and disappointed. I pray that you have more hills than valleys in this life, like the one you are walking through now. I pray that when you face disappointment, you will rise. You will gain strength. You will gain perspective. You will learn. You will grow. I love you."

To the parents who have children in travel sports, or if you have walked in similar disappointment with your child, I know your heart breaks for her. You wish you could protect her from all sadness and heartache in life. It won't be easy. Be strong for her. Lift her up. Pray for her.

Parenthood will be filled with many, many joys. You will laugh and love in ways that you would never have imagined. You will also struggle in ways you couldn't fathom because of your love for that child. Parenthood and the love we have for our little ones change us and our world in an overwhelmingly beautiful way. They show us what is truly important in life. I would not change a thing. These children that we longed for and prayed for make it all worthwhile.

Parenthood and the love we have for our little ones change us and our world in an overwhelmingly beautiful way.

Jenny's Story
Open Mind, Open Arms

Jason and I met in college and got married a year after graduation. We talked about starting a family because we always knew we wanted children. We briefly discussed adoption, but it was not our first choice. We thought we would only do that if God led us to go that route in the future.

Two years after we married, we found out I was pregnant. This was going to be the first grandchild for both sets of parents. We were thrilled, immediately starting to prepare for the baby. Around fifteen weeks, we went for the first sonogram and found out it was a little boy. However, they could not find a heartbeat, which devastated us.

We continued trying to get pregnant for over a year without success, so we began to explore medical explanations for why I was not getting pregnant. The doctors said that because we had gotten pregnant once before, it was promising that I would eventually get pregnant again. I couldn't help but think that this was taking far too long.

After a few more years of not conceiving, we decided to pursue adoption. We talked about being foster parents, but we didn't feel good about that option because we wanted a child we could adopt, and we knew that was not always the case with fostering. I had heard how hard it was to give back a foster child to the family once you had the child for a while, especially if the situation at home for the child was hostile or unsupportive. To spare our hearts any potential grief, we decided to do an international adoption from Russia. The process required us to hurry with preparations but wait for long periods with no updates. I contacted our case worker every couple of weeks for any news. She was terrific, but the process was slow.

One day, when I was at work, our case worker called, so I knew it had to be good news. She told me that she had a referral of a baby girl named Marina matched to us. She said she would send me an email with her picture and medical information. I was elated! After all the waiting, it finally seemed to be happening. Jason came to my office to see, expressing relief, excitement, and fear all in that moment. I was emotional as I looked at her pictures for the first time. It seemed unreal that I was looking into the face of the child God had picked for us. I printed out and laminated the picture to carry around with me and show it to everyone. We finally had a face and a name to go with the prayers we had been saying for ages.

We had to make two trips to Russia. We first flew over when Marina was around seven months old to meet her in a small room in the orphanage. We got to visit her three times on that trip. It was hard to leave her after that, not knowing how long it would be before we could bring her home, but that was the program's rule. We were told we would go back in a month or two to get her, but it ended up taking three months before we were able to return. They called us the week before all the paperwork expired to come back to Russia. The timing the Lord had for these events was perfect. It was summer, and my husband was off from work as a college professor.

This international adoption process was expensive, especially counting the trips, but we felt the Lord was providing for us. On the second trip, when we went to pick up our daughter, a family friend had won tickets to travel anywhere in the world. She had heard about our story and generously donated her tickets to us. Then, we got a call from the airline saying they would upgrade us to first class both ways. I guess this friend had called and told them our story, but I do not know for sure. Having never flown first class, and first experiencing it on a ten-hour flight, was exceptional. It was little things like that flight where we felt the Lord's hand at work. He was kind to us, not having to provide that comfort but doing so anyway.

We were in Russia for two weeks before we went to get our daughter. I was very emotional as they brought her into the same tiny room where we had met her the first time, now knowing she was ours. We even celebrated her first birthday while we were there. It was wonderful to finally be parents to our little girl.

When Marina was three, my husband and I decided to be trained to be foster parents. It was a hard choice, but our finances would not allow us to adopt internationally again. We finally realized that many kids needed parents even if it was only for a short time.

The first call we got was for a two-month-old infant. We had her until she turned one, and she went back home. Giving her up was hard, but knowing that we helped her and her family was fulfilling. I felt like the Lord grew us through the experience. We had to trust in Him more than ever before. I got to know the girl's family a bit and felt the Lord speak to me that this process was about relationships, not about me wanting more children. I knew that there was something bigger in store for us. I had to let my fears go and let the Lord work in his unique way, but it was not an easy mindset.

After that little girl, we fostered a brother and sister, Isaac and Autumn, whom we ended up adopting. They were two and six months old at the time. Due to the circumstances, we did not get to interact with their families as much as we had with our previous foster child. These two children were a joy. It seemed so easy for them to transition into our family.

We had another sibling group that came and went. It was not a good fit, and unfortunately, we had to admit that it would not work for our family. It was difficult, but since we already had children in our family, we saw things differently when introducing new kids with their own issues.

We had three kids at this time, which seemed to be a complete family to me, but we still wanted to remain foster parents, even if it were for kids who would come and go. We had a little boy, Joseph, who was three years old and ended up staying with us for only two months before returning home. Then, a couple of months later, we got a call saying that he was back in the system. We were asked if we could take him back. We said we would; however, we were starting to homeschool our children and could not transport him back and forth to visit his mom. If that continued to be his plan, then we would not be able to take him. He did not end up coming to us, and for a while, I questioned whether I made a good choice.

Joseph ended up coming back to us when he was five. That time, they were looking for an adoptive home for him. Now he is in our family. Unfortunately, he went through hard times in that period, which broke my heart. I wondered how life would have been different for him if we had taken him when he was three.

Then we had a little girl, Hannah, come into our home when she was nine months old. I was a little overwhelmed with the thought of caring for five kids. I was having a hard time with the idea of juggling them all. One day, I was discussing this with a friend of mine, and her response was, "Why not?" After I thought about her words, I realized she was right. We had room in our house, enough love, and we could afford to support more children. We ended up adopting Hannah and Joseph at the same time.

At this point, I was no longer thinking about biological children. I had made peace with not getting pregnant and adoption as the avenue the Lord wanted to grow our family. I loved my kids as much as I could have loved a child born from me. Little did I know, my husband had still been praying about biological children.

Later that same summer, after we had adopted Joseph and Hannah, my period was late. I was forty-one, so I wondered if I was going through perimenopause, but I ended up texting my husband, asking him to stop by the drug store on the way home from work to pick up a pregnancy test. I told him that it probably was not pregnancy, but I wanted to be sure of it. When he got home, I took the test right away. It was positive, and I was shocked. Luckily, my husband had bought a box of three tests, so I took another, which also showed up positive. The Lord was unfailingly kind. He didn't have to do this for us, and again, he provided anyway.

I worried because of what had happened years prior during my first pregnancy. There was a day early on where I was spotting a little, so I called the doctor, who said that there was nothing to worry about if it was just a little. I got out my Bible and tried to find comfort in what God was telling me. I knew I could not go through nine months of worry. I had to let go of my fear and affirm, "Lord, even if this pregnancy doesn't come to provide a healthy baby, I have to be okay with that." I felt genuine peace after praying it. The pregnancy went remarkably well and I was not sick at all. We found out we were having a girl and were excited once again. The day Hallie was born was one of the best days of my life. All the other children loved her right away. The amount of love in my now-huge family filled my heart.

While I was pregnant, we did not get any calls to foster children. After having our daughter, we wondered if we should be done with being foster parents. Having six kids was plenty and more than I ever thought I would have. At one point in our infertility struggles, I didn't think I would even have one.

When Hallie was about a year old, we got a call that Jason's brother was dying after suffering from ALS for some time. We traveled to be with him and family as he left the earth, one of the hardest things I have ever done. When Jason and I were driving back home, I checked my email, and one of the social workers I knew had emailed, reporting that a baby was just born. He was in the hospital; he had been exposed to drugs and alcohol in the womb and weighed only 4 pounds. In the email, the social worker asked what we thought about him. I burst into tears and immediately asked God what He wanted us to do. Our family was going through an emotional time, and the Lord set us on this path. Again we thought: Why would we refuse? Is it ever the right time for anything? If we always waited until we felt it was the right time, our lives would not be nearly as exciting or fulfilling.

I had a trip with Marina planned the following week, as she turned thirteen, and I wondered how we could make all these changes happen. Jason said he would go to the hospital and visit the child in the NICU. I wondered how he would juggle that while caring for our other five children but ended up emailing the social worker back, asking what we needed to do. Jason met Ethan before I ever did. He visited the hospital and held the child for the first time. Ethan was able to come home when he was eleven days old. He was the youngest baby we had ever gotten through the foster system. He never had visitation with his mom, so I felt like the Lord handed him to us. Since he was exposed to harmful substances and underweight, I often prayed for his brain and health. He is now three, and his only issue is delayed speech.

We are finished growing our massive, loving family now. We told social services that we were done fostering. Our family is complete and I am amazed by how it all happened. Our families are gracious, caring for all our kids as if they had all been born to us. I have heard people say that they couldn't love children that weren't theirs, but I think anybody could if they truly wanted.

Coming to terms with God's plan for me has been crucial in my life. I must trust that He has a much better plan than I could have conceived. But when we live in the present, when things seem terrible, it is hard to see His plans. We walked through the grief of losing a baby, possibly never having children, and not being able to have what we dreamed. There is nothing wrong with being sad about loss. I had to trust in God even though I disliked some of the experiences I walked through. We can get stuck in a place of despair, leading us to miss out on the full potential of life, or we can grow into a desire for more for our lives. God can take our greatest hurts and use them to build a more beautiful life than we could have imagined.

I feel that the Lord has used my experiences to help me see how important it is to live with open hands, not clinging tightly to things of this world. All that we have is His, and we are to be stewards. He has shown me over and over that He is in control of our family and has a purpose and plan for our lives. When I got married at twenty-three, I never pictured it looking as it does now, being a mother of seven amazing children. It is not always easy to live open to what the Lord has for us, but I never want to be so self-focused that I miss out on a freely given blessing from God.

Alice's Story
Dreams Come True

We all go through our lives with unique hopes, dreams, wants, and desires. When we are young, we think about what we want our lives to be like. I wanted to be a teacher, get married, and have a family. I thought I would meet the perfect guy and I did. Lloyd and I were very much in love. We dated for three years, got married and were very happy.

For the first five years of marriage, my husband and I were very close. We did everything together and were best friends. We mutually felt that it was time to start a family. Fifty-five years ago, when I was twenty-seven years old, we learned that we could not have a biological family of our own. We wondered what we were to do. We could feel sorry for ourselves, and I certainly did. I felt strongly that it was my *right* to have a child. It seemed that everyone could have a baby, but I couldn't. Back in those days, there was no IVF and few alternatives to conceiving naturally. I went to the doctor, but he couldn't give me anything to change my ability to become pregnant. After this news, we had no clue what to do next. We didn't know where to turn. We didn't even know anyone who had adopted a child.

We were open with family and friends about our inability to conceive. We needed the support, which all our friends happily gave. By this time, most of them had children. They knew I was distraught about not being pregnant when it seemed that everyone around us was. It was a reminder to me every time I saw them of what I couldn't have. I wanted to be supportive of my friends. I was happy that they were pregnant. I wanted them to have a wonderful life and build a family, but it was difficult for me each time I went to a baby shower or a christening. Every time, I felt that I was not enough.

We wanted a child badly and to give them love. We also wished for the child to love us. We were ready to be parents in every way but could not fulfill our desires.

Fortunately, there was an attorney teaching at the school where I taught, so I went to him to ask about the adoption process. He led us to the Children's Bureau, which I didn't know much about at the time. That is where we decided to apply for adoption.

It is necessary to understand that this was a time in history when we had homes where unwed mothers were sent. It was considered a shame for these girls to be pregnant, not only for the girl but also for her parents. The pregnancy was something not to be spoken about.

Girls came to these homes during their pregnancies and spent a few months there until giving birth. Looking back, I think that is tragic.

Lloyd and I went to a general meeting at the Children's Bureau, where couples were invited to hear about the adoption process. This was an eye-opening experience for me. When I walked into that room filled with other couples in the same shoes, I realized that I was not alone in this.

When we applied to adopt, I had individual sessions with the social worker, as did Lloyd. We also had some sessions together. Then we had a home visit to ensure our home was acceptable to bring a child into. Next, we had to have three sets of friends write a letter saying that we would be good parents, listing their reasons for saying so.

Around the time we thought we might be getting a child, we said that it didn't make a difference if we got a boy or girl. We had even said that we were open to getting twins. Thankfully, God didn't give us twins because He probably knew we wouldn't have been able to handle them.

Believe it or not, the adoption process took nine months, the same as if I had carried a child in my womb. I was teaching school that year, which ended June 7. Scott was born on June 11, and we got him on June 18. When we went to pick him up, we put on our nice clothes and drove to the Children's Bureau. When they handed him to us, I knew it was the greatest blessing God could have ever given us. We loved him instantly. There was no difference than if he was biologically ours. I thanked God daily for the blessing that He gave us so that we could have a family.

Two years later, we adopted again. This time we got our daughter, Dawn. I don't know what we ever did for God to bless us twice, but I am overwhelmingly grateful. I felt that adopting them was a blessing to the children as well. However, later, I came to realize that both adoption days were the happiest of my entire life but were the saddest in the life of two other women. I hoped and prayed all those years that those women would someday be able to have a child to raise and love themselves—even that they were the same sex. I found out years later, after adoption records were opened, that this indeed was what happened.

We were very open with our children and told them from the very beginning that they were adopted. We read stories to both of our kids about adoption and they knew their history.

One year, I chaperoned a field trip with my daughter's class. My daughter was in the very back of the bus, and I was up front with the teachers. A friend of my daughter yelled to me, "Dawn isn't adopted, is she?" and I proudly replied, "Oh yes, she is!" Dawn was excitedly telling everyone that she was indeed adopted. We had talked about it so much that she thought it was *better* than being born to us. I was always pleased and comforted to know that this is how she viewed being adopted.

Dealing with infertility and the feeling of not being enough was tremendously difficult. Still, ultimately, Lloyd and I were able to establish the family that we had dreamed of in our youth. To me, there was no difference in how I love my children. I could not have loved them more, even if I had carried them myself.

Becky's Story
Something's Not Right

Charlie and I married later in life at thirty-five years old, so I immediately wanted to start having kids. When I did not get pregnant after a while, we tried various methods of having a child, including artificial insemination and in vitro fertilization. No doctor could tell me what was wrong with me. I did get pregnant through in vitro twice, but there was never a heartbeat after eight weeks. We had already started talking about adoption prior to these pregnancies. We found an adoption agency and thought we might do an international adoption.

When we didn't think things could get worse, we experienced even more loss. We had four people who had been close to us die within two weeks, including two in a murder-suicide. It was a tough time in our lives, so we took a break from trying to have a baby and from considering adoption after those losses.

During this break, I got pregnant on my own. I went to my gynecologist after taking a pregnancy test and he and I both cried because we were so happy for this to happen naturally. On my fortieth birthday, I had an ultrasound appointment and there was no heartbeat. It was the worst birthday I had ever experienced. At that point, I had to stop trying to get pregnant or looking into adoption completely. I was distraught and melted into my couch. We got a dog because I needed something to cuddle. I needed time to heal after losing these pregnancies.

After this time, we decided to do a domestic adoption because laws had changed and international adoptions were becoming more complicated. I had always said that I wasn't up for open adoption because I thought it was a bad idea, but Charlie always reminded me to be receptive to all options and not jump to conclusions before I got all the information.

We went to a meeting about adoption. A birth mother spoke to the group, and her speech changed my preconceived notions. She told us a story of how she went out to dinner with the adoptive parents and the baby. As the baby was throwing a fit, the birth mother thought, *Thank goodness, I'm going to a movie with my friends later.* That was the turning point that made me realize that open adoption was possible. I had always thought the birth mother would feel that she made such a horrible mistake and would want the child back, but in this instance, she was grateful that she had plans to hang out with her girlfriends later instead of taking care of the child.

We got serious about writing our adoption letter after that meeting. This letter is given to potential birth mothers to tell them our story. The adoption agency sent out our letter and we got a couple of responses. It was apparent to us that one would not work out. The other one sounded promising but ended up being a scam. Luckily, we had not gotten very far into the process with that mother, but it was still disheartening. The third response was from a birth mother named Brittany. The moment we received her letter, it was probably the closest I have ever felt to Charlie and to God. We cried together. We prayed together, which wasn't our norm at that time. We wrote our response to her together. Brittany said that although it was an open adoption, she really didn't want contact. At this point, we would have said yes to anything, so we told her that was okay.

She asked some questions about our lives, and we sent back our answers. After that, she asked to speak with us over the phone. It was scary to do that, but it went well. She then wanted to meet us in person. A month later, we arranged to meet at a mall for coffee. She came with handmade frames holding the ultrasound picture. That was how she told us that she had picked us to be her child's parents. There were many tears shed that day. We shared family photos with her and she shared hers with us. We learned that she was nineteen and had only dated the birth father for a couple of weeks when she got pregnant. She was on her way to break up with him when she realized she was pregnant. He was an angry man, and she was a bit afraid of him. By the time we met, she had cut off all contact with him and he had signed paperwork giving away his parental rights.

Brittany told me she wanted me to come to doctor appointments with her, so I drove to her hometown two hours away as often as I possibly could. I became extremely close with her during this time. She became a part of the family.

Charlie and I were there at the birth and I held Brittany's hand as she labored. When Matthew finally entered the world, I was the first to hold him. Charlie and I spent the first two days in the hospital, and the three of us cared for him together. We were so thankful and blessed to have that time with each other.

The adoption agency warned us that the birth mother would cut ties before we were ready, and she did. We found out it was because she was having more babies. We still see her, but not as often as we once did.

The birth father did reach out to Brittany asking for updates, so I told her to direct him to the adoption agency. He did so and asked for a picture. I said that I would send a picture if he provided a family history. I sent the picture to the adoption agency but never heard back. I later found out that the adoption agency had filed for bankruptcy. I will probably never get that family history.

When Matthew was a baby, he had typical baby problems. When he was a year old and began to walk, I noticed that he walked on the insides of his feet, and it looked like his legs were caving in on the interiors. It looked abnormal. His birth mother was very flexible, but nothing out of the ordinary. When he was two years old, I put him in gymnastics. When he was made to scoot along the uneven bars, he complained that his feet hurt. I decided to take him to an orthopedic doctor.

After evaluation, the doctor thought Matthew had a connective tissue disorder. I asked him what we do about it, and he said that we probably didn't need anything done at that point. He said we could do orthotics for his shoes, but he didn't think that would help. We decided that we could go down that road to see if it would provide relief. I took him to get fitted for the orthotics, but because of the cost and Matthew's ever-growing feet, we decided against this option.

When Matthew was three, I took him to his first dental visit. They didn't do much at the appointment besides brush his teeth and do a simple examination. The dentist felt his jaw and when Matthew opened and closed his mouth, it made a clicking sound. The dentist said, "I think he has a connective tissue disorder." I told him that he was the second person to tell me that. He said it might be Ehlers-Danlos syndrome, but the only way to know for sure is to get genetic testing done. He also mentioned that there was nothing you could do about it if he indeed did have it.

At Matthew's five-year-old well-check, we learned that he had grown nearly 5 inches in a year and his wingspan was greater than his height. The pediatrician said that it was time to get genetic testing done, which we did. That is when he was diagnosed with Marfan syndrome.

The sad part is that Brittany's family doesn't want to face this diagnosis or talk about it. The geneticist said they could get a swab from the birth mom with no blood work, but she wouldn't get that done. Physically, you can't tell that anyone in her family may have it, but if you didn't know how old Matthew is, you would simply think he is tall and skinny. If you look at the physical characteristics of Marfan syndrome per mayoclinic.org (tall and slender build, disproportionately long arms, legs and fingers, a breastbone that protrudes outward or dips inward, a high, arched palate and crowded teeth, heart murmurs, extreme nearsightedness, an abnormally curved spine, and flat feet), Matthew does not exhibit many of these traits.

I am so grateful for that, but he still sees several specialists and we spend lots of time at doctor's appointments.

One of the biggest blessings in all of this was that I could get a job at my church the same month that Matthew was diagnosed. I believe that was God's timing. I felt so alone when Matthew was first diagnosed. Nobody understood. All of my mom friends had their own problems they were dealing with. Unless you have a child with a diagnosis like this, you can't understand the impact on your life. Having other staff members from my church who could hold me up when I couldn't hold myself up was irreplaceable. This job landed in my lap at just the right time. If I didn't have this job, I would have been sitting at my house by myself, scavenging the internet for information. To work somewhere where each week we have a devotional and pray for one another is meaningful. I am grateful that I can come into the office and cry if I need to after an appointment. The support system has been a tremendous gift to me.

Going to my first Marfan syndrome national conference was the biggest blessing of all. I learned important terminology and what questions I needed to ask at Matthew's appointments. I have learned to question why the doctors are doing what they are doing and then continue to ask questions along the way. Matthew may be adopted, but he is my kid, and I know him backward, forward, and upside down. I must trust my gut on what was wrong and relay this to the specialists.

My biggest prayer is that Matthew himself will be able to find the blessings with his diagnosis. Currently he can't see any good in his condition because he is teased for how tall he is. He also always seems to be friends with the shortest kids in his class. We are part of a support group in our state, but we only know of one girl his age in the entire state with the same condition. I hope that he can eventually meet some friends at the annual conference, but he is not quite old enough to be chatting with others online. I hope that he won't feel so alone in this diagnosis by being part of the support group and attending the annual conference.

Even though Matthew doesn't see Brittany often, I am grateful that we still have some connection. I am thankful that Charlie encouraged me to consider an open adoption because it was wonderful to be a part of the pregnancy and birth. I am pleased that Brittany remains part of the family.

Going through infertility, adoption, and Matthew's diagnosis was much easier with loving souls at my side. I am grateful for having tremendous support from my husband, church family, and support group as we continue to manage Matthew's health problems. I have people who can hold me up when I cannot stand alone, which is incredibly valuable. Despite the hard times, I feel completely blessed.

Michelle's Story
Doing What's Best for My Son

My first child, Henry, was born when I was twenty-four years old. On that day, I remember him crying nonstop. On day 3, we brought him home and he continued crying and screaming, hours on end. I remember my husband saying to me, "You are the NICU nurse, fix this." I wondered if the problem was perhaps that I was a new mom and didn't know what I was doing. I couldn't figure out what was going on with him. I questioned why I had a baby at such a young age. After months and months, we realized he was simply a difficult baby.

When Henry was about three, we had other issues with him. He became defiant and unruly. I remember one instance when he scaled the pantry about six shelves up and said, "Look, Mom," as he was retrieving snacks from the top shelf. At this point, I also had a one-year-old, so I thought I was an overwhelmed mom who didn't know how to handle this. I did speak with the doctor, and I was told that he was just a typical toddler.

Fast forward to the age of five. I began noticing how Henry was different from his peers. He was a happy child, but my motherly intuition was picking up things nobody else noticed. He was having struggles with his sister and with sports, primarily soccer. His competitive nature was heightened, and he often experienced emotional swings. I brought up these issues to the doctor again and was told that he was fine since he was not having any problems in school.

When Henry was seven, I again explained his intense emotions to his doctor and said we couldn't figure out his behavior. On our doctor's recommendation, we went to see a psychologist. It was hard to take my seven-year-old to a psychologist. Within five minutes, she told us that my child had attention deficit hyperactivity disorder (ADHD). She recommended medicine for Henry. It was difficult for me to accept that my seven-year-old needed medicine, but we went ahead and started it. About six months into the medicine, we decided to take him off because we felt we had lost who our son was. He had become quiet, which we thought we wanted, but we also saw that he had withdrawn himself, turning many of his previous emotions into sadness.

We kept Henry off of meds until fourth grade. At that point, we started him on three medications because we felt we needed to try something else. He was always a good student, but many of his stronger emotions came out on the playground before starting these meds. Once beginning the new medication, teachers began asking what we were doing because he was a different kid entirely. They could see he was now calm and he began handling negative situations better. We had questioned at one point if he even had ADHD because his grades had always been good, and he didn't have any issues in the classroom. Typically, that is where ADHD presents itself.

I did step away from my job as a nurse that year to be a stay-at-home mom to balance Henry's home life. I was there in the mornings to get him ready for school and there after school to help with homework. My additional assistance was what he needed.

A few more ADHD symptoms appeared in fifth grade, including poor organizational skills and not turning in homework. Henry's backpack was often filled with papers he had shoved down in it. That year, we discussed all these habits with his teacher, who ended up being an angel to us, as she was a parent of an ADHD child herself. She helped put together a picture checklist of tasks Henry needed to do to be more focused and organized. After her help, we didn't have any other issues for the rest of the school year.

In sixth grade, Henry began middle school and had to make new friends. That seemed to be when our efforts started falling apart.

There were more pressures, he began missing assignments, and I was constantly emailing back and forth with his teachers. Teachers said he was lazy and asked why he needed his mom to help him. I knew how capable he was of doing things at home, but I couldn't see him in the classroom. I asked if he was engaging in class and he was. He also wasn't acting out, but rather, he was quiet, often shutting down. Teachers agreed that he was a good kid but thought he was lazy.

Around January, I grew tired of the weekly emails with teachers. I started looking for a way to get him more help in the classroom. I consulted a friend of mine who was a special education teacher in another school system. I believe she was another angel on our path. She pointed me to a website showing me the exact information that I was looking for. I found out that I needed to put in writing that I wanted my son thoroughly tested. Looking back, Henry had been diagnosed with ADHD within five minutes of the psychologist meeting him. There was no official testing, only me telling the teachers what I thought should be done. I advocated strongly for my son to be tested. Because he was behaving more as an introvert at this time and quietly shutting down, I wondered if he might have autism. I only wanted to figure out what was going on with Henry. As a parent, I had the right to have him tested in seven different areas and I chose for him to be tested in four areas, including autism. The school questioned why I was having him tested for autism because they didn't see any signs. I replied that I didn't care; I wanted him tested for it.

The results came back with Henry having slower mental processing speeds but a high IQ. He was close to autism on the spectrum but the school wanted further testing to decide for sure. The results were a solid acknowledgment that I wasn't imagining what was going on, and that I noticed things the teachers did not. He was falling through the cracks. We ended up getting him an IEP (Individualized Education Plan). There were two parts of his IEP for the teachers to check with him. The first was check-in and check-out every day at the beginning and end of the day on his anxiety level. The second was for a teacher to check in on him five minutes into each class and see how he was doing.

In seventh grade, he began using this IEP. This was the year when many physical signs of his stress appeared, including losing weight and feeling ill. Henry had always been a small child, and I worried about him. He was generally the smallest kid in class. The second nine weeks into the school year, we noticed some of the same issues he had experienced in the sixth grade. Often, he was shutting down and being introverted. I began emailing teachers again. Luckily, Henry had a special education teacher help him, and she started learning more about him.

In February, Henry began missing assignments again. Math class was the biggest problem. He was taking advanced math and the teacher eventually said that he wasn't cut out for the class and would need to sit out the rest of the year and retake it the next year. Yet in his standardized testing, the importance of which is so often emphasized, he was performing off the charts. His processing was simply slow. I had to reteach all of his lessons at night because he struggled to grasp the concepts in class. At this point, he was begging me to home-school him. *Begging.* He would say things along the lines of "You just get me" and "I'm more comfortable at home." He was also eating lunch alone. I had asked the school to look out for him, and yet, nobody was.

One evening that February, when Henry got home from school, I told him that he needed to get his homework done and study for the next day's test. He had an emotional outburst the likes of which I had never seen before. He exploded, "I just can't do this anymore! I can't do life anymore! I shouldn't even be here anymore! Do you think I'll amount to anything?" Listening to him in this rage was extremely difficult. I met him on the stairs. He looked at me and sadly explained, "I try to be a good friend and everyone walks away from me." It is terrifying to have a thirteen-year-old boy (especially one who has access to the internet) say things like he doesn't have friends and doesn't want to be here anymore. Yet I needed these events and this explosion to begin the exploration of what more was out there for him.

I told him I didn't care about his academic success at that point. We told him that he only needed to go to school, even if he failed, but he had to go no matter what. I joked, saying he had to go to school so that I didn't go to jail. I told him not to be stressed. We affirmed that we would work together and find a better solution for him. I looked at home schooling options, but I knew one piece that he needed was socialization. I saw home-school gym options, but I thought he needed more. Then I came across Hawksbill Learning Center, which is a school for ADHD and autistic children. I had come across this school when I was looking at options when he was going into sixth grade (before we decided to do the testing). When I initially came across this school, I saw that it was a school for autistic kids, and at that point, he still hadn't been tested, so I had initially ruled it out. We also looked at a Christian school because he had always maintained a strong faith. Throughout the years, we would sometimes tell him we couldn't help him right now, but God could. He would pray and write in a journal about this faith.

In March, when my husband, Henry, and I visited Hawksbill Learning Center, you could physically see Henry walk with lifted shoulders. I believe he walked differently because he saw that there was another potential option for school. Before this, he was unaware that there was another option. We sat down with the head of the school and Henry said he would love to try this school. He got to come in for an entire day as a prospective student. Henry was able to try out the school, and the school to try him out. The school doesn't accept everybody. Many of these kids do need help, but the school wants the proper fit of students to truly work one-on-one with these kids. At the end of the shadow day, I asked how the school was and Henry said that it wasn't school, it was camp. I asked him what he meant. He replied, "You know how on the first day of camp, you sit down and learn everyone's names? That is how it was. There were ten of us. I sat at a table with them and they wanted to know who I was, and we went around all day together."

He remained at his regular middle school until the end of the school year. Toward the end of the year, he started getting physically ill. He would regularly go to the nurse's office and throw up. In May, we checked in with his psychologist, and sure enough, these were physical signs of stress. He had lost 11 pounds in three months, which is especially concerning because he was small to begin with. He had seen something different at Hawksbill Learning Center that he liked, and when we put him back in his school, the environment caused him anxiety, fear, and stress.

A week after the check-in with the psychologist, we got the call from Hawksbill Learning Center confirming that they would love for Henry to attend the school. I remember crying and thinking about how I was going to get my kid back.

As we prepared for the transition to his new school, we prayed that Henry would be a leader in this school. There were kids with more intellectual and physical problems at this school than Henry. We knew he was intelligent and that he could help other kids by being a leader.

In July, he went to a Christian-based camp for a week. They always give character trait awards from the staff who get to know the kids. He had been going to that same camp for years by this time. They always gave one kid the leadership award, similar to the MVP or model student for the camp. When they gave awards this year, they awarded Henry the one for leadership. At that point, we knew that Hawksbill Learning Center would be the place for him to be a spectacular leader.

Henry is now an eighth-grader at Hawksbill. He has been doing exceedingly well and gets straight As. He still forgets to turn in an assignment now and again, but that is typical of many children, especially those with ADHD. They have him placed in advanced math. The staff mention to us how thankful they are that Henry is at their school, and that he is a huge asset to the school. They refer to him as the big man on campus. Everybody wants to be his friend. He is invited to social outings and sleepovers with friends; he hadn't been invited to sleepovers since fourth grade. To see my kid struggle for such a long time and now be thriving and considering college and a career as a meteorologist is just so sweet and satisfying.

I feel that God had to take Henry to his lowest point to show him that he is made for something more. I hate that He had to do this to a child. It has taken me nearly four decades to realize that for myself. Henry is an incredible kid and I am glad that people see that in him. ADHD kids are unique and don't have to fit the mold. There are other options for them. My son now knows that he doesn't have to live in fear or stress. He can verbalize his problems. He's gained back the weight he lost. He never used to smile, but now he does. He is growing. He looks "normal." This change makes me wonder if all of the stress affected him physically and caused him to be so tiny for so long. He stands tall and is no longer a cowardly introvert. He is an entirely different kid and completely comfortable being his quirky, wonderful self.

I realize that sometimes we have to go through all kinds of pain to find our path. I have never felt God more present in my life than I have walking through this journey with my son in the past two years.

Kristen's Story
Big Lessons in a Beautiful Journey

Although my third pregnancy seemed normal, I felt like something was amiss throughout the nine months. My motherly instinct told me that something was different this time.

My first child was breech, so at thirty-six weeks, my husband Brian and I had a consultation, including an ultrasound, to figure out birth options. We found out the amniotic fluid was extremely low, so we opted to have a cesarean section. Because this happened with my first child, we also had to go in at thirty-six weeks during each subsequent pregnancy to ensure the fluid level was adequate.

At this appointment in my third pregnancy, the technician took a long time at the ultrasound, finally saying that she was having difficulty getting a good measurement on the femur. She left the room to have the doctor look over the results to ensure the amount of amniotic fluid was acceptable. She was gone a long time, causing me some concern, but when she came back in, she reported that the doctor thought the fluid level was sufficient so I could leave. I had a feeling I should ask more questions, but since she said it was fine, I proceeded to go.

We had a planned C-section since I'd had C-sections with both of my other children and had significant scarring with those. The surgery went well and Russell was healthy after birth, so he did not have to go to the NICU. When we got to the recovery room, I fed him for the first time. I noticed his arms were not very long and it wasn't easy to get him in a comfortable position to burp him. I initially thought it was odd but didn't give it any additional thought.

When my husband and I took him home, I began to feel ill. Brian took me to the emergency room the following morning and we took Russell along since I was nursing him. They discovered I was leaking spinal fluid. They patched the spot leaking fluid and I instantly felt better. That day also happened to be Russell's first well-check, so we went from the hospital to the pediatrician.

At that appointment, the pediatrician was aware of what I was dealing with earlier that day. He told us that Russell looked great but that he would have us come back in ten days for a weight check, which I did not remember having to do with my other two children. At the appointment to weigh him, the doctor examined Russell and asked if we had noticed anything different about him. I questioned what he meant, and he asked if his arms were shorter than my other children's arms. I said no, even though I knew since the first time I went to burp him something was unlike my other kids. The pediatrician then told us that he believed that Russell had a form of dwarfism because he had some telltale signs. My husband and I had no idea that two average-sized people could have a child with dwarfism, plus we already had two average-size children.

I am generally emotional after I have a baby, but my world stopped that day. The doctor used terms that sounded extremely scary: kyphosis, achondroplasia, and sleep apnea, to name a few. He suggested we go see a geneticist and a handful of other specialty doctors, but we were first sent directly to the children's hospital for a full skeletal scan.

We got the results later that day: Russell's diagnosis was achondroplasia, a form of dwarfism. The pediatrician suggested that we call him if we had any questions and not get on the internet. He said that everything would be fine, but we didn't need to be overwhelmed and frightened by all the information that could be found on the web.

I wish I could say that our only reaction was "He will be short and that is okay," but this stopped us in our tracks. We had no idea what this diagnosis meant. How would this change Russell's life and our lives? Would he be able to chase his dreams like my other children? Knowing, when your baby is only ten days old, what the mark on his back will be for his entire life, is hard. We had never met a little person or had any interactions with someone with dwarfism. We had a lot to learn.

Russell also had sleep apnea, so he rarely slept, which also meant I rarely slept. On his worst days, he would wake up every seven minutes. In the few months following his diagnosis, there were some dark days. Since we did not know anybody who had a child with dwarfism, it was lonesome. Our extended family was terrific, but it was hard not to have the support of others who have walked in the same shoes.

When we found out that Russell was a little person, we saw a geneticist who gathered an in-depth medical history from my husband and me, along with detailed information on my pregnancies, including medical notes from my OB-GYN. The geneticist saw the note in my chart stating that Russell's femur was measuring small at my thirty-six-week appointment. They had caught it that day, but for whatever reason, did not tell me. That wouldn't have changed anything in the long run, but had we known going into the birth (when I was still able to sleep at night), I might have handled the news differently. It wouldn't have changed how we loved him, but we might have been more prepared, having more time to research before he arrived.

We were initially unsure whether we should tell our other two children about Russell being a little person. We didn't know if they would understand because they were so young. One evening at dinner, we told them, at ages four and three, and their simple response was "okay," and they didn't question any further.

We moved to a new state when Russell was fifteen months old. It was a difficult time because we had to explain to new people about his dwarfism. We also knew I was pregnant with our fourth child. We learned that every person has a 1 in 2,500 chance of having a little person, even with no family history of dwarfism, because genetic mutation simply happens. Even though we were back at the same odds that everyone else has for that mutation, we were still a little nervous about this pregnancy, so we had some additional testing done.

We were grateful for how Russell completely changed our parenting perspective, particularly how we viewed our children and how we gauged success. Having our fourth child pushed us to not baby Russell as much as we might have. Our desire for all our children became for them to be good people, work hard, and be kind to others.

Many nights I cried and prayed for God to take my legs and make Russell average size. I tried to negotiate with God with what I thought needed to be changed. There were hard days, but I eventually realized that Russell was perfect just as he was.

Before he entered school, we were allowed to pen a letter to be mailed to every kindergarten family explaining that Russell has achondroplasia. We asked that the parents speak with their children to make them aware that he is small but is supposed to be in that class. We sent the letter because kids, especially when younger, are inquisitive. Their curiosity isn't something to be embarrassed about. Once it was explained that Russell was short, they were okay with it and let it go. Every teacher Russell had was so supportive. We made clear that we didn't want the teachers to baby him. We have explained that he prefers to keep a low profile and not be singled out.

We read the book "Wonder," with Russell and he can relate to Auggie wishing he was "normal" and wouldn't get noticed or singled out, and I can relate to his mother because I have sat on Russell's bed with him at the end of hard days when he says, "I don't want to be a little person anymore."

It is hard to realize that we may never know his worst days. When he gets older, I must trust he can handle whatever he faces and that whoever he goes to for help will be a good support for him. Some people stare or point, but we ignore that. If someone asks a question, we are happy to address it. Brian and I know that we will never understand what he goes through. For example, if I went into a grocery store today, nobody would ever remember me. However, every time we go into a grocery store with Russell, he gets looked at and spoken to because people know him. People call him by his name, and there is good and bad with that. It is lovely when people refer to you by your name, but I often ask Russell after someone speaks to him if he knows who spoke, and often, he has no idea. As much as the media has improved by including a handful of TV shows that portray little people, there is a slim chance that you will run into someone in your day-to-day life that has dwarfism.

Russell is the same on the inside as anybody else; his outside is just different and he cannot do anything about it. Is he going to be the last kid picked for a team? Probably. He will always compete with average-sized kids. If he wants to play a sport, he will work hard and play it. He can still participate in most activities, but some things look different for him. No matter what he attempts, he always gives his best effort and has a good attitude.

Next year, he will be in middle school, which is hard for any child, but I feel it will be particularly daunting for Russell. I have to know that this is his life and he has to deal with whatever comes his way. I hope that we can help him handle whatever he walks through so that when he is out on his own as an adult, he has had enough experience to understand that bad days happen but are not the norm. Hopefully, the Lord has given him some thick skin because he will need it in the real world.

We have met some adult little people who have been good examples for Russell to navigate the world as he gets older. God has placed exceptional people in our lives. We have met other little people and families through the LPA, Little People of America. Russell has a great community and I pray that continues as he gets older. I also pray that his average-size friends who know him today take the knowledge about Russell out into the world when they are grown.

At the end of the book *Wonder*, the principal talks about how our courage, kindness, and character are the most necessary traits to live a rich life. I not only want Russell to live with these values but all my children. Having Russell has taught us what characteristics are most important and that we need to be kinder than necessary.

Having a son who is a little person has its challenges, but I believe we are better people from what we have learned along the way. This may not have been the path we dreamed Russell, or my family would travel, but it remains a beautiful journey.

Evelyn's Story
Different Than Normal

Both of my children were different from the time they were born. When my son, Jacob, was in kindergarten, he had the best teacher. She was wonderful. She understood that something was wrong with him by the middle of the year. During story time, he would fall asleep. When he did not fall asleep, the class would be talking apples and he would be talking oranges. This is what tipped the teacher off that something was not right with him. We had his hearing tested and he did have 30 to 35 percent hearing loss, due to fluid in his ears, so we got tubes placed. That helped the hearing, but after the tube placement, the teacher thought additional testing needed to be done because he still was not having logical conversations in the classroom.

We agreed for him to be tested. A student-teacher led that testing. My husband and I went to a meeting to get the results. When we walked into the room, there was a long table with twelve people around it. The student-teacher started explaining that she had a terrible time with Jacob during the testing. He didn't want to come with her so she told him that they would go for a walk, then ended up in her office for the test. When she started administering the test, he began to cry. This teacher told him that he couldn't leave until the testing was done so he needed to stop crying. After testing was completed, the student-teacher concluded Jacob was going to be a murderer and a rapist. My son had just turned six! I was baffled by this seemingly far-fetched and illogical projection of my first-grader as an adult. All the people around the table agreed with her statement.

The example she gave for their conclusion was that when she had shown him a picture of bears on a bicycle with a picnic basket and asked him to tell a story about what was on the page, the story he told described a scenario with a lot of blood and guts. I explained that he recently saw his dog get killed by a car in front of our home.

We discussed the testing more, but the conversation went from bad to worse. He was labeled as "other health impaired." I was determined not to cry. When my husband and I left the meeting, we looked at each other and wondered what had just happened.

The next day, we got a call from a parent advocate who was in the meeting. She said she couldn't believe what we had been told and was astonished that I kept my cool. She apologized that professionals had already written him off at six years old. That lady was a mentor to me for several years. Her son, who was now a young adult, was mentally challenged, so she wanted to help others in the same boat. There were more resources available to help us than when her son was growing up, and she gave us a list of who to speak with and places to call. She explained that I needed to fight for what we wanted and needed for my son. She told me that God had put her on my path and I agreed. I felt she understood my feelings and could help us get my son what he needed. She was an angel to my family.

The meeting at the school was the beginning of a long road. When Jacob was in fourth grade, I had frequent meetings with his teacher. The day after one such meeting, Jacob came home with a note from that teacher stating she was reporting him for touching a female student inappropriately three months earlier. I went ballistic because if this were true, I should have been notified immediately, and we had been having regular meetings with the teacher, including one the previous day.

Shortly before this time, I got a job as a special education assistant in a private school. I decided to bring my kids to that school with me. Jacob began at the new school for fifth grade, which was great timing since all kids were transitioning to middle school that year anyway. He functioned well there. He was identified as ED or emotionally disturbed in middle school. In high school, he ran cross-country and track. His teachers and coaches embraced who he was and loved him. He did well and graduated from high school. That same year, the new diagnosis of Asperger's syndrome, a disorder on the autism spectrum, was created, so we tried to have him evaluated for this but did not have any luck in doing so. When he was twenty-one, he had his first schizophrenic break and was diagnosed with paranoid schizophrenia. He now resides in a group home, as he can no longer safely live by himself.

When my daughter, Sarah, was about eighteen months old, she fell playing ring-around-the-rosy. When we pulled her up, her shoulder and elbow went out of joint. The doctor was able to put it back in. By the time she was three, she could put her shoulder and elbow in and out of place on her own. She was very clumsy, and if she fell, it would go out of joint. We didn't think much of it.

By first grade, her arm had atrophied and she ended up needing physical therapy. We were often told that her pain and weakness were all in her head and that she complained to get attention.

At the age of twelve, Sarah opened a can of peanuts and when she went to set it down, she hit her pinky finger and thought she had broken it. She was put into a splint. This incident started pain through her arm, neck, and down one whole side of her body. We went to a couple of neurologists and to a children's hospital trying to find answers. After some time and a couple of preliminary diagnoses, she was finally diagnosed with Complex Regional Pain Syndrome. What that meant for Sarah is that her nervous system went crazy when she got injured. Usually, when you are hurt, your brain says "Ouch!" and you pull away from the painful stimulus, but with CRPS, the pain is constant and heightened.

Sarah went through a period when she could not keep clothes on because they hurt, and sheets on the bed caused pain all over her skin. Her body shut down and the only thing she could move was her left arm. The single place we could touch her where it wouldn't hurt was on the tip of her nose. We had to wait one month to get to see a specialist. During that time, she writhed in pain. I had to do range-of-motion exercises on her so she wouldn't atrophy. She and I both cried during those movements.

She finally got into a rehabilitation unit at a local hospital. They had to make a special spot for her because she was a minor. We met some wonderful people during her stay there and she got fabulous care and therapy. Sarah was able to walk out of rehab. We felt so fortunate because we had feared she would live the rest of her life in a wheelchair.

She continued to have health problems that medical professionals couldn't identify. Sometimes she would fall onto the floor with no apparent cause. She spent more time with tutors than in school. We came to accept that this was simply part of her life. Her ability to walk seemed cyclical. She had many diagnoses, did various therapies, and was in and out of a wheelchair through the years. She graduated from high school. She tried a holistic approach for a while and it worked well for her for about five years when she was a young adult. She was able to be a nanny for a family for eleven years, but she had many ups and downs during that time. She now uses an electric wheelchair all the time.

Both of my kids' conditions are genetic. My husband and I both went through a period of feeling parental guilt because of their problems.

We have two children very different from "normal" or "regular" kids. My family doesn't look like most families. I had always been taught that you play the hand you were dealt. My mantra has always been "God's got it." My husband was mad at God for about sixteen years because of our children's conditions and didn't go to church during that time. For me, I could not have gotten through any of this without God. When I was a child, I received a wall hanging with the poem "Footprints in the Sand." That poem and the image of God carrying my family and me during the tough times were what got me through. I believe that God sent angels in the form of humans to help us and be a part of our lives right when we needed them most. I chose to find the good in the tough times with our kids, and often, it was the people surrounding us, supporting us, and showing up when we least expected that was the true blessing.

Mandy's Story
Finding Joy in Simple Things

Jocelyn was born a normal full-term baby even though she was not very active in my womb. I went into labor naturally, but after I had an epidural, her heart rate kept dropping. Doctors ended up doing an emergency C-section because her umbilical cord was wrapped around her neck. When she came out, she was blue but quickly started crying and breathing on her own. Even though her arrival into the world gave us a bit of a scare, her doctor said she was a healthy baby.

She had a bit of delay with a few milestones, such as standing, but every child does things on their own schedule, so I was not worried. Her pediatrician noted she was a little behind, so she was placed in First Steps for therapies from ages one to three to get her caught up to her peers.

At age three, Jocelyn was at day care and had a seizure with convulsions, turning blue during the episode. That seizure lasted about a minute and she was rushed to the emergency room. She had an MRI done, but we were told the seizure was related to her having a fever of 105. They also noted that she had a little fluid on her brain, but we were told that was nothing to worry about.

A few weeks later, Jocelyn vomited a foaming substance several times throughout the day. My mom came over to help me because I was having a difficult time tending to a sick toddler while caring for my infant son, who was two weeks old at the time. While my mom was there, Jocelyn had another seizure. It started with her arm rhythmically moving, followed by her entire body erratically moving, lasting thirty to forty minutes. We called 911 and the paramedics transported her to the hospital.

After the second seizure, which so different from the first, we were told Jocelyn had epilepsy. She had another MRI, which showed a change in her brain from just weeks before. The doctor said he believed that she had a type of leukodystrophy, a genetic disorder that affects the brain, but there are thirty-nine different types of leukodystrophy, and it was not clear which form she had.

When she got to first grade, she could not keep up in the regular classroom, so she entered the skilled-life classroom and did well. She was a social butterfly and had many friends. We finally got referred to a neurogeneticist when Jocelyn was six and got the diagnosis of Alexander disease. The odds of having it are 1 in a million. It was not hereditary, but rather, things didn't develop properly when she was growing in utero.

With Alexander disease, the white matter in her brain is destroyed while fibers accumulate causing physical and mental delays and seizures. As the white matter changed in Jocelyn's brain, it affected her functioning. We were told that the life expectancy of someone with this condition is teens or twenties, and occasionally, they can live to be in their thirties. Since learning of our daughter's diagnosis, we have been doing all we could to manage the symptoms, but there is no cure for Alexander disease.

Around this same time, Jocelyn began behaving aggressively, biting, kicking, and screaming for hours on end. There was no trigger for the behaviors, so we called the neurologist who suggested giving her an extra dose of anti-anxiety medication. She had always been anxious, but the additional medication didn't help calm her. A couple of hours later, when she still had not calmed, the neurologist requested we take her to the emergency room. Nothing was medically contributing to her behaviors, so the physician suggested taking her to a stress center. That center would not care for her because of her age and her neurodegenerative disease, and we could not find anyone else to help. It took us years to find the care that Jocelyn needed. She continued to have fits of aggression, including trying to break out the car window, and biting. It was a trying time because we often had to ensure she did not hurt herself or anyone else during these episodes.

Other than these behaviors and an unsteady gait that she had always had, she had not exhibited any other disease progression. She was healthy with no decline for several years.

In 2016, she began to have paranoid behaviors and would startle easily. She did not want to be alone. She stopped going to the bathroom and had accidents. By this point, we had a third child, and it was a challenge to care for Jocelyn, clean up her messes, ensure her safety, and care for our two other children. In one instance, we had asked her to clean up her room and she didn't want to do it, so she purposely collapsed to the floor, breaking all the metatarsal bones in her right foot. This made mobility more difficult.

That was the starting point of a physical decline. Jocelyn had a caregiver during this time period, but she left the agency and we could not find anybody else who could help. We had one caregiver for a short time and while in her care, Jocelyn fell and cut her knee open. She ended up getting cellulitis in that leg, and while she was hospitalized for that, her left lung collapsed. That led to pulmonary issues.

We talked with the doctor about how it was becoming too much for my husband and me to manage Jocelyn's medical care while we cared for our two other children and worked at our full-time jobs. Her doctor admitted her to the children's hospital and had her evaluated for a couple of nights. She was then transferred to the behavioral health unit at a nearby children's hospital because they dealt with children with neurological diseases and behaviors. They adjusted her medications, and monitored her for a week, and then discharged her. After a few days at home, we again saw an escalation in her behaviors, and she returned to the children's hospital for two weeks. Upon returning home, she continued having accidents and paranoid behaviors. She started having increased difficulty walking and fell often.

We signed up to be part of a research study on Alexander disease. She ended up going to the children's hospital where the study was being conducted. We learned that her startled responses were actually a type of seizure, abnormal firings in her brain causing the startled responses and behaviors like biting and hitting. Her meds were once again adjusted and the new medication has worked miracles in controlling the behaviors. She also had brain surgery to drain fluid that was on her brain, but none of it improved her walking or toileting.

Because of her behavior, we tried to get her into a skilled nursing facility for kids and adults with mental and physical needs, but we were told she was too mobile. She would have been at risk for eloping from the facility or hurting one of the other residents. Once she was no longer able to walk, she was admitted to that facility.

I hate that she isn't home, but she loves it at the facility and it is the best place for her because of all of her medical needs. It was the hardest decision we ever had to make. I think any parent would want their child to be in their home. I cried as we got her settled in her room, but the staff reassured us that she was in good hands and would be getting great care. We bring her home for a couple of days at Christmas and she enjoys being home, but by the end of her stay, she says she is ready to go back to be with her friends.

Shortly after being admitted to the facility, she had to be hospitalized because her oxygen levels had dropped. She was doing well but the levels continued to drop and she had to be intubated again. When I got to the hospital, twenty people were working on her. A doctor came over to us and told me that it wasn't looking good. They had one more medicine to try to see if she would respond to that, but there was a chance she wouldn't make it. She did pull through that day and was put on a ventilator after a few days. Things continued to fluctuate. They extubated her because she got better, but she declined again and had to be re-intubated. She ended up being intubated for thirty days and was hospitalized for six weeks. Up to this point, she had been eating by mouth (although she had some swallowing issues for years due to a lack of muscle control in her throat related to Alexander disease).

After being intubated for thirty days, she was no longer able to eat by mouth. Because Alexander disease affects the muscles, she had problems swallowing and having her food go all the way down. They did a swallow study after this prolonged intubation and determined that she couldn't get any food to go down, so she needed a feeding tube. We were told that she could regain some strength in her throat and a new swallow study should be done in a few months. She did pass a swallow study, so we allowed her to have soft foods like pudding, but within two weeks, she was back in the hospital with pneumonia because she had aspirated her food. We gave her the choice at that time of continuing to eat by mouth with the potential for more hospitalizations, or just using her feeding tube, and she chose the feeding tube. I think getting the tube was harder on me than her because I enjoyed taking her snacks when I visited.

My husband and I have been able to reach out to others dealing with Alexander disease so we can try to help them. We know what it's like to feel alone in a diagnosis. We didn't meet another family with Alexander disease for many years. When we did, it was such a relief to know that we weren't the only ones. Jocelyn is now sixteen, but unlike most sixteen-year-olds, she is pure and innocent and takes delight in the simple pleasures of life. She loves to get her nails done and visit with friends and family. She is a great example to appreciate what we have and what we are able to do.

We have learned so much from Jocelyn. She taught us to appreciate the smallest things because that is how she is. She is very simple and does things at her own pace. Even though she has had many medical problems, she is a joy, and I love the perspective she has given my family and me.

Cristy's Story
Fighting for Answers

When my daughter Brooklyn was in the fifth grade, she began getting sick unusually often. She constantly had a sore throat. I had her tested multiple times for strep throat, and it always turned out negative. Her pediatrician finally sent her to an ENT, and by the time we got in to see him, her throat no longer hurt. He told us her throat looked fine, so he guessed she was having allergy issues. We scheduled her for allergy testing. After being tested for over one hundred possibilities, the only thing she was found to be allergic to was dust. At this point, she had been on numerous meds, including allergy meds, but nothing seemed to help. I took her back to her pediatrician and explained that she wasn't allergic to anything, so he took her off all the medications. After this, she would still have random spurts of sore throat, followed by its equally random disappearance.

One weekend in January, she was at a birthday party and wasn't feeling well. She called me to come to pick her up early, which I did. The following day she couldn't physically get out of bed. Her knees were stiff and hurt so intensely she couldn't bend them. She also had a sore throat, her stomach hurt, she was sensitive to light, the joints in her fingers hurt, and her head hurt, but she did not have a fever. I took her to the doctor that morning and he thought she had mononucleosis. I had to take her to the hospital for testing, along with a strep test. Both came back negative. They said that perhaps the mono test was taken too soon after the onset of her symptoms and may be showing a false negative result. They told her to go home and rest because mono was still a possibility. After a week, her symptoms hadn't changed and she hadn't gotten any better. She still hadn't had a fever, which puzzled the doctor because she was tested for mono again with no change in her numbers, meaning it wasn't mono. The doctor thought it might have been a virus and said to go home and rest.

She was sick in bed for eleven days and didn't do anything. Most of the symptoms had disappeared, but her legs remained stiff and she couldn't straighten them. Nearly every day she showed different symptoms. I also took her back to the pediatrician, and I was given a referral to a rheumatologist. At this point, she could no longer walk. Her knees were bent, so we had to help her walk. I carried her on my back up and down the stairs in our home. The rheumatologist thought it could be arthritis caused by an infection, so the specialist put her on a different medication and instructed us to come back in two weeks. Brooklyn continued to have bouts of pain in her head, throat, and fingers. I strongly requested she get an MRI to rule out rheumatoid arthritis in both knees. It came back only as edema/swelling in her knees, but not arthritis. The rheumatologist said she couldn't do anything else for us, so she sent us to a pediatric orthopedic doctor. At this point, I was doing research online to figure out what was happening with my daughter's health. The orthopedic doctor looked at the MRI and didn't see anything besides the swelling. He then did an x-ray, which also didn't show a problem. He decided to put Brooklyn on a different medication. She was on several meds at this point and she said the pain never went away no matter what pain meds they gave her.

The orthopedic doc sent us to physical therapy. The physical therapists focused on helping Brooklyn's knee pain. They put her on crutches because she still couldn't walk. After two weeks of physical therapy, the orthopedic doctor put her on different anti-inflammatory meds because the others were not working. He thought there might have been tendonitis in her knees but said the therapy and this new medication should help. At this point, the therapist was stumped by her condition, not understanding why she could not straighten her knees. By the end of two months, they managed to get her legs straight. Brooklyn was supposed to wear braces at night, but she said they made the pain worse. She would cry and take them off in the middle of the night. We stopped using the braces after three or four weeks. We went back to the orthopedic doctor and switched her meds yet again. He was beginning to suspect other possibilities; he couldn't figure out why she was experiencing that much pain. He began researching nightly on his off hours and said he might want to send her to the Cincinnati Children's Hospital. I asked if there was anything else they could do, to which he responded that there was a surgical procedure they could do involving the nerve in the knee. After researching, I saw that this would be very painful and much could go wrong with this procedure. Brooklyn didn't go back to school for an entire full day for a month because she could only stay there for a short time before ending up in the nurse's office crying in pain.

My husband and I were discouraged, as was the doctor, since he couldn't figure out why she was experiencing so much pain. My husband and I started discussing Brooklyn's condition with people we knew in the medical field. Two different people recommended one acupuncturist in the area. Around this time, we were also waiting to meet with an infectious disease doctor. When we finally managed to see that doctor, she ran many tests, which all came back negative. The infectious disease doctor then questioned whether this was all in Brooklyn's head. My motherly instinct told me that this was not the case, that there was something physically wrong. That doctor took her off every one of her meds. Brooklyn continued to have pain and still felt horrible, even though her legs were straight. It hurt for her to walk. She cried every single day. After that appointment, we decided to take her to the acupuncturist to see if we could find another way to help instead of the surgery or going to Cincinnati Children's Hospital for further testing.

The acupuncturist felt all over her legs, which no other doctor had ever done. The acupuncturist noted that the problem wasn't Brooklyn's knee; it was tendonitis in her tibia and fibula. That isn't something anybody else had noted. Right before her first acupuncture session, Brooklyn said her pain level, on a scale of 1 to 10, was a 10. Right after the first appointment, her pain was down to a 5. We went back the next week for another treatment and her pain receded to 2½ to 3. After five appointments with the acupuncturist, she wasn't 100 percent without pain, but she was close to it. We planned to go to Hawaii for our summer vacation after that fifth acupuncture treatment. The acupuncturist said she could walk on vacation, but she couldn't run, and she had to continue using ibuprofen. The plan was for her to have one more acupuncture session after we got back from Hawaii.

Two days before we left for vacation, Brooklyn told us her ear hurt. I took her to the doctor since we were preparing to fly. Her doctor didn't see anything wrong, so he thought it could have been a virus. We left for our vacation, and for the duration of the flight, Brooklyn was dizzy, her head and ears hurting. She was miserable. She wasn't any better once we arrived. After two days, I called her doctor, and they gave her a prescription for medicine for the dizziness. Then, a day later, I knew that the issue was something more because she couldn't even lift her head. I took her to urgent care, and they told us that she had a double ear infection. The flight could have made it worse. She was also dehydrated. She got two meds for the ear infection plus the meds for dizziness. She felt terrible for the whole trip. We flew home, and she cried again because of the pain in her ears. I called the ENT as soon as we got home and he was able to see her the next day. He told us that Brooklyn's ears had cleared up, even though they were still causing her pain. Her throat was neither hurting nor red. The ENT sent her to the neurologist. Once we made it there, the neurologist thought it could just be everything all together, but he did put her on a new medicine for headaches, with the possibility of migraines being the issue.

About a month later, Brooklyn began complaining about her throat again. I took her back to the ENT, but of course by the time we got in to an appointment, the pain had stopped. Our normal ENT was on vacation, so this ENT was new to us. He suspected that she had tonsillitis. He looked over all the information in her chart and instructed us to bring her to him instead of the pediatrician the next time Brooklyn got sick.

Since there were still ongoing issues during this time, I Googled everything I could to figure out what was going on with my daughter. This was around the end of August. By the end of September, Brooklyn no longer wanted to eat because her throat hurt so badly. I scheduled an appointment with the ENT for ten days later. During this time, she couldn't eat anything; she said it felt like she was swallowing knives. Her symptoms began to show up again—throat pain, joint pain, headaches, etc. Once we finally got in to the ENT, he briefly looked at her and asked, "Are you ready to get your tonsils out?" They scheduled the procedure for two painful weeks later.

After it was over, she took weeks to recover from the surgery, but all of her symptoms disappeared. She has been healthy ever since. It was tonsillitis causing all the issues over the past several months, along with tendonitis in her legs. She was sick for far too long.

When the doctors could not find the answers, I am grateful that I maintained that the problems were physical instead of imaginary. I am glad that I listened to my motherly instinct and kept pursuing an answer to what was making her so sick. Even though the road was tough and long, there were so many blessings along the way. I am thankful for the friends leading us to the acupuncturist who helped alleviate some of her pain. It was a blessing that the regular ENT was unavailable and that the ENT who filled in for Brooklyn's appointment is the one who finally came up with the correct diagnosis. Most importantly, we are greatly relieved that we finally found out what was wrong with her and that she is healthy once again.

Kirby's Story
Special Needs, Special Gifts

If someone had asked me before my wife and I had children how I would feel if my child were autistic, I would have said it terrified me. Then along came my son, Luke. From the time he was little, we had a feeling he was different. He didn't match the charts for when a child should walk and talk. My wife, Melissa, and I sought help from physical and speech therapists, who all assured us that Luke was not autistic. After all, he made eye contact and babbled. It wasn't until he was in kindergarten that we finally had a diagnosis: high-functioning autism with ADHD (attention-deficit hyperactivity disorder). The evaluation was done at Duke University and the results were no surprise to us. We learned there was a spectrum for autism and Luke was near the high-functioning end. He is neurodiverse, while his older brother, Jack, is neurotypical. There had been challenges all along, but we finally had a name for them.

As we searched for occupational therapy for Luke, we eventually found ABA (Applied Behavioral Analysis) therapy, which uses motivation rather than punishment. Luke was guided by positive talk and rewards and was taught life skills. Still, we wondered what the future would hold for Luke. Would he ever be able to live on his own? Would he find a job? Like all parents, we wanted both of our children to succeed in whatever endeavors they chose.

At a diversity and inclusion conference I attended, I was dismayed by a great deal of conversation on racial and gender inclusion, while there was no mention of the inclusion of people with disabilities. After the conference, I realized I wanted to raise more awareness about this issue somehow, especially about how it relates to employment. Melissa and I spent time researching and learned that 80 percent of those with autism were either underemployed or unemployed. Even those who had college degrees were often unable to get a job. This spoke to how corporate America needed to be educated on how to bring those on the autism spectrum into the workforce.

Employers need to recognize the strengths these individuals have and find a way to leverage those strengths. Since those with autism have different ways of viewing situations, they are innovative in solving specific problems in areas other haven't been able to. They see the world through a different lens and are focused, detail-oriented, and creative, while having an incredible work ethic. Employers should not be overlooking these strengths. Certainly, people on the autism spectrum can have challenges, but we all do, and if given a chance they can bring great ideas to the table if their diagnosis isn't seen as a weakness. There are a few large companies that have targeted programs in place around hiring individuals on the spectrum. They have discovered that if it is done the right way, the company has great benefits to gain by leveraging people's strengths.

In the summer of 2019, our son Jack and I decided it would be fun to run some 5K races. One of the races was a charity 5K in which we could choose which charity we wanted to support by running. Because of Luke, we chose to raise money for Esteamed Coffee, a tax-exempt nonprofit organization that was launching a coffee shop employing people with disabilities.

After the race, Jack and I approached the organization's tent, where we met the two founders. After introducing myself, I offered to volunteer. They had a great mission and I wanted to be a part of it. After chatting a bit, they asked me if I would like to join their board and I accepted. Their biggest need at that point was fundraising for the coffee shop.

At my second board meeting that August, I pitched an idea for a fitness endurance event to raise both money and awareness for the nonprofit. I'd always wanted to participate in such an event, so I offered to ride a bicycle from coffee shop to coffee shop across North Carolina, splitting the funds raised between Esteamed Coffee and other, comparable shops. I was still forming the idea in mind, but as we spoke, it became more concrete. The other board members asked if I could announce it at our September fundraiser. They also agreed that the endurance event should happen by the end of the year. By the time I addressed the 150 people at the fundraiser, there was no turning back.

The mental and emotional expenditure needed to plan the event was more than I could have imagined. We had to find sponsors, locate all the places we would visit during the ride, and find willing participants. I also had to assemble a crew to follow me. And then there was the physical challenge of getting into shape. I hadn't ridden a bike in years. I didn't even own one.

I bought a bike and started riding, often 50 or 60 miles at a time, even in the pouring rain. Those training miles built my confidence in my ability to complete the undertaking. I even took a week off work to train for the event.

In the meantime, I started talking about my upcoming ride with my coworkers. I was amazed to find all kinds of people who were willing to help. One coworker was a videographer and made a professional video to use as a promotional tool for the event. After he sent it to some of his connections in the media, I was inundated with requests for interviews. Many news channels along my route wanted to run stories on the fundraiser.

We planned our path and itinerary for the December ride by connecting the dots between coffee shops that employed differently-abled persons in the state of North Carolina. It was an incredibly long route, winding 412 miles through the state over four and a half days, with stops at seven different coffee shops. Until the news media showed up, I hadn't realized how much visibility and awareness this event would raise for these small shops in their communities.

We were treated like royalty at each stop we made. It was remarkable how incredibly welcoming the people were. That alone was worth the ride, but I felt fortunate to have the media there to raise awareness of what each shop was doing. At the end of the day, this media attention was less about the money raised and more about the visibility that it brought. It did attract subsequent donors too.

By January, we had the funds needed to open the doors of Esteamed Coffee. From that standpoint, the adventure was a huge success. It was a daunting task and physically taxing, but the outcome was fantastic.

I tried to put myself out there to do what I could to raise awareness and let others know there is a path for kids on the autism spectrum. I wanted to help create that path for Luke and others like him to find employment as adults. I wanted them to know that there were, in fact, companies that would value them and offer them jobs.

I'm continuing to do research and trying to understand what it takes for a corporate initiative to successfully hire people on the spectrum and figure out what jobs would be the right fit. At the same time, we need to figure out how to support and prepare those with autism for employment. What does it take to help those on the spectrum find a place to land? If autistic people want to work, we need to build bridges between them, their caregivers, and corporate

America. Where are those companies? How do we prepare them? How do corporations have to adapt? Ideally, hiring people on the spectrum would make quite a dent in the current unemployment statistics.

How did I feel when I heard my son was autistic? I felt love. It didn't change a thing for me about how I felt about Luke. Having a child with autism can be quite a challenge, but we honestly wouldn't change a single thing about him. He is creative and makes us laugh and I love watching his joy and passion for cooking. There is a place for Luke and others like him. Because of him, I'll continue my quest to do what I can to make employment better for those with autism. Even if it takes riding another 412 miles.

5

End of Life

After an unforgettable six-week camping vacation, my father-in-law, George, began experiencing increased fatigue and back pain. He and my mother-in-law had logged thousands of miles driving to the southwestern United States. When we saw him at Christmas that year, he frequently napped during our visit. It was normal for him to take an afternoon nap, but he napped more throughout the day during that visit.

He went to an orthopedic doctor after the new year and was referred for an x-ray and MRI, with an expectation that they would find the problem and perhaps he would get a referral for physical therapy. Unfortunately, a cancerous spot was found, so he contacted his urology oncologist (because he had bladder cancer years prior) for advice. Immediately he was referred for further testing to determine if it had metastasized from his bladder cancer, which it had not. That would have been unexpected since it had been more than five years since he had bladder surgery.

The next step was to get him into radiation to reduce the size of the tumor, which was causing pain on his spine. He did get immediate relief with that treatment. Further tests identified small-cell lung cancer that had metastasized to his spine and other areas. It was a fast-growing cancer with a poor prognosis. When George finished radiation, he ended up with pneumonia when we visited him over spring break. He had one good day when we got there and we took family pictures that day, for which we are so grateful now. The next day he was hospitalized and stayed there for the remainder of our visit. I desperately wanted him to get better because I could not imagine him not being here. I wanted him to live forever, or at least long enough to see my kids grow up.

He was treated for pneumonia and then decided to do chemo-therapy shortly after that. He tolerated the treatments well for a few days, but then he deteriorated. At the end of the month, he had a quick decline. My family was on our way to my son's soccer game with another family in a town an hour from home when my mother-in-law called to tell us that George had taken a turn for the worst and might not live much longer. We decided to go ahead and allow my son to play the soccer game. After the game we drove home and my husband quickly packed up and drove the 600 miles to be with his parents. He got there in time to say goodbye. I was grateful for that.

George and I had a special relationship, and we had many mean-ingful conversations. After he passed away, I thought back to a chat I had with him during our Christmas visit. He was sitting outside on the deck and said, "Deanne (he pronounced my name Dee ANN ee), I am tired." I told him to go inside and lie down. He said, "No. I am TIRED," with a strange emphasis on "tired." I did not understand at the time what he meant, but I now believe he was telling me that he was tired of fighting, tired of the pain, and did not want to stick around when he wasn't able to do as much as he used to do.

I am so thankful that my kids have fond memories of their grandpa. They had many fun and memorable times with him. Even though George didn't get to see them completely grow up, they were old enough when he passed that they never forget him. I like to think that he is looking down on them and watching them with a grand-fatherly pride. I hold the memories of him dear to my heart. I am so thankful for the many years I had him in my life. I miss him so much, but I could not have asked for a better father-in-law.

I wrote this in memory of George:

> Memories of you taste like strawberry milkshakes,
> Feels like you leaning in to tell a story,
> Smells like roasting marshmallows,

Looks like my kids running into your arms,
And sounds like you saying my name as only
you did.

Laura's Story
Finding Love after Loss

My husband, Jim, died unexpectedly when I was forty-four years old. I was left a widow with five children ranging in age from five to seventeen. It was difficult for all of us, and we all had different methods of grieving. I got my children involved in a grief center that had a program designed for kids. I also was part of this group, and through it, I learned that there was neither a "right" way to grieve nor a timeline for grief. My dad had died a year and a half before my husband, so I understood grief. However, this time it was different.

About a month after my husband's passing, I remember sitting on my bed and realizing that I could see myself remarrying. I couldn't imagine *not* having marriage as part of my life. I felt God putting on my heart to feel no guilt or regret in wanting a new husband. I knew that day that I would eventually marry again. In the meantime, I grieved ceaselessly.

After a period of grief, I did date a few men I met through online dating. It is tough to be in your forties and reenter the dating world. I had been married for twenty years. After a few years of casual online dating and not finding anyone I wanted to date seriously, a couple down the street—friends of mine—told me that they would be happy to arrange a date with a good friend of theirs, Tom. He was a single man who had never married or had children. I decided to go for it. On the night of the date, I walked to my neighbors' house, where we had all agreed to meet for our double date. Wondering how to introduce myself, I decided that the awkwardness of meeting someone that my friends had set me up with called for a simple handshake. To my surprise, Tom met me with a huge bear hug. Because of his warm introduction, we were comfortable with each other right off the bat. The double date with my neighbor friends, which included archery and dinner, was quite fun. Tom was easy to get along with and had a great sense of humor.

The next day, the neighbor who had arranged the evening asked if I had a good time on the date. She said Tom was asking for my number. I agreed she could give it to him. Tom and I began texting frequently. Our schedules were busy, so we didn't have a chance to go out again for three more weeks. It was apparent early on that he would at least be a close friend. Our relationship then progressed swiftly, and within three or four months, we both knew that we wanted to get married.

Tom told me that before we announced to the family that we planned on getting married, he wanted to ask my late husband's dad if he was okay with Tom marrying me. How many guys would do that? Tom was the sweetest man I knew. Jim's parents remained closely involved in our lives after Jim passed away. They only wanted what was best for my kids and me, so my former father-in-law gave his blessing for Tom and me to marry.

My kids all took the news differently, just as they had grieved differently. When Tom and I married, I kept my first married name and hyphenated it with my new married name because it was important that my first husband remain a part of my life and my family. I tell Tom that I am not married to a ghost, but I want his memory to be present for myself and the kids. Tom wants to hear stories of my first husband. He tells me that he doesn't want to replace Jim. I make sure my kids know that they can say anything about their dad without me stopping them. Tom and I both want them to know that they can tell him anything they want. Tom harbors no jealousy. Tom says he believes that this was supposed to be his family, and I feel he deserves one. He was single for a large portion of his life and had no children. He wants to be a part of my kids' lives but gives me space to make some parenting decisions alone, especially regarding my older children. I also want him to be supportive and help me with some parenting.

I would never wish this journey on anyone, but I realize now that I had to have a loss to have Tom in my life. I genuinely believe that my dad and my first husband sent Tom to be my new husband. I have to maintain a childlike faith that I cannot begin to explain. I have gratitude for Tom being placed in my life. My story is bittersweet in many aspects. I couldn't change one thing without changing everything in my life. I have no remorse, grief, or guilt in remarrying because Tom is a gift. My journey makes me smile now.

Britt's Story
Unexpected Loss and More Love

When my twin daughters were four and my other daughter was two, I had my hands plenty full, and we weren't trying for another pregnancy. I was trying on a dress in October for a wedding I would be a part of that December, and it would not fit. I couldn't believe I had gained weight. I didn't know I was pregnant at that time, but I soon started showing more symptoms and found out when I was fourteen weeks along. Life at that time was so busy that I didn't notice until then. I hate to admit it, but I was upset and angry at first because the pregnancy was not in our plans. I already had three little girls, I was working full time and was stressed. I have always been an emotional person, but looking back, I cannot believe that I was angry.

My husband and I eventually came to accept that I was pregnant and that we would soon have four kids ages four and under. When we told my parents, their reaction was less than warm because they did not understand why we were okay with having four kids. They were far from the only ones who thought that we were crazy for this reason.

I was thirty-six when I got pregnant, so the doctor asked if we wanted to do advanced testing. We decided not to test because we never had issues with our other children. At twenty weeks, I couldn't make it to the ultrasound, so I rescheduled it for four weeks later, the earliest they could get me in. When we were at the appointment, the ultrasound tech was cheerful as she began making conversation, asking us if we wanted to know the gender, but then her demeanor sharply changed. She quickly said that she was going to get the doctor.

The doctor came in, taking his time checking out the baby on the ultrasound. Finally, he informed us that our daughter had severe spina bifida and hydrocephalus. Because of where the sac was on the spinal cord, she would never walk. Understandably, this news was a complete shock. The doctor told us that since we already had three young kids, we needed to figure out how this arrangement would work in our lives. We went through many tears, constant prayer, and much planning for the logistics of our daughter's future. Our house was not handicap-accessible. We had to consider that our car may not be suited for her. We soon noticed everything we took for granted up to that point.

I was feeling fine at that time in the pregnancy. We went back to the doctor four weeks later for another ultrasound. There was only a very faint heartbeat, and the doctors did not fully understand what happened. My daughter ended up not making it. I had to deliver her naturally at thirty weeks, a truly awful experience. She was a beautiful baby, and for weeks, I kept thinking about how I would have had four daughters. I became angry again, this time at God, my husband, and what felt like the whole world. Why did this tragedy have to happen to me?

Once the news of what happened to us spread, many friends went radio silent toward us. I guess people didn't know what to say or how to talk to me, so they didn't reach out at all. I felt alone and more depressed than ever before. I did have my other three beautiful daughters, but they were confused about where the baby went. I struggled through some dark times that year. Once I started talking to people about our loss, it was comforting to find many others who had also lost a baby and walked in similar shoes.

After I spent some time in this depressed state, my husband came to me and said he thought we should have another baby. I instinctively tried to shut that down. There was no way I could go on that roller coaster again. However, my husband was very persistent, trying to convince me that another child was the trick to pull me out of my despair. He made it clear that another kid would not mean forgetting the daughter we lost but rather healing my broken heart.

I eventually came around, and once again, I became pregnant. I spent those forty weeks anxious, not enjoying the pregnancy because of the level of worry I felt. We did the testing and got frequent ultrasounds. After nine months, we had a healthy little boy.

I don't know why my daughter passed away and doubt I ever will. I don't understand why God allowed this to happen to me. However, I do know that I would not trade my little man for the world. He is a mama's boy. He is the most kind-hearted little boy, and with him, our family feels complete.

Experiencing those difficult stages of emotion got me where I am today. At one point in my life, I did not want kids at all, but I never felt complete until my son came along. I had to lose my girl, but if I'd had her, then I never would have had him. There was overwhelming darkness at times, but my son has brought much-needed light into our family.

When people go through something as tragic as loss, it can be hard to see more than a day in advance. Time truly does heal all wounds, even the most painful of them. I know that God has a plan for us, and even if we don't understand it in the present, we have to trust that when one door closes, He will soon open another. I had to have hope to escape my darkest place, something I did not have for a long time. Still, I held on, persevering day by day until His true plan for us was revealed.

My kids are teenagers now, pushing my buttons and driving me crazy, but I am wholly grateful for each of them and never want to take a second I have with them for granted.

Kirsten's Story
Cancer Is Hard, So Is Family

In 2013, my dad was diagnosed with cancer. Before he became severely sick, my two sisters and I wanted to be as helpful as possible, so we sought ways to assist him. We wanted the best result for our dad.

As we were trying to navigate this path, I felt that my sisters and I returned to the original roles we once had as children in the family. Kim saw herself once again as the middle child. I felt like the baby of the family, with everyone talking over me. My family did not view me as an adult because I hadn't lived near them since I had grown up. Kelly behaved as the oldest child, pressuring herself to do everything for the family, although that was not being asked of her. It was helpful for me to consider how these family roles were going to function throughout the process of my dad's disease. It became apparent that communication between us was going to be especially difficult. I wanted the family unit to come together for Dad. We had always been a loving family, but this time, working jointly for this cause was very different from the typical fun get-togethers at Christmas. We had to pull together to help Dad, and Mom too, as she was having a tough time as the primary caregiver. Cancer is taxing on everyone.

My mom, my sisters, and I were each dealing with the situation differently. I believe a moment from God transpired when I accepted that I was not the sister people would listen to when it came to helping Dad. This realization changed me. People generally think they have to be the hands-on help, but I realized that there was another way to benefit those around me. I began speaking through other people, such as the palliative care staff because they held my mom's ear. For example, I called the palliative care team to explain that Mom would not tell them she felt highly anxious. I understood that Dad would get better help if the staff could nudge Mom to acknowledge that she needed some help. I realized an argument with my mom or my sisters was not going to be helpful for anyone. This led to an unusual dynamic in the family. Typically, they would push my buttons and I would react accordingly. I was the youngest and used to being belittled. As a child, I thought that speaking louder was the way to get my point across. The long-term blessing from this awareness is that I have a new way of communicating because I was forced to speak differently due to our need for cooperation for our dad. This situation radically changed my thought processes and responses to my sisters and my mom.

When my dad was told that he had roughly six months left to live, I flew out to where he and my mom lived to help care for him and give my mom a much-needed break. As soon as my mom left for a short vacation, my dad's health dramatically declined. The next day, the hospice staff told us he had about three months remaining, and by the following day, they said he had only a month left to live.

I was very fortunate that my husband gave me his blessing to stay with my family once my dad started to decline, while he took care of everyday life at home. I am incredibly thankful that he cared for the kids and dealt with their schedules, even though doing so was hard for him. This gesture allowed me to not worry about them while I was away. During this time, my church family brought my husband and children meals, and neighbors offered to assist with carpooling and other tasks to help lighten my husband's load while I was hundreds of miles away. Other people being present to help my family was an enormous blessing. People are often lovely and willing to take time out of their days to help others. It was comforting knowing that we were not alone in our suffering.

If, during this time, I had focused on how exhausted we all were and how upsetting it was to see my father wasting away, or even what I needed to be doing at my own home, it would not have been beneficial. I would have been miserable if I had argued with my sisters and mom over decisions instead of counting my blessings. Not finding beauty in situations would suck the life out of me and lead me to be angry. I chose to spend my dad's last days with him and loving him, not arguing over who should do what. I decided to accept my sisters and mom for who they were and honor our uniqueness. I had to be intentional to find the good in those times, and that made the last days with my dad filled with love rather than misery.

Stephanie's Story
Celebrating in Grief

When I was a young adult with two little children of my own, my brother Geno died. This was the first time that most of us in my large extended family had experienced someone young dying unexpectedly. Even though Geno had cancer and was given only three to five years to live, we truly thought he would be the one who could beat cancer. We were all in denial, including Geno, until the end. His death rocked the world of every member of my large, unusually supportive, loving, and close family.

About two weeks before my brother's passing, when we had been told his health was declining, we held a party in the garage with many of his friends to celebrate him. My brother was a smoker and the garage had become his place to retreat. Getting into the garage for his smoke breaks became an ordeal because he had had a stroke, leaving him with partial paralysis. As a result, he used a wheelchair. We would dress him warmly (his last months were during the winter in the Midwest and the garage only had a small space heater) and gather his coffee, smokes, and lighter and take it to the garage for him.

Some people may question how we could have a party when someone is dying, but "party" is a loose term. It was more of a gathering to celebrate who my brother was and how he chose to live. After his funeral, we sang, danced, and drank wine. The song "Only the Good Die Young" randomly came on. We bawled. But he would have wanted us to continue to dance and sing and drink because that is who he was—the life of the party. He was so full of life and always tried to make people laugh. I remember my whole family sitting around in the days following his death and mentioning how it sucks that he isn't here and won't be here, but we would carry on as if he was. By us living like him, it helped us to process the grief better. In the weeks and months that passed after he died, we would say that we didn't want to forget him. The way my family dealt with the loss of my brother ended up being the standard for the way we dealt with any loss after that.

During Geno's last weeks of life, I was very active in his doctor appointments. Then after he passed, I was involved in the funeral process. I assisted my parents in things that most people don't ever consider: picking out the burial plot, learning about the embalming process, and assisting with the funeral components. I helped with the agonizing details that very few think about in advance or want to deal with in the moment. All of this made his passing more real.

One way I processed the loss of my brother was by making a video to honor and remember him. The year after he died, I searched through videos and pictures I had of him. My husband, Bryan, a technology genius, helped me put this video together. I chose the content—the photos, videos, and songs—and he compiled it all and edited it. My goal was to have the video done by Christmas to give to my parents as a gift over the holidays. This became one of the primary ways in which I processed my grief.

In my hometown, there is a race that raises money for cancer care, and my aunt started a team in memory of my brother. Every year after we've run this race for Geno, we go to my parents' home and my dad gives a speech about Geno and then plays the video that I made. It is another special way that we keep his memory alive.

Two years after my brother died, my husband, Bryan, had his dad coming into town for a visit one weekend. His dad was a doctor and frequently traveled, so Bryan didn't get to see him very often. That weekend, Bryan wanted to take his dad four-wheeling in a Jeep since this had become one of Bryan's favorite pastimes. Bryan always emphasized safety, but at the same time, he was a thrill-seeker. He researched everything to the nth degree and would ask for experts' advice when it came to off-roading, so I was never worried about him engaging in the activity. He had taken me Jeeping a couple of times and I trusted that he would never do anything to jeopardize anybody, let alone himself. He was in love with life and couldn't wait to wake up the next day to see or do the next thing.

He did take his dad Jeeping that weekend when he was in town. On one of the trails, something on Bryan's car broke on the driver's side front wheel. He was going at a low speed when it happened, and his buddies helped him get on a flat surface to assess the situation. Bryan worked on it and thought he had fixed it. His dad offered to buy the part to fix it entirely since they sell parts at some Jeeping locations, but Bryan insisted that he had fixed it enough to get home. Besides, the part was way more expensive at this off-roading site than it would be at home. Bryan also didn't want the day to be tainted for his dad. He didn't want their day together to be anything less than fun. This is how much he loved his dad: He tried to roll out the red carpet for him and enjoy the day together. He didn't want to spend the day getting and installing a new part. Because of how well we all know Bryan and how careful he is, nobody was more forceful about him getting the new part and getting it fixed before driving home. Unfortunately, it was not fixed well enough, and on the way home, the wheel popped off, causing the Jeep to flip. Bryan's dad was in the car and survived, but Bryan did not.

When my husband died, my children were ages fourteen, five, and one and a half. I was a widow with three young kids. It's a club that nobody wants to join. I will never be the same; I have no idea how I endured the days and weeks after he passed away. My mind went into autopilot. Having experienced my brother's death two years before, I was quite familiar with what was happening. I would have never imagined in a million years that the things I helped my parents with for my brother's funeral would help me with the funeral for my husband just a short while later. I remember speaking with Bryan's grandmother after Bryan's funeral and saying that I didn't know how I would make it in this life now. She told me, "You don't need to know how you are going to do it; you just do because those kids of yours need you."

My large, wonderful family was so supportive, present, and helpful again during this time and they continue to be to this day. They are the biggest blessing in my life by far. It doesn't seem right to say that there was a blessing with my husband dying, but I had no choice but to look for the blessing rather than continually wallow in my sadness. Because of this, I try to remember to be grateful for how close and helpful my large family is. The way my family dealt with Geno's death became an example to me for how to deal with the grief of losing my husband. I've taught my children to celebrate their dad, which we do on his birthday, the anniversary of his death, and on Father's Day. I made a video to honor and remember him, as I did for Geno. We laugh at what he would laugh at and cry about the things we miss. Even though my boys were so young when he passed away that they don't have many memories of him, we talk about him and keep his memory alive. I tell them stories, as do other family members, to keep him a part of their lives.

It took much time, even years, to allow myself to grieve. After he first died, I would sit by the window crying and imagine him coming home. I couldn't fathom him never walking through the door again and never being in our life. I attended a Bible study at my church by Kelly Minter called "Ruth: Loss, Love, and Legacy." I remember mentioning in the first class that I didn't want to do this study because I didn't want to cry and think about Bryan. However, I find it funny how God puts things right where and when I need them. I dug deep during that study, but I did skip some classes because as much as I don't mind being vulnerable, I don't enjoy crying much in public. I didn't think I would get through class without being a mess. I still worked on the lessons each day and found the Ruth and Naomi story inspiring. Their relationship example, being the mother-in-law and daughter-in-law, can be compared to how close and dear my mother-in-law is to my heart.

It is a blessing that the relationship with my mother-in-law and father-in-law has stayed close through the years, and I would even say has gotten stronger. We need each other so that we can continue to have a connection to Bryan. My kids and I want to be a part of their lives. I would speculate that the same holds true for them, that they want to remain part of our lives since we are a link to Bryan. My father-in-law has even attended the party in Geno's memory, which was special for him. Bryan and I used to marvel at our in-laws and say we are so lucky that we love each other's families. Since my husband's passing, anyone I've dated had to understand that family is important to me, including my in-laws. I've only dated a couple of men since my husband died. My in-laws met one of the men, and it indeed was difficult for them to see me with another man, but they were very gracious. That is a testament to how strong our relationship is. The continued relationship with my mother-in-law and father-in-law was one of the many ways God has put things or lessons or relationships in my life that have allowed me to find joy despite the overwhelming sadness. It has energized me to focus on what I do have rather than what I don't.

My walk with Christ has strengthened since the loss of my brother and my husband. Through all the pain I felt, I had no other choice but to turn closer to God to ask Him to help me find my way. The most significant blessing is that I'm more aware of how much I need Him. Unfortunately, when life brings us to our lowest, that is when we cling to God more, and through this, He scoops us up and draws us into Him. The loss of a brother and husband is more than anyone can handle alone, but with my family and God, I can continue to celebrate their lives and find joy despite all I've endured.

Lynsey and Grant's Story
Henley, Heartbreak, and Hope

Our daughter Henley was born in 2008, and she was a normal, healthy little girl for the first eighteen months of her life. In August 2010, our world was turned upside down with our daughter's diagnosis.

She had some incidents of vomiting over a few days, but she did not seem to have any other symptoms of a virus. After she would vomit, she appeared normal. Then, on Friday that week, she vomited throughout the day, atypical for most illnesses. By Saturday, we realized this was not normal, so we took her to the emergency room. Although we were there for ten hours, they didn't run many tests. The doctors thought it could be Esptein-Barr virus or mononucleosis. We wouldn't have those test results back for ten days, so Henley was discharged.

We had to take our very sick little girl home with us. On Sunday morning, she could barely lift her head off the pillow. Grant, a chiropractor, rarely says we need to go to the doctor, but he said we should take Henley back to a hospital after seeing her in that state. He had palpitated her belly and felt a lump that had not been there the day before. When we stood her up, we could see that her stomach was severely distended. Her grandparents came to watch our son while we took Henley to a different hospital. There, she had a chest x-ray and an abdominal x-ray done.

I will never forget sitting in that room in the ER when the doctor came in pale-faced and could barely speak. He showed us the x-ray of her lungs, which were covered in white spots. We immediately knew this was not how they were supposed to look.

We headed up to the oncology floor after speaking with the doctor. We found out she had a tumor on her adrenal gland. The next day, she had surgery to place a port and to take a biopsy of the tumor. We were holding our incredibly sick daughter and had to place her into the arms of someone we didn't know. This was the first time in my life where I had handed my child over to someone other than family. My son, Cooper, was three and Henley was eighteen months old. We had family living nearby, and they were always the ones to help us when we needed someone to care for the kids. We were scared to death as our daughter went off for surgery. We didn't know what we were facing.

Suddenly, Grant and I simultaneously felt shivers all over, along with an unbelievable sense of calm. We knew at that moment that we needed God in our lives. God had always been a part of our lives through prayer and belief, but we never attended church. We said we were Christians, but we were not active in our faith. We knew the only way we would get through this was with Him. We felt His presence. An overwhelming sense of peace came upon us. I knew at that moment that our situation wasn't going to be okay, but at the same time, it somehow was. We both felt what we knew was the Holy Spirit coming into both of our lives at the exact same moment. During this frightening time in our lives, when we knew there was something wrong with our baby, we felt a peace that could only come from God.

We learned that Henley had stage 4 neuroblastoma. When they came back with the pathology reports, we were told that it was covering her body. We remained hopeful and Henley started treatment immediately. We now know that the doctors never expected us to leave the hospital.

I don't remember much from the meeting where we were told what to expect from the treatment process. What stood out most to me was that my daughter would have a chemo treatment, most likely leading to hearing loss, potentially even deafness. I went out of that meeting and prayed constantly. I thought that I could learn sign language if she became deaf. Although they told us our daughter was dying, all I took from the meeting was the potential for hearing loss from the treatment.

I repeatedly prayed that day that if God was going to take our daughter, to take her now. She was eighteen months old, and I didn't want to get closer to her and love her more just to have her taken away all the same. I am now so thankful that God does not answer all prayers. We would not be the people we are today if God had granted my request and taken her that day. With the support of our family, our community and God, we would not take a single minute for granted.

Family, friends, and community came together to support Henley. We have lots of local family and were never alone. We experienced so much love, assistance, and encouragement during this challenging time in our lives.

We found a surgeon in New York City who did neuroblastoma surgeries. We started treatment, and Henley had surgery there. Her tumor near her adrenal gland was wrapped around many essential arteries and veins, making it an extremely complicated surgery that lasted nine hours.

We spent time in New York after the tumor was removed. There was a neuroblastoma team at that hospital. After the surgery to remove the primary tumor, she was very sick for a while. The treatment protocol was a little different since the cancer center was privately funded. They were doing a new study using stem cell transplants, and we took part. It was a hard decision to transfer her care to that hospital, which was 700 miles from home. There were occasions when I was away from home for weeks at a time. I knew Grant had a medical practice to run, but we made the arrangement work for us. We met some awesome people who became some of our closest friends. All in all, we were quite grateful that we had transferred her care there.

At one point, Henley was entirely cleared from detectable cancer, but that only lasted a few weeks before she relapsed. Her type of cancer was very aggressive and hard to completely eradicate. She relapsed in the brain, which was very rare. At her hospital, they had a treatment for curing neuroblastoma in the brain with a 96 percent success rate, the only place in the world with this treatment. She had brain surgery to place a port in her brain for the treatment. Unfortunately, even though this treatment has a high success rate, it did not work for her. She struggled with cancer in the brain for a long time, to the point where we ran out of treatment options. On the scan, we could see half of her brain was covered in blood. Her doctor, who never gave up, looked at us and informed us that she wouldn't make it.

After we were given this devastating news, they could not keep Henley down. They told us she should not be able to walk or do all she was doing because she should be dying. They kept us there at the hospital, even though she was acting normal. We finally asked if we could take her to the Ronald McDonald house. They told us she could collapse and die, to which we responded by saying we were willing to take that risk because we would rather be there instead of in a hospital room. Besides, she was acting normally. They agreed for us to take her home and make her comfortable. She looked fine to us, so we went to the Central Park Zoo for a while before heading home, enjoying the outdoors and even grabbing some ice cream.

When we got home, we decided to take a trip out West because we thought we would be starting the process of hospice soon. We would know when Henley was done fighting—and she was not done fighting. My sister and brother-in-law lived in Colorado, so our whole family spent a week exploring the mountains there. Henley was not under any treatment; we had no plan, unlike what we had been dealing with for quite a long time. While visiting there, we functioned like any other family on vacation, and we had the most amazing week.

We went on a hike near a cliff, and Cooper, who was just five at the time, made a cross out of sticks, placed it on a rock overlooking the mountains, and knelt down and prayed. He then brought us all together in a circle to pray with him. We prayed about our next steps and we felt very clearly in which direction we were being led.

While still in Colorado, we contacted a doctor in Michigan who was doing some cutting-edge research with neuroblastoma. She said she would be happy to do whatever she could to help. We got back from Colorado and went to Michigan to begin a new treatment there. We ended up doing this treatment with Henley for over a year, which cleared her of her brain cancer, a welcome surprise after being told the year before to go home and put her in hospice. This treatment allowed her to enjoy life. We had to travel there once a week for the day for treatment, and we would return home that same evening.

Looking back, I would maintain that this year was one of our best with Henley, but at the same time, we genuinely thought we

149

had said goodbye to her a couple of times. One day, she played in our backyard playhouse, using the pretend phone to call everyone she knew. She would say hi and tell them she loved them. I thought it was a little strange, and now I wonder if she knew she was not well and was telling everyone goodbye. That night, she became very ill and we took her directly to the children's hospital in Indianapolis. When they gave her an antibiotic for sepsis, she went into full-blown seizures. We were told that her kidneys were not working well, so we were to say goodbye to her. Family flew in, and we said our farewells. For a couple of days, she was touch and go. I grieved for her. I thought about how Cooper would start kindergarten soon and that maybe God needed me to be home more for him. Perhaps it was okay that this was her time. Then, she survived. I was drained, wondering how we were still in this fight, how I had to keep going. It was a weird moment. Grant did not grieve that time because he was hopeful for her recovery. After Henley lived through sepsis, I remember saying to my mom that I would have to grieve for her all over again someday.

It seems crazy, but there were times that year that she was absolutely her best. When we had to stay in Michigan, we often went to a beach there and Henley loved the "hot pool," or as most people call it, a hot tub. We had the best time, enjoying each moment as a family. She taught us that if we felt a whim to do something fun, we should go ahead and do it. We had to live in the moment continually with Henley. We lived for the now and if we were blessed with tomorrow, it would work itself out.

As we approached our ten-year wedding anniversary, Henley was still the best she had ever been, so Grant and I decided to go on our first vacation without the kids since their births. A few days before leaving, we took Henley to have her routine labs drawn. We saw her doctor there, and I told him how Henley was doing outstandingly well and that I didn't want to awaken from this dream.

Two days later, walking became difficult for her, and she complained of leg pain, so my mom and I took her to the children's hospital in Indianapolis. They took some x-rays and said we should take her up to Michigan to get scans as soon as possible. This was not abnormal because Henley was under the care of the specialists there. She had relapsed eight times, so here we went again for yet another relapse. On the way home from the hospital, I had to pull over for a funeral procession. Feeling uneasy, I looked at my mom and said, "This is it.'" I knew this time that we were going to lose Henley. Instead of heading to Mexico for vacation, we took Henley to Michigan, where we were told she was covered in cancer. It was back in her liver and adrenal gland where it started. They told us to take her home and make her comfortable. Before we left, she had radiation for pain so she could walk. We got a video of her running down the hallway as we were getting ready to leave to go home. She begged us to go to her hot pool. We told her we couldn't go this time, so she asked her daddy if she could have a hot pool at home. The next evening, after Grant got home from work, we went and bought one. Less than a week later, we had the hot pool delivered; it happened to arrive the same day as her hospice bed. That night, we held a big party and all of our family and very close friends came. Henley enjoyed the hot pool the entire day. We tucked her into her bed that night after having a wonderful day together, unaware that this evening was her last.

We awoke early to a bloodcurdling scream from Henley's room. Grant rushed into her room, then returned to inform me that we were going to lose her that day. Henley was incoherent. I felt as if her spirit had already departed, her body soon leaving us as well. She passed away later that morning. The hardest thing was watching Grant reverently carry Henley down the steps and out to the SUV that carried her away.

We had tried to make the best of each day we had with Henley when she was able. Through our experiences and the memories we made, it was evident that God was alongside us the whole way. We were able to learn so much, and we grew significantly as a family. It was one of the most stressful times of our lives, but our burdens were lessened as we brought God into our relationships.

One of the most significant benefits of this terrible journey with the ultimate loss of our daughter was an unbelievable perspective. We knew that our story here on earth was just a blip on the scale of eternity. We realized that this was not the end, and for Henley, this was just the beginning. I am so grateful that she is now whole and with Jesus. The worst day of my life was the day we lost her, but I can see how amazing and special it is that she is where she is now.

Every year before school starts, we write down Cooper's age, grade, teacher, favorites, and one wish. Every year after Henley passed, Cooper's desire was for Henley to come back. This year, his wish changed, and it took my breath away. His wish was no longer to bring Henley back because he realized that Henley was happier in heaven. He is wise beyond his years. We have gone through much counseling to get to this point. I agree with Cooper that I would not bring Henley back. We were blessed with her for four and a half years, and she taught us more in that short time than any person could in a lifetime. She is truly home now, and as much as it hurts to accept, we know she is in the place she is supposed to be.

We always wanted a third child. When Henley got sick, we knew there was no way we could bring another child into our lives at that point. After losing her, I was scared to death to bring another child into this world. I did get pregnant but had a late miscarriage at fourteen weeks. I got pregnant again shortly thereafter and miscarried again. Cooper knew about the first miscarriage but not about the second. He had lost his sister and then lost a sibling-to-be in miscarriage and that was more than enough for a young boy to process.

Then, I got pregnant with Crosbee. I had to go through frequent counseling because I felt that she was dividing our worlds. I wanted her and could not wait to meet her, but she would not know Henley while Cooper did. She was going to have a life that neither of my other two children had. For instance, if we could visit a park with Cooper and Henley, it was a miracle. Rarely were we able to do normal family activities. I felt like Cooper grew up in a hospital. Once Crosbee was born, I realized that I shouldn't have worried because she completed our family. She did not divide it; rather, she became a tremendous light. She has healed our weary, broken hearts.

There are still recurring dates and memories where we again feel the hurt and pain of losing Henley, but we now tend to see the blessings: our community that came together to support us more than we could have imagined, our family being so much more tightly knit, and being able to live life centered on what is most important. Before Henley's sickness, I thought that we had a perfect life: I was a stay-at-home mom, Grant had his own practice, a job he loved, and I had a son and a daughter. It took a tragedy to make me realize that life is so much more perfect now that God is the center of all that we do. We saw people trying to fill themselves with possessions, money, or whatever it may be to try to feel complete, while we discovered that we feel whole with God central in our lives. That is the biggest blessing of them all on our long and painful journey.

6

Gleaning the Good from the Bad

When I discussed this book idea with my friend Karen, she used the term "gleaning" to describe how we find the silver lining in our misfortune. At that time, I had no idea what gleaning meant, but she explained that it is gathering the usable crop that is left over from the reapers during harvest. Gleaning from our stories is picking through the excess pain in whatever we have experienced, trying to find something good that we can keep and use. I loved this idea and have clung to it ever since she explained it to me.

Gleaning from our stories is picking through the leftover pain in whatever we have experienced trying to find something good that we can keep and use.

Picking through the rubble and mess in our life to find something usable may seem like a huge hassle. Why would we do that? Is it worth the effort? My friends, finding those pieces of goodness amid the mess is a gift for your mental, and dare I suggest, physical, health. It transforms us so we can move through our pain to a point of contentment.

When my first child was born, I had planned to breastfeed him exclusively. Unfortunately, after meeting with a breastfeeding expert, I learned I had a physical problem that caused a low milk supply. This made me sad, especially directly postpartum. I had

154

to supplement with a bottle after each breastfeeding. This made for long feeding sessions followed by pumping in an attempt to increase my milk supply, which meant even less sleep for this new mama. I was thankful that during the late evenings and on the weekends, my husband could take over bottle feeding and I could go to sleep while he cared for our son.

I have to admit that not being able to exclusively breastfeed my children is one of the biggest disappointments in my life. I wanted the bonding. I wanted the ease of not having to clean bottles and make formula. I wanted the nutrition for my baby that my own body could produce. I had to get past the disappointment and sadness and realize how thankful I was to be able to give my baby a minuscule amount of breast milk, that formula was an option, and that both of my children were healthy. In the end, it did not matter how they got fed, just that they grew and thrived.

I am certain I did not wish to glean anything good from my disappointment in the throes of sadness and exhaustion. When things don't go according to my expectations, I feel dissatisfied, mournful, and often bitter. I just wanted things to be how I had envisioned. I often need time to mope and grapple with my sadness before moving on, and it may be the same for you. I could not be cheerful in the face of my misfortune, but by accepting and becoming content with the situation over time, I could relax and enjoy my sweet baby boy.

Mai Xia's Other Story
Love, Loss, and Healing

My family had only been living in our new home in the suburbs of Indianapolis for two years when my mom died in a car crash. What is especially sad is that she was the passenger in a one-car accident, and my dad was driving drunk. When we came to America from Laos via Thailand, my dad had given up opium because he had to, but he picked up alcohol in its place. He never talked about everything that happened in Laos, but he had many demons that he didn't know how to deal with, so he tried to drown them. I decided to move out of the family home after her death. I felt I was becoming too codependent living in that home. I was constantly checking the house and car for bottles and monitoring my dad's drinking. Every time the phone rang, I was scared he had killed someone, and eventually, I decided I couldn't bear it anymore. It's important to understand that leaving like that is strongly frowned upon in my culture, but he wouldn't tell me that directly. Instead, he had my brother talk with me, letting me know he felt that the community would think he was a bad father. I just explained from my perspective: I had a college degree and a job, so I was buying my own home.

I did move out. At this point, all my friends had moved away or gotten married, so I started going to a church closer to my home in the suburbs. My sister told me that she knew of a church that was starting a life group. I spoke with the singles pastor of that church, who told me there was an all-women's group and a coed group. I was so desperate for friends that I joined both groups.

While I was still in college, I was busy with church and Intervarsity Christian Fellowship. I kept asking God during that time to send me one guy who would become my husband, nothing more. One gentleman, Bob, whom I met in my current life group, became a friend. He was quite open about his life and was yearning to know God. One Christmas he even called to wish me a merry Christmas. I thought his behavior was a bit strange, so I called my girlfriends, asking if he had called them as well, which he hadn't. We continued hanging out with our group of friends. Finally, in April, I told him to meet me for dinner to chat. During dinner, I told him that I felt a vibe from him that he wanted to be more than friends. When I said that, he was genuinely shocked. He replied, "No, you are like my buddy, my spiritual mentor." I politely gave him a heads up for meeting women in the future, that women often get emotionally attached. I went home that evening and prayed. I was thirty-one years old and still hadn't dated. Understandably, I was annoyed with the Lord. I felt like God was saying to me, "Are you only serving me for what I can give you?" I also felt like He asked me, "What if I don't give you a family? Or a husband?" I thought, *All right, God, I hear you and will serve you even if I don't ever get a husband or children, but if that's the case, I will need you to take all of those desires away from me.*

In July, Bob and I started participating again in life group. I began praying for the Lord to change Bob's heart toward me. Then, my prayer became for God to change my heart toward Bob if he wasn't the right person for me because thinking of him was painful. Then, my prayer became for the Lord to bring someone else into Bob's life because I cared for him as a person. My experience was a lengthy process. Unbeknownst to me during that time, Bob had never seen me as a potential date until I said something to him at that dinner in April. He then talked with pastors and male mentors, telling them he liked me, but he didn't want to mess up our friendship. He knew I had never dated, and he had never before been in a Christian relationship. He was trying as hard as possible to figure out his feelings.

At Thanksgiving that year, Bob went to Kentucky to visit family, and he ended up coming home early. He asked me if we could get together. We went to dinner and he said he wanted to talk about something. He informed me that he would like to start dating. I asked him what had changed between April and now, and he said that he had never thought about a relationship with me until I said something. He said he went to a men's conference and he told a friend about me and the situation. The friend told him that I sound like an incredible girl, and that if he didn't want to date me, he had a friend he would like to introduce to me. Bob thought, *Oh no, I don't think so.* The light bulb turned on in his head at that time. He realized that I was someone he wanted to date.

At dinner that night, he put everything on the table about his past. He told me he hadn't done this with any of his past relationships. After hearing all he had to say, I told him I would pray about it, but I thought we could make it work. This was the beginning of our relationship. We dated for six months, were engaged for ten months, and then got married. We were ages thirty-three and thirty-five and knew we wanted to have kids quickly because we were older. After six months of marriage, we started trying, and I got pregnant very quickly. I had a miscarriage at ten weeks. Bob and I had originally planned to go on a mission trip to Nicaragua in July, but I had to back out of the trip when I found out that I was pregnant. After losing the baby, I was able to go ahead with the trip. While we were there, a pastor prayed over us to get pregnant and I actually became pregnant on the trip.

At twenty weeks along, we went for an ultrasound to find out the gender of the baby. The ultrasound tech didn't say anything during the ultrasound, and I knew that wasn't a good sign. I asked what was wrong. She said that there were markers that she wasn't pleased with and that she would have the doctor chat with us. Bob and I started praying. We prayed over the room that nobody else there would receive bad news that day. Two Bible verses kept going through my head: "The Lord gave and the Lord hath taken away; blessed be the name of the Lord" (Job 1:21 KJV) and "Consider it pure joy, my brothers and sisters, whenever you face trials of many kinds" (James 1:2 NIV). At the same time, I asked God how I could get joy out of this.

We were moved to another room, and the doctor had a chat with us. We were told that our baby had markers of Down syndrome. We also learned that she had a hole in her heart, pulmonary arteries in the wrong place, and other health problems. We were told we had the choice to end the pregnancy, but we decided that we were keeping the baby no matter what happened.

We started going to a specialist each week, including a pediatric cardiologist. We were grateful that we got to see "pictures" from ultrasounds of our baby girl each week. During our appointment at twenty-six weeks, we learned that the baby was going into heart failure. I asked if there was anything we could do to save her. We were told that there was nothing they could do, even if they delivered her that day. We just had to go home and wait for the baby to die. I noticed decreased movement two days later, so I returned to my OB for an ultrasound, which didn't detect a heartbeat. My doctor told me that labor could be induced or we could go home and wait for my body to take care of it spontaneously. Initially, we went home. Two days later, I told Bob that I couldn't bear the thought of carrying a dead baby around in my body. I went in to be induced. We named her Rachel Ann. When she was born, she was only 1 pound and 2 ounces. She was tiny, but everything on the outside of her was formed. We were able to hold her for as long as we wanted. We took pictures and had handprints made. We felt such overwhelming peace during this time. I felt all the prayers from the people praying for us while we were there; however, it was devastating to go home without a baby. I went to the hospital pregnant and came home with empty arms.

We had Rachel cremated and held a service for her at church. The same pastor who had performed our marriage ceremony led the service for Rachel. I remember him saying during the service how he didn't understand why terrible things like this happen. I felt that way often after Rachel died. I simply didn't get it. Bob and I wondered if we would ever have kids. Our pastor said that day that he could tell Bob and I were ready for children, and he wished he could give us a dump truck load of kids. We did feel prepared for kids; we were even ready financially. There were times when I felt God had cheated me a bit. I had felt the same way when I was single for so many years. I felt God was withholding gifts from me. I thought about how I had served God my whole life and didn't understand why He wasn't giving us a child. Then I felt like the Lord was asking me, "Do you only do things for me so you can get things from me?" Growing up, I had a false sense of theology and thought that if I do what I'm supposed to do and follow the Lord, all would be good and bad things wouldn't happen to me. That simply isn't true. When bad things happen, was I still going to believe all I said I believed or was faith all a show? Even though my prayer for Rachel was for her to be completely healed, she wasn't healed as I had hoped: She was completely healed, just not on this side of heaven.

Even though it was such a difficult time, it drew Bob and me together. My husband proved to me that he was the godly man that I thought he was throughout this trial. It strengthened our marriage and drew us closer to God as nothing else could. I wish this tragedy didn't have to happen. I wish it were great things that drew us closer to the Lord. It is in the valleys that we cling to Him and we find out what we really believe. I wouldn't wish this on my greatest enemies. It was okay for me to cry and scream and mourn. It was okay to be mad at God. When I went through hard times, there was a different level of reality and solidity in my relationship with God. I built confidence in my faith. I learned that I don't have anyone else to count on and lean on as I do with God. It was a helpless situation and the only thing I could do was rely on the Lord. That mindset is where He wants me. The greatest blessing in all of this is seeing the strength in my husband. He is such a godly man, who loved these babies, and I could see the care and love he had for me. I had waited a long time for this man and I know the Lord had put me with the right person.

We were blessed later the same year that Rachel died with a healthy son. He was even born in the same room as Rachel. We praised God that we finally had a healthy child in our arms.

I feel like where there was once sadness, God brought joy to my husband and me through my new son. We have a second son now as well and feel truly blessed. We went through some unbelievably heartbreaking times but knew that God was with us through it all, drawing us near to Him.

Angie's Story
Fortune Found in Multitudes of Misfortune

When my husband and I got married, we had been together for six years and were ready to start a family. We did not conceive very quickly. We tried numerous methods attempting to bring a child into our home. After a while, my husband sat me down and said that if our objective was to start a family, we should consider the route of adoption. I was not entirely sure if this was what I wanted. I typically cope with struggles by doing research and gathering knowledge. I weigh out all the choices, along with all the consequences. That is how I got comfortable with adoption being a way to bring a child into our family. After six years of failed attempts to have a child of our own blood, we adopted our daughter, Jordan.

Bringing our daughter into our home ended up feeling very natural for us. We went through the process of international adoption. To start, we traveled and stayed in her country of origin for two weeks and waited for the completion of all the paperwork to bring her home. When they brought Jordan in to meet us and I held her in my arms for the first time, I felt like God was in the room with us. The experience was stunning. When we were on the plane traveling home with our daughter, I thought, *This is when we find our fortune in our misfortune.* We realized that the objective wasn't to conceive; rather, we wanted to start a family.

Two years after adopting our daughter, we were shocked to find out that I was expecting. We were in such disbelief that my husband wouldn't believe it until we went to my doctor's appointment. The team of doctors who had worked with us for years as we tried to conceive now decided to go ahead and do an ultrasound at the first appointment. We found out that we were having twins. It was a shock because it was natural. We had tried so many things for so many years, including in vitro fertilization, and the doctors could not explain why we couldn't get pregnant. This pregnancy was difficult because one of the babies had a growth restriction and wasn't doing very well. I went on bed rest for three months. We were going to do a C-section two months early, but two weeks before the scheduled C-section, we lost the baby that had not been growing well. We made the choice to try to carry the other child longer. We had done enough research to know that we could continue to carry both to give the other baby a better chance. We did not know anyone else who had experienced something like this. None of the experts could have prepared us for this. It was arduous. When we lost that child, I asked that nobody else be around for forty-eight hours so I could take the time to cry and grieve on my own. I didn't want someone to say that it was okay. I chose to grieve and not to be okay. It wasn't that I didn't want people to help; I just needed to move through it on my own. On the day of the scheduled C-section, we decided that we had mourned so long for the loss of the one child that we would focus on celebrating the birth of our son, Gabe.

We worked hard on getting him healthy for the first six months of his life. He was a preemie and had sleep apnea, which left him hooked to a machine. It was during this time that I was blessed again and became pregnant with my son Zach. I was grateful that this pregnancy was easy. It brought our family together to work through infertility, adoption, loss, and new babies. We had so much to be grateful for with our three children. We had a family just like we had dreamed. Life was good.

Then, a few years ago, I was diagnosed with breast cancer. At first, the doctor was not diagnosing it as cancer. It was a lump that the doctor thought should be a cyst, but I wasn't convinced after doing some research, so I got a referral to another doctor. Nobody had done an ultrasound, so I requested one be done and the doctor said he would do whatever was necessary to figure out what it was. After five months of having what was believed to be a cyst, I learned that I had breast cancer. That new doctor empowered me to move through it and make my own choices. I researched to learn all I could about the options that were laid before me. At first, I didn't surround myself with people who understood the disease because doing so would mean acknowledging it was real when at that point, I was still in denial that I had cancer.

The doctors gave me information and laid out some choices of treatments. I chose to do a mastectomy because I thought it gave me a chance to live longer. Then the next step was chemotherapy. For some reason, that was a more troublesome decision for me because chemo can cause other problems. I questioned what it would do to my body and what it would mean for me long term. My husband and I challenged chemo strongly and I went as far as calling the company that produces the chemotherapy, asking many questions. I also learned that if I took the chemo, I would have to start medication, leading me to even more research. There are side effects and possible risks of taking that medication, such as blood clots and cervical cancer, so I had more risks to weigh against each other. Luckily, both of my grandmothers had taken that medication, so I had a base of information there. The third choice was to have a hysterectomy, leaving me with a broader selection of meds to take. These three treatments, mastectomy, chemotherapy, and a hysterectomy, were the routes I chose.

After making decisions about what treatment options we were going to use, we wrote them down and gave them to family. We did not let anybody know when we were dealing with infertility, but with my breast cancer diagnosis, we let people in after I had come to terms with the diagnosis. Not only did I need the support, but we had three young children who needed it. We also didn't want people questioning our choices and trying to influence our decisions, which is why we wrote down our plan beforehand. I didn't want to be judged by friends or family for what I chose.

The community helped us, especially so that my kids could remain kids while I went through surgeries and treatment. When I first got the diagnosis, I didn't think so much about what I had to go through but was thinking about how my family would have to navigate this with me. My heart was broken for what they would have to go through, even more so than myself.

What was my process working through treatment? I broke everything down into stages. First was the mastectomy, which took about six weeks of healing. Then, when it was time for chemo, my husband sat down with me and said that chemo was my choice, not my sentence, and that I did not have to do it. He knew that saying these words would empower me to go through with it, knowing it was my choice. After he said that, everything clicked for me. I knew I had moved through everything else, and I could push through this. I did start to surround myself with women. The nurse at the school my children attended was going through breast cancer as well. We saw each other at oncology appointments, and when she finished her last chemo treatment, I sat in the same chair she had just sat in to do my first treatment. It was refreshing to move through the process together, which helped make it normal.

How did I get through it? I pictured myself at the next stage, which empowered me to push forward. To stop, wallow, and ask why it happened to me feels defeating and would cause me to spiral into despair, so I avoided that.

I was part of a Moms in Prayer group at my kids' school that prays for the kids and teachers. I was hesitant whether to share my diagnosis with them, but my husband reminded me that if I were to share that information with anyone, that would be the group in which to share it. The day that I decided to share, there was a sheet on the table with the theme for the day and it was Jeremiah 29:11 (NIV): "'For I know the plans I have for you,' declares the Lord, 'Plans to prosper you and not to harm you, plans to give you hope and a future.'" It was at that time that I felt flooded with God's presence. I needed to hear those words. It was positively overwhelming to hear.

One blessing in this experience was that before my cancer diagnosis, one teacher that all three of my children had had at some point in elementary school had experienced breast cancer. We prayed for her during her illness and treatment. It was encouraging that my kids could see her on the other side of the treatments and healthy, proving to them that cancer could be fought and beat. We also explained to my kids that not everyone is okay after having cancer, and we didn't promise anything, but we also focused on people that had moved through this and were healthy.

I look back and know the things that got me through these difficult times were faith, prayer, gratitude lists, and research. I do a solid amount of research to know the facts and become knowledgeable about what I'm facing. Then, I can list things I need to pray about because those are things I cannot control. I take the stuff outside of my control to God.

This process helped me to realize that things that happen to me aren't personal. I need to surround myself with supportive people who will let you tell them how much things really suck right now. The experience also showed me the importance of having a game plan. Everybody suffers through terrible times, but I had to have a plan to work through my time of suffering.

Today I am healthy and doing well. I love the life I have with the family I have always dreamed of having. Although I have undergone much pain in my life, I have certainly been fortunate.

Melissa's Story
Overcoming Trauma and Addiction

When I was three and a half and my little sister was fourteen months old, my mom died at the age of twenty-nine. She had been on a weight-loss diet for a high school reunion she was planning to attend. Back then, it was common to go to the doctor when you wanted to lose weight. My mom's doctor prescribed medication, including diuretics, to help her shed excess pounds. After taking the meds for a while, she went back to the doctor saying that she didn't feel well and thought something was wrong. The doctor convinced her that she had just hit a plateau in her weight loss, everything was fine, and she was feeling normal things someone would feel when dieting. We now understand that the diuretics were too strong for her. They caused potassium to be pulled out of her body, giving her hypokalemia. That led to cardiac arrhythmias, which then caused a heart attack the night after seeing the doctor.

The night my mom died, I had gotten up, gone to my parents' room, and tried to wake my mom to tell her I wanted a drink. I shook her a few times and couldn't rouse her, so I woke up my dad, and he told me to try again. I repeatedly tried to wake her. Finally, he told me to get the water myself. I remember going into their bathroom, using a step stool, and getting a glass of water. I don't know how long I was in there, but it must have been a considerable amount of time because there were paramedics in the house when I came out of the bathroom. My dad was sitting on the couch with his head in his hands. I didn't understand what was happening, but somehow, I knew my mom was not coming back. Later that day, one of my mom's best friends came to get my sister and me. That friend talked with me about what happened and I told her that my mom went to heaven. I don't remember talking to my dad in between all of this. My memory flashes to the blanket, gurney, EMTs, police officers, and my dad sitting on the couch with his head in his hands.

My dad remarried when I was five and a half. My stepmom was our caretaker, but she was also busy with a clothing store she owned. My dad was never around because when he wasn't working, he was gambling or golfing. When there were troubles in my life or I was missing my mom, there was never anyone to talk with to explain that I was hurting. I remember a handful of times my dad came and sat by me when I was crying. When I would start to explain to him what my issues were, he would say, "Well, you think you had a bad day..." and would proceed to tell me how bad his day had been. I recognized that there was no reason for me to go to him with my problems. I was feeling abandoned and lonely, and thus, I kept everything to myself.

As I got older, I started to blame myself for my mom's death. I remember looking in the mirror every day wondering how different life would be if my mom were here. I remember seeing my friends with their moms, longing to have that mother-daughter relationship. I wanted the hugs, the push to do my homework, and the feeling that someone cared about me. I would tell myself, "Melissa, what if you had just woken up earlier, caught the heart attack, and mom would still be here?"

I had knee surgery around age fourteen. I was given pain pills for recovery after the surgery. I accidentally started taking the meds incorrectly. Instead of taking one to two pills every three to four hours, I took three to four pills every one to two hours. During this time, as I was incorrectly taking this medication, I realized that my internal dialogue had changed. I wasn't going through the routine of blaming myself for my mom's death, nor wondering how different life might be if she were still around. What was the difference? The pain pills. It became a slow downward spiral of addiction. The only way I knew how to cope, how to get out of bed, or how to smile was with mind-altering substances. I didn't realize I had a drug addiction; I just knew I felt better with the medication. It also alleviated the knee, back, and neck pain I had been experiencing. I thought I needed it. I was addicted for many years.

With urging from my family, I went to an alcohol and drug treatment facility for addiction recovery. I thought they would let me have my pain pills while there since I had MRIs and CAT scans showing what was causing my pain. Of course, I was wrong about that. When I left that facility, it was one of the hardest times of my life because the life-altering pills were the only coping mechanism I'd had before my inpatient stay. I felt that the treatment facility detoxed my body safely, but afterward, I was sent back into the world without many tools to deal with my new reality. Yes, we did have classes and different techniques taught while I was there, but I was coming out of such a blurry state of mind that nothing stuck with me about how to cope. I was beginning to feel things that I hadn't felt in a long time. I did enter an outpatient program at night after being discharged from the inpatient program, but I felt I was missing my best friend. The pills were the one thing that had made me feel better throughout my day. Everything remains fuzzy for me from that time, but I do remember thinking I didn't know how to live. I thought the therapy, including listening to everyone else's pain, wasn't what I needed.

I stayed sober for about six months. I honestly didn't believe I had a drug addiction. I tried to hide my relapse for a while. I genuinely told myself I was fine. Then I had a fast downward spiral.

One morning my husband woke me up, told me to get dressed and come downstairs. It was just like on the TV show "Intervention," where loved ones gather and explain why going to a treatment program is necessary. My aunt and uncle were in my living room, along with a man I didn't know. I surrendered entirely after they read letters they had written to me. My aunt drove me to an addiction recovery center in Tennessee, where I stayed for thirty days.

I was part of a relapse group at that facility. We focused on someone different in our cohort each day. On the day I was the participant holding the attention, the therapist had us engage in an activity together. A woman from class was sitting on the ground in front of me. I had a belt wrapped around my waist with a rope attached to it and one of the men in the class had the end of the rope. The therapist explained that the woman in front of me was playing the role of my mom and was saying "Melissa, Melissa." The guy would pull the rope, preventing me from reaching my mom. This activity made me finally realize that her death was not my fault. I was only three and a half when she died, so I should not hold myself accountable for her passing. Afterward, I had a good healthy cry and did a lot of processing.

I was at this treatment facility on my twenty-ninth birthday. That day, I was eating dinner and had my back to the kitchen area. Everyone else had gotten up to put their trays away, and I was still sitting there looking out the window having a pity party for myself, thinking I was a total piece of crap. I had a three-and-a-half-year-old daughter at home. I would probably have been out to a nice dinner if I was at home with family and friends, but here I was in rehab. Suddenly, I heard some girls behind me singing happy birthday. That, for me, was my aha moment. I thought this was the best birthday gift I could have ever received. My aunt and uncle paid for this rehab for me. After being in rehab twice, I saw people leave before they completed treatment because insurance would no longer pay. I remember saying, "Thank you, God, that my aunt and uncle can afford this. I am so grateful to be here. There is nothing else that I needed for a birthday besides this." After I had my daughter, I feared seeing my daughter at age three and a half because I would be able to see how young I was when my mom died. It dawned on me that day that I was twenty-nine and my daughter was three and a half, the exact ages as my mom and I when she passed away. It was clear to me at that moment that I was exactly where I should be.

I am happy to report that I am sober and have been since this intervention and treatment. I do not ever want to relapse. Even when I had a C-section for my twins, I used only Tylenol and Advil for recovery, and when I had kidney stones, I only took IV Tylenol to deal with the pain. I am incredibly proud of myself for that.

After having the twins, I was extremely busy caring for them and my toddler. It was a blessing to be busy because I was not think-ing about my trauma or sobriety as much. My faith grew during this time as well. I was able to see Jesus in the people who came alongside me and loved me during this time.

I am also blessed to have a husband who loves and supports me and is an amazing father to our three children. God knew I needed him. I don't know what I would do without Zach. I have been with him since high school. He has seen me endure so much trauma and pain, and he has stuck with me through everything. He has been the only consistent thing in my life and has shown me that I can be loved unconditionally.

I have been undergoing trauma therapy to deal with the linger-ing agony of the loss of my mom. I have learned that the body pain that I endured for years was a manifestation of the trauma of losing my mom. The result of my loss was not just tears and emotions but included physical symptoms of back and neck pain. I have had to heal emotionally to heal physically.

Through therapy, I have new ways to deal with anguish from my past and any current problems I face instead of using pain medication. I have learned that I get to choose today what I allow to hurt me. The trauma of losing my mom consumed my life and changed who I am, but I'm now happy, healthy, and so fortunate to have a family that loves me and supports me through it all. I have been able to share my story and my faith with others as they, too, trudge through traumas. Even though the path to this point has been long and difficult, there was goodness, faith, and love that came from healing from my trauma.

Susan's Story
Close Call

On Saturday night, November 5, 2005, I was at home with my husband, Tim, and sixteen-year-old son, Ryan. When we were getting ready for bed, I watched the nightly news and saw that we had a severe thunderstorm watch overnight. Since it was not a warning, I went to bed and thought nothing more of it. Around 2:00 a.m., I woke up to a horrendous noise. I could not explain what it sounded like and had no idea what the noise could be. There was also such constant lightning outside that I thought it must have been morning when I first opened my eyes. I yelled to my husband over the loud sound, "What is that noise?" He didn't know either. Disoriented, we both grabbed for our glasses. I walked toward the master bathroom trying to get my bearings. As soon as I got to the doorway, I heard glass shatter. I quickly reacted by kneeling by the bedroom wall and covering my head, just as I had been taught in elementary school disaster drills. That early childhood lesson had stuck with me. Within twenty seconds of crouching down with my arms protecting my head, I could see the sky and felt rain hitting me. I still couldn't figure out what had just happened since I had been pulled out of a deep sleep and was a bit disoriented.

Tim was fine and so was I, but then, panicked, I thought, *Where is Ryan?* He should have been in his bedroom, which was separated from ours by just a small hallway. However, I remembered that he was watching TV in the great room when we went to bed and wondered if he was still there. Neither Tim nor I could get to his room because of the sheer volume of debris in the way. We started shouting his name. My husband found his cellphone and tried to text Ryan. While texting, we persistently yelled for him and finally heard him reply, "I'm okay, I'm okay!" Somehow, Ryan was able to make his way to us even though we could not get to him. As soon as I saw him, I started bawling. I was so grateful to see that he was alive and well.

At this point, we still didn't quite understand what had happened. The glass that we had heard shatter was from our master bathroom window. The windows in our master bedroom remained intact. We raised one of the windows. A neighbor of ours came by and asked if we were all okay. Before I answered him, I asked him what happened, and he said, "A tornado." I didn't think it could have been a tornado because I believed that nobody could survive one. I had always heard that a tornado sounded like a train, and whatever the sound was, it certainly didn't sound like a train. Even now, I cannot equate the sound to anything I have ever heard.

The neighbors had come out of their homes and were congregating in the street on this warm November night. We crawled out of our bedroom window and joined them. Everyone was in their pajamas trying to make sense of what had happened.

After a while, we got in touch with Tim's parents, who live across town. Their house had not been affected whatsoever. They drove to our neighborhood to get us. Before taking us to their home to await daylight, they took us to my parents' house, less than a mile from our home. My dad was in hospice care there. I was worried that if the tornado had struck their home, he wouldn't have survived. When we got to their home, we couldn't even tell there had been a storm. They had lost power, but they had no damage, not even a leaf displaced from their tree. We arrived at their home around 3:00 a.m. My mom answered the door and I explained what had happened. She had no idea that a tornado had come through our town.

We returned to our home at daybreak to assess the damage. When we drove up, we saw there was extensive damage. Our house had not been flattened. We still had most walls on our house, but most of our roof was gone. The wall from our great room that held our fireplace was now in our backyard. I shudder to think what would have happened if Ryan had been in the great room during the storm. It was the room that sustained the most damage.

We didn't lose any clothing, pictures, or personal items. We did lose a lot of furniture, trinkets, and the contents of our attic. We were fortunate that everything destroyed or ruined was easily replaced. The whole experience was a major inconvenience, but we knew people who had lost loved ones. We learned that before the tornado hit our neighborhood, it had hit a mobile home park. Twenty-five people died that night in the tornado, twenty of whom lived in the mobile home park. We had merely lost insignificant possessions, and I didn't feel we had any right to complain about anything when many lost considerably more.

We learned that the damage was so extensive to our home that it would have to be bulldozed. Members of our church, friends, relatives, and even a few people we didn't know helped us pack what could be salvaged from our home. The weather was mild for that time of year, but rain was predicted two days later so we knew we had to get our things out of the home in that short amount of time; otherwise, it would be ruined even further by rain.

I don't think most people think about insurance until you need to make a claim. We were very grateful to have excellent insurance. I was told by the insurance adjuster to write down everything that we had lost, a task that seemed insurmountable. Hurricane Katrina had happened just a month earlier. Our insurance adjuster disclosed that he needed to get down to Louisiana because they had far more claims related to the hurricane. We settled on a dollar amount instead of itemizing our claim. I was thankful that I didn't have to worry any longer about identifying every single item we lost. A burden was lifted when we were able to resolve our claim this way.

I like to say that after this tornado, it was both the best of times and the worst of times. It brought out the best in people, but it was nevertheless a rough situation. People died and had their homes destroyed. Our home had to be torn down and rebuilt. Many local restaurants were providing meals to those in need. The generosity of people was overwhelming. People everywhere wanted to do *something* to help. My fellow employees had a "rebuilding shower" for me. They gave my family checks, gift cards, and gifts to help with our displacement and home rebuild. My son's soccer team even bought us a Christmas tree and decorations since we had lost ours in the storm. We were reminded that people are unbelievably kind, generous, and thoughtful.

My husband, son, and I never felt sorry for ourselves. We knew we had to put one foot in front of the other and get through it the best we could. Even through the loss we experienced, I am grateful because we could replace what we lost unlike many folks around us. I don't doubt that God was looking over us that night. After going through an experience like this, we can easily identify our priorities in life and see the good that came out of this catastrophe.

Madison's Story
Changed and Stronger

The day after my fifteenth birthday, I was sexually assaulted. I didn't tell anyone about it when it happened. Then, in my junior year of high school, I was dating a guy named Evan. Around six months into our relationship, I was sexually assaulted by him. After the assault, he expressed a lot of guilt. He kept saying that he was sorry and it was just a misunderstanding. Because of that, I kept doubting what had happened to me and feeling that maybe this was not what I thought it was.

When I was assaulted, I specifically said no. I believe he knew what he had done, but I don't think he understood that it would affect me the way it did. The morning after it happened, he wanted to talk about it. He picked me up and we talked in his car. I think he was trying to save face. He cried while I rubbed his back and consoled him, and I told him it would be okay. As soon as I did that, I realized that our relationship couldn't continue and I needed to do something.

It was at this time that I first talked about either of my assaults with anyone. I told a youth group volunteer at church and a guidance counselor at my school. I started group and individual therapy sessions. Despite all of this, I decided to stay with Evan. He and I had an unspoken rule to forget what had happened.

One day, when Evan and I were having lunch together, I noticed that I was eating more than usual. I didn't feel full despite all that I was consuming. I immediately thought that I should take a pregnancy test. I took one that night, and it was negative. I told my mom about it and said I was going to take another one in the morning. I'm not sure why I told her. She was surprised and disappointed, but not necessarily mad. She was reasonably caught off guard.

The next morning, I took another test and it was positive. I sat down with my dad afterward and told him that I was pregnant. He said that we would get through it, that people have done it for thousands of years, and we would work through it too. He hugged me, and I went to school. It felt unreal; it didn't feel like it was happening to me.

While sitting in class, I found it hard to focus. I kept thinking about how somebody was growing inside of me. I told Evan that morning that I was pregnant, and he immediately told everyone he knew. We went to a large high school, so I didn't expect it to be huge news. I was in art class and overheard a few popular girls say that they heard that Evan got a girl pregnant and that she would surely be kicked out of school because of it. I leaned over to them and said, "Hey, that's me."

One girl said, "No, it is someone else. She is in my gym class."

I said, "That is also me."

Luckily, that was the only time I had to face somebody talking trash about my pregnancy. It was jarring that they could denounce my pregnancy so readily. I was not prepared for that.

I am pro-choice, but at my first ultrasound, I saw the heartbeat and knew I would keep my child. Before that appointment, I dreamed that I gave birth to a girl who came out wearing a pink dress. I knew that she was mine, and I needed to have her. She was the choice that I made.

When I told one of my friends that I was pregnant, she said she would have an abortion if she were me. I told her the choice

I made was to keep the baby. I had somebody to care for. All my other friends were incredibly supportive and happy for me. They were excited and wanted to see the ultrasound pictures. I had much love and care from an abundance of people in my life. If I didn't have the help and approval of my family and friends, I might have gotten an abortion. I am lucky because I have a loving, supportive family. This decision wasn't going to ruin me. I wasn't destined for a life of poverty. I believed that this was going to be something good in my life because I was in a situation where it can be.

Evan ended up cheating on me when I was five months pregnant, and we broke up. I continued to feel very angry that he did this to me, and to this day, I continue working through those emotions with my therapist. I decided to let him be in my daughter's life, even if he and I were not going to be together. I spent the majority of my pregnancy without a boyfriend.

Not everything about my situation was positive. There was a lot of shame in being a pregnant teen. I did wrestle with my faith, despite the support I had been given. During my pregnancy, I was not expecting the physical discomfort that carrying a baby could cause. I was also struggling emotionally. I would lie in bed and wonder, "Why me? Why now? Why, God? Am I really living this?"

At first, my grandma had a hard time accepting my pregnancy. Once Isabella was born, her feelings quickly changed. Grandma is now happy to have a great-grandbaby. My grandpa once told me that back in his day, the pregnant girl would be sent to an abbey and the baby would be put up for adoption. He said that unwed mothers were considered fallen women. I told him I would be just fine and that I was *not* a fallen woman.

A group of friends showed up at my house to give me an impromptu baby shower. Everyone was wonderfully kind. One friend offered to be there if I needed to vent in the middle of the night. This was meaningful to me, especially since I was still a teenager who felt the need to rant. People made sure I was safe, healthy, and happy. Most never questioned my decisions. Everyone showered me and Isabella with goodness and kindness.

It has been tough dealing with Isabella's father, but he is a great dad. His family is so sweet, helpful, and generous. Isabella has three sets of grandparents and ten uncles. Evan sees her regularly. She goes to see her grandparents at least once a week. We share childcare and it has been surprisingly awesome so far.

I was able to graduate early. After I had my baby, all my friends were in school finishing their senior year while I was at home alone with Isabella. I felt a bit lonely, so I reached out to a friend from theater class; we started hanging out more and became close. Her friendship has been an enormous gift to me.

My friendships have changed, as has my faith. I have come to understand that faith as a parent is different from faith as a child. I have so much more to be thankful for, more to worry about, and more to pray about. I pray for God to protect my family. I feel that God has put good, kind people on my path for a reason. My daughter and I need them.

I have been to many sexual assault support groups to help me heal. I hear stories of horrible things girls have been through, but I see those girls as some of the strongest people I have ever met. They have been quite a blessing to me. We often say we are better than what happened to us. Also, I believe that I am happier than I ever could have been if I had not had my daughter. I am convinced that all things work together for good, even when bad things happen.

Heather's Story
Full Circle Support

Martin Luther King Jr. Day of this past year is seared forever into my memory. The five months leading up to this day were extremely difficult for me. I tried a new career path, which didn't work out. To call it a disappointment is an understatement. I was going through therapy to process the change of direction in my life and discover my purpose and path.

During this time, a good friend of mine, Charity, was battling colon cancer. When I got up on MLK Day, Charity and her son, Johnny, were on my heart. I had not seen Charity in about a month;

however, she remained in my thoughts and prayers every day. We had made arrangements that I would take care of Johnny that day. He was off from school, and we didn't want him confined at home all day while his mom was feeling ill.

As I went downstairs to make myself a cup of coffee, I thought about another friend of mine battling breast cancer who was to start chemotherapy the next day. The thought hit me hard because so many in my life were hurting. I went upstairs and snuck back into bed to have a few more quiet moments before the busyness of the day. I saw a relatively vague text from my preschool teaching partner, but I sensed something awful had happened. I learned that one of our preschool students from two years earlier had unexpectedly died of an infection. It was the second preschool student we had lost since I began teaching there five years ago. When I learned this news, I completely lost what was left of my calmness. I had the whole day planned out, but I was crippled with heartache. I tend to be a person who keeps going no matter what comes my way, but at that moment, I just couldn't.

Feeling overwhelmed, I called another friend of mine, Andrea. I wanted to ask if she would go work out with me before I picked up Johnny because I needed to be with someone. When she answered the phone, I barely got out one sentence before breaking down. She was on her way to take her son to the doctor, so she told me she couldn't go work out at that time but offered to meet up later. About ten minutes after I got off the phone with Andrea, my doorbell rang. She was standing at my door. She sat with me for two hours while I cried. She listened to me and prayed with me. It was an experience I will never forget. I would not have gotten through that day without her.

While I tried to process the sadness of two friends with cancer and the loss of a preschool student, Andrea said some things to propel me forward to face some of the other grief I had been dealing with, including the loss of my career path. She showed me how I could reach out to others to help them just as she was helping me. In the next few months, I did end up reaching out to a few people who I knew could use a listening ear, and talking it out was very helpful, both for them and me.

MLK Day was an excruciating day. When I finally did go pick up Johnny, we were trying to figure out what to do. Since it was a cold winter day, we decided to see a movie. When figuring out which film to see, I made sure we steered clear of any tear-jerk movies because I didn't feel like crying one more tear that day. We decided on *Spiderman*. I thought I'd be safe with an action film, but dang, I ended up crying three times during it! Who knew an action film could make me tear up?

What came out of this time for me was the critical importance of having someone to count on to come alongside me during times of pain. I also learned to be vulnerable enough to let friends play that role in my life. Our society is wired to make us feel like we need to be strong on our own, pulling ourselves up by the bootstraps when we're feeling down. This day taught me that sometimes, I need the encouraging words of trusted friends to work through my problems. I also learned that I need to know when to be fully present for someone else. Andrea was generous enough to give that to me. I needed to know when to throw my daily schedule out the window for someone else.

Fast forward to later this summer. A friend of mine stopped by the church, where I work my second job. She updated me on her mother-in-law's condition; she had been battling cancer for many months. My friend had just popped in, so I knew she needed to talk. We found a quiet space and I listened to her. She asked if I would visit her mother-in-law in the hospital and pray with her. I had a full schedule for that day, but I knew I had to rearrange my plans because it was important that I do this for her. I had never before gone to pray with someone who was within days of dying. I felt led by the Holy Spirit to do this so keenly I wasn't even nervous. I prayed the whole way there, and I was at peace with doing this for my friend and her mother-in-law.

The experience came full circle for me. I could be fully present for someone who needed me, just like Andrea had been fully present for me in my time of need. I am incredibly grateful that I could bless someone in the same manner I had been blessed.

Bambi's Story
What a Child Should Never Endure

Warning: This story contains rape and abuse.

I will never know who my father is, my dad or my uncle because they are both dead. Three years ago, I learned the truth—that my dad held my mom down while my uncle raped her. A short while later, she discovered she was pregnant with me.

My childhood was filled with abuse and violence. I lived in unfathomable conditions. The man who called himself my father raped my sister, his biological daughter, when she was four years old. My memories of him include him drinking, doing drugs, and beating my mother.

When I was about eight years old, my mom escaped and moved in with my first stepfather. He was an evil man. We lived in poverty in a trailer with no utilities or running water. I had to use a bucket for my toileting. Not only were the physical conditions of our home deplorable, but so were our family relationships. One day during a fight, my stepfather chased my mom with a machete outside of our home because my mom accused him of trying to seduce my sister. He narrowly missed hitting mom's head with the machete as my sister and I watched out the window. Another time, he made a bonfire outside of our trailer and burned our few belongings. I was afraid to fall asleep at night, not knowing what he would do next.

Unable to be without a man in her life, my mom moved on to my second stepdad as soon as she left the first one. At first, he was kind and caring. Then one night, while my mom was gone, he offered me alcohol. I was only thirteen, but he said I was old enough, so I drank it. A little while later, he tried to rape me. After getting away from him, I ran to a friend's house and called the police. When my mom got to the police station, she refused to believe me and called me a liar. She blamed me, which was devastating because I needed her support then more than ever. My stepdad left town and my mom signed away her parental rights. During that year, I was in and out of foster care and group homes. I started self-harming by cutting myself, so I was sent to treatment centers and put on various medications. They were trying to fix me, but medications couldn't heal me. All I wanted and needed was therapy and my mom.

When I ran away from foster care and was first put in a group home, I also decided to run away from there. It was a cold night and I felt totally abandoned by my mother. Vulnerable and alone at the age of thirteen, I trusted a man I met who said he would take care of me. Rather than protecting me, he trafficked me. He not only became my pimp but introduced me to crack cocaine as well. I quickly became dependent on the drugs to help me get through turning tricks.

I was under his control until I was nineteen. I tried to escape many times, but he would always find me, beat me, and take me back with him. Finally, I got away from him when I tried to jump out of a moving car. He was beating me in the backseat as we drove past the police station. I told him either I was going to jail, or he was, but he needed to leave me alone. By this time, I was completely addicted to crack and my days were filled with doing drugs and turning tricks. I had to stay high in order to be with fifteen or more men each day. I didn't want to be a prostitute—nobody wants that life. I was using my body to make money to survive. I promised myself I would never have a pimp again after what I had been through for those six years.

I continued using drugs and prostituting myself after my pimp was out of the picture. One night, when I was standing on a corner, cold, hungry, and coming off a high, my grandpa drove by. As excited as I was to see him, I was mortified he was seeing me like this. I was hoping he would get me some food and a warm bed to sleep in that night, so I got in his truck. He told me my grandma missed me and worried about me, so I asked him not to tell her I was working the streets. He took me to a convenience store and bought me some food since I told him I was starving. I devoured the food while explaining I had nowhere to sleep. When I asked him to get me a room at a cheap motel, he agreed, but instead of handing me the key, he walked into the room with me and locked the door. My heart stopped. My grandpa told me that I would have to work for that room and if I did, he would never tell my grandma about anything that happened that night. Crying, I said I no longer wanted the room. He raped me anyway and warned me not to tell my grandma, assuring me she wouldn't believe me if I did.

At twenty-two, I got another pimp. He was a dope man and promised me that I could sleep and get all the drugs I wanted as long as I gave him all of my money. I fell for that, and he ended up treating me worse than my first pimp. I was making more with prostitution than I used in drugs, and he also had me robbing people. I made plenty of money for him and he did all kinds of horrible things to me, including putting a gun loaded with one bullet in my mouth and pulling the trigger, laughing the whole time. By the time he was sent to jail for pimping and pandering, I was pregnant, and the child was possibly his. He thought I set him up, so he had me jumped when I was five months pregnant with my daughter. I protected my belly during that beating and, luckily, did not lose the baby. A week after that attack, I was still heavy into drugs and got arrested for the first time for possession, which was a blessing in disguise.

If it had not been for my incarceration, my daughter might not have made it into the world. In prison, I got off drugs and had prenatal care, so miraculously, she was healthy when she was born. I gave birth to her in shackles in the prison hospital. The first person to hold my girl was a prison guard. I was able to hold her and be with her for only one day. Then my sister came and got her while I went back to my cell. It was a hard reality for this first-time mom. One month later, I left prison behind.

With drugs no longer a part of my life for four and a half years, I replaced them with an addiction to food. After having my son, I weighed 300 pounds. Since I was frustrated with the gradual speed of my weight loss after his birth, I turned to ice, which was the new crack cocaine. A PTA mom during the day, I ran an escort service at night, all while doing drugs once again. I ended up back in prison, for five years this time. My sister took care of my kids each time I was imprisoned, and by the time I got out, they had grown and changed.

In 2016, I was offered a spot in a Women in Recovery program. The judge gave me a choice—either attend this program and change my life or he would send me to prison for twenty-five years. I chose the program. It wasn't easy, but I wanted to change. It is a prison diversion program that had everything I needed, especially trauma therapy. During this time, I learned to love myself, establish healthy boundaries, and realize that I was not my past. When I got into the program, I had blamed myself for my grandfather raping me, but came to accept that I was the victim. I was also a victim every time I turned a trick. I didn't want to be a prostitute, but I was doing it to survive, especially during the years between thirteen and eighteen. I was still a child! The program helped me heal from PTSD (post-traumatic stress disorder) from incidents I encountered while turning tricks. I had to heal from all of it.

Graduating from the Women in Recovery program in twenty-two months was a fantastic experience. Eighteen months into the program, I came up with the idea of the nonprofit I would eventually start: Angels Against Trafficking. Narcotics Anonymous taught me that I could not keep myself in recovery unless I shared about it. My idea was to show ladies who were prostitutes and drug addicts that I loved them and cared for them.

Two and a half years ago, a judge awarded me custody of my son because I was clean and doing everything the court needed me to do. My daughter didn't want to come home with me, and I wouldn't force her, although it hurt my heart. She decided to stay with my sister. I hope she will forgive me someday. All she has known of me was that I was a prostitute and drug addict, and so for her, it didn't matter that I was clean for over four years. She must get over the anger and hurt, and I understand that.

For now, I am raising my son and am grateful to have left behind a life of trauma, cutting, drugs, and prostitution. I am no longer suicidal. Instead, through my nonprofit, I help others who are still stuck in that life to feel loved, and I give them hope that no matter the circumstances, things can get better. Although I in no way condone the sex work, I give out condoms to keep them safe. I also feed them and have a clothing closet for ladies in need. I didn't expect my project to be a big deal, but as more and more people hear about it and support it, it's become one. The girls on the street don't feel judged when I interact with them since they know I've walked in their shoes.

My story has shaped who I am, a strong, caring woman. If I can help anyone escape the world of sex trafficking by sharing my story, then I've found a purpose in it and for that, I'm forever grateful.

Amanda's Story
Loss of Mom and Marriage

My mom and I were always very close and had a great relationship. In 2011, she started having gastrointestinal issues and was told by her doctor that she needed to have her gallbladder removed. After that surgery, she continued to have problems and was diagnosed with pancreatitis. She was prescribed medication that should have made her feel better, but it didn't. My mom was overweight but never had any major health issues before that time.

She had to be her own advocate and push the doctors to give her additional tests to see what made her feel so poorly. It had been six months since the onset of symptoms. When she finally got a scan done, a tumor was found on her pancreas. A biopsy revealed she had stage 3 pancreatic cancer. Unfortunately, she was not a surgical candidate because the tumor was attached to one of the major arteries.

We were familiar with pancreatic cancer because my mom's father had died of it just six years earlier, within two weeks of diagnosis. We knew it was a terrible disease, one of the worst cancers to get because it is aggressive and often not found until advanced.

When we met with the doctor to figure out treatment options, we were told they could do nothing. We were given zero hope. We were crying as we left, but my mom was positive despite the bleak outlook.

We got two referrals for other opinions, so my mom received chemotherapy for a couple of months. She was in and out of the hospital because the chemo was so potent. She was told that because she was strong and healthy, she was given the most aggressive chemo. Throughout the entire treatment process, my family tried to make it fun and hopeful for mom. We made up songs to entertain her and gave her fun gift baskets to enjoy during her chemotherapy sessions.

After those treatments, her tumor had shrunk significantly, so we had a glimmer of hope. The only way to survive pancreatic cancer is to have Whipple surgery, which involves removing a huge portion of your pancreas and GI tract. It is a complicated surgery but is touted as the only hope of surviving this dreadful disease. Most people do not survive even after that procedure because the aggressive cancer comes back. At first, mom's doctor suggested that she see a surgeon to do the Whipple surgery, but then advised to try radiation first. She ended up having radiation and chemo simultaneously. It was intense, but Mom was always so hopeful. She often said that perhaps God was using her to be a witness to other people. She never complained about having this dreadful disease or the grueling treatments she was receiving.

After the radiation and chemo combination treatment, scans revealed cancer had spread to her liver. I began to question whether we should have done the Whipple instead of those treatments, but we couldn't worry about that and needed to focus on the next steps. Mom was given a new chemo treatment for a few months. Then she started having fevers and delusions and was often disoriented. I took my mom to what I thought was a chemotherapy treatment, but instead, we were told that there was nothing else they could do for her and it was time to call in hospice.

One of my mom's sisters came to help me while mom was home with hospice services. I didn't realize that home hospice did not mean 24-7 care. The hospice staff came once a day to check on mom while my aunt and I provided the rest of the care that mom needed, including bed baths, incontinence care, and morphine doses for comfort. When she was no longer talking, we knew she was nearing the end. Mom was stubborn and wanted to hold on, but my brother and I told her it was okay to go to heaven. She was in hospice care for a month when she passed peacefully at home. I thought I was prepared for her death since I knew it was coming, but I was devastated when she was gone.

My mom and I had worked for the same company. After she passed away, my boss encouraged me to take some time off to grieve. He, too, had lost family members to cancer, thus he knew the importance of taking that time. I had to admit that I was concerned about going back into the office because I didn't think I could handle conversations about my mom, so I took an eight-week leave of absence to mourn and process my grief.

My boyfriend asked me to marry him a month after my mom died. I knew I should have said no, but I was still emotionally distraught after my mom's death and wanted something to look forward to. None of my friends had lost their parents at that point, so I felt like nobody understood what I was going through except for my boyfriend, who had lost his dad four years earlier. I found out I was pregnant two months after Mom passed away. I got married and had my daughter, Lola, who was a huge blessing to me.

When it was time for me to return to my job after my leave of absence, my boss sat me down and asked me if I truly wanted to return to the same job. He knew I was not completely happy in my current position. He reminded me that life is too short not to do what I want to do. I was inspired to search for a new job outside of that company.

I found my dream job and we moved to a new state so I could start a new career, but around the same time, I felt like my husband wholly changed and our marriage crumbled. Several red flags had warned me not to enter marriage, but since I was pregnant, I thought it was the right thing to do. As much as I wanted our marriage to survive, I was miserable.

I was still grieving my mom and began grieving this marriage that wasn't as I dreamed. I wanted to work it out for Lola because I didn't want her growing up in a broken home. I wanted to be sure I had tried my best to make it work. We did go to marriage counseling, but I realized I needed better for myself. I thank God for revealing what was wrong in the marriage so I knew I should leave my husband, but I was also mad at God for quite a while when I was experiencing the loss of my mom and my marriage. I believed it was okay to be angry and to express emotion since God made us emotional beings. After working through my feelings, I knew I needed to trust in Him and know He had a greater plan.

After my divorce, I decided to stay in this new state with my dream job, even though my family was two hours away. I joined a new Bible study and often listened to worship music. This helped me feel that I was not alone, even though I often felt lonely in this big new city. Drawing near to God was the only way for me to heal.

I met my now husband online. On day one, I knew I would marry him. I had heard people say similar statements before and I thought they were crazy, so I was surprised to find that I felt that way after my first date with Brian. I believed God had orchestrated our meeting. We have an extraordinary relationship. He treats me like I should be treated and he loves Lola and she loves him. He is a God-loving man and he treats us like gold.

Even though Brian never met my mom, they have very similar personalities. They are both goofy, loud, and loved by all. Brian always says that he would have loved to meet my mom because he thinks they would have gotten along so well. They totally would have!

A blessing that came from my mom's illness is that I became very involved in the Pancreatic Cancer Action Network, a national nonprofit whose mission is to increase awareness, advocacy, and survival rate. My husband encouraged me to become part of the local chapter and I have met some of my best friends through this organization. We have all walked through the same thing and now can help other families. God put me in a position to lead others and to make an impact in my community. It has become a massive part of my life and I love the people and the way we give back.

If it weren't for my mom passing away, my boss encouraging me to find my dream job, and having the courage to stay in a new city after my divorce, I would never have met Brian or become part of this phenomenal organization. As much pain as the loss of my mom and marriage caused me, I can clearly see I was blessed after all I lost.

7

Finding the Silver Lining
from a Distance

My dad was a coal miner. Yes, I was a coal miner's daughter. Don't get the idea that we were Loretta Lynn poor as I grew up, but we were not well-to-do either. When I was in sixth grade, my dad got laid off from his job. Miners often went on short-lived strikes, but unfortunately, this layoff due to lack of need for coal production lasted longer than usual. My dad was laid off for three years, which for me was during those troublesome middle-school years of sixth, seventh, and eighth grades.

Luckily, my parents had our house paid off at that point and the only debt we had was payments for our piano. But let me tell you, being poor during middle school was tough. Really tough! For one thing, we did not have the money to buy new school clothes. One summer, my aunt Jeanie took my sister and me school shopping and got us a few outfits. I remember feeling so good in my new stirrup pants and button-down floral shirt on the first day of school. Clearly, I was a fashion icon! But seriously, that kind gesture from my aunt made a lasting imprint on my life. I remember her generosity and kindness every year when I take my kids shopping for school clothes.

My dad finally got an interim low-paying job in a factory, and my mom, who had always been a stay-at-home mom, got a job in a retail store to keep food on the table and pay the bills we had. Those two jobs didn't mean we had the funds to go out to dinner or buy any extras, but we had what we needed to get by. Buying more than the necessities was not something we could do with our limited income. For example, I wanted to try out to be a cheerleader at my school in seventh grade and it was mandatory to wear a specific color shirt and shorts for tryouts. I did not own either, and my mom got upset because I couldn't understand why I couldn't buy new shorts and shirt. On a side note, I did not make the cheerleading squad. I obviously thought my enthusiasm would outshine my inflexibility and uncoordinated nature and, shockingly, it did not.

During the years while my dad was laid off, one set of my grandparents would bring us fresh and canned vegetables from their garden, along with meat from the grocery store. My other set of grandparents gave us eggs and veggies from their farm. Those things helped us immensely.

I had a great-aunt who loved going to yard sales, so she bought us clothes regularly from these sales. God bless her! She was trying to help and was so kind and generous, but any kid in middle school will tell you that they do not want to go to school wearing someone else's worn-down clothes, especially when other kids are wearing the latest Nikes or Guess jeans. Middle-school years are hard and kids are mean. I certainly was never popular and didn't want to be popular, but I didn't want to be picked on for my clothes. I already was bullied a bit about my buck teeth. We couldn't afford braces while my dad was laid off and I was desperate to get my teeth straightened. I would tie dental floss around my front teeth while I slept to try to fix my smile. Just so you know, it didn't work.

Perhaps the most humbling experience in those three years was when a family from our church with kids about the same ages as my sister and me brought us several bags of groceries around the holidays. I was mortified when they came and I tried to hide in the corner, pretending that they did not know they were at my house. However, once the family left, I was so excited to look through all of the goodies they had brought. I was thrilled to get fresh oranges! Buying fresh fruit was not something we did because fruit is more expensive than chips or snack cakes. As embarrassing as it was to have peers bring us food during our time of need, it was truly appreciated.

Looking back, it is one of the moments in my life that made me want to work in social services.

The day we found out that my dad was going back to work in the coal mine, we actually jumped for joy and cried happy tears. We ordered a pizza to celebrate, which is something we usually couldn't do. One of my first thoughts was, "I can get braces!" which I eventually did.

While going through that time with my dad laid off, I would never have said anything good was in that experience. Sometimes the silver lining does not present itself for months or years after the trial has occurred, which is what happened here. With enough distance, I can see how this period in my life shaped who I am. I am grateful for what I have, give to others when I am able, and am cognizant of how others feel when they are going through a similar experience.

Ali's Story
What Can I Learn from This?

Warning: This story contains rape.

Twenty years ago, I was a manager at a Fortune 1000 company. Human resources informed me that one of my employees had falsified information on his resume. Unfortunately, this wasn't discovered until after he had already started the job. He didn't have the requirements for his job, so I had to fire him.

When I dismissed him, I felt that the exit interview went well. He appeared to take the news in stride. We discussed other job options within the company that he did have the qualifications for, but I explained that he would have to interview for the other available positions. Once he completed his degree, he could try to be rehired for the position he had just been let go from.

That night, my coworkers got together at a local bar, as was common on Thursday evenings with the office staff. I decided to stop by and have a drink with everyone, and the man I fired also happened to be there. I didn't stay long and announced I was heading home. That man said he was leaving as well and asked if he could give me a ride since we lived one street apart. Because he had worked for me for a month, I felt I knew him well enough to agree to the ride. He said he wanted to ask me more questions about the other available job. We chatted the entire drive to my place. He asked me if I thought he should interview for the other job, and I encouraged him to do it, but also to finish his degree and perhaps get his old job back. I explained that if he saw his future with the company, he should go for it. He expressed appreciation for my taking the time to discuss it with him.

The conversation was relatively casual and comfortable, and in addition to discussing the job, we chatted a bit about his personal life. He mentioned that he was trying to get back in the dating pool. There were no red flags or alarm bells so far that warned me to be wary of this man.

He walked me to my door and kissed me, which was fine because he was attractive. He proceeded to make me exceedingly uncomfortable, so I explained to him that was not what I had in mind and told him to leave.

He refused to go and kept pursuing me even when I repeatedly said no, which led to him raping me. It was degrading and vile. I had my period that day, so he had to take out my tampon, which added an additional foul layer to the horror. When he was done, I told him to leave. He suspected that I would call the police, which I told him I would, leading to him to stay, ensuring I could not.

The whole scene was a nightmare. He kept me captive in my own home. He stayed all night and would not allow me to go anywhere or do anything. My blood was everywhere, and I was terrified. I didn't have my phone in my room so I could not call for help. I thought if I pretended to be asleep, he would leave, but that didn't work. Finally, as dawn approached, I told him that I had to open the office that morning, and if I didn't show up, everybody would know something happened. Finally, he left.

I didn't know what to do because I had to go to work. I took the hottest shower I could physically endure because I felt so violated. I proceeded to cut off all of my pubic hair because I felt as if his physical presence was still on me. I needed to rid myself of any possible reminders of him.

I called my dad and started crying. Even though I could barely speak through my sobs, he could sense that something horrible had occurred and asked if I had been raped. I told him I had, but I didn't know what to do because I had to work. After talking it out, I decided to go to my office.

I opened the building so staff could get in, then called my comanager and told him that I could not work that day. He said that I sounded terrible. I explained that I had been raped and had brought myself to work but couldn't function well enough to do my job that day. He arranged for another manager to come so I could leave.

I called a coworker friend of mine, and she helped me decide to go to the hospital. Even though it was many hours later, it seemed the right thing to do. Because I had showered, gotten rid of the hair, and had gone to the hospital hours later, all evidence was destroyed.

Later, I found out that everyone at the office knew who had done it to me because he came in to work that day and asked where I was. The staff knew he had been fired, so they deduced that it was him who had raped me.

A friend drove me three hours to my parents' home. It was an incredible gift that I was beyond grateful for, as I needed to get away from my own home and to get love and support. I was so sleep-deprived that I fell asleep on the couch in my parents' sunroom. My brother came home to see me after he found out what had happened. He tried to hug me when I was sleeping and startled me so badly that I began to fight him. I didn't initially recognize him in my state of trauma and exhaustion. That was only the start of how this violent act would change me forever.

I was a mess for a long time after this. I wanted to die and often questioned my judgment. I had many other questions I wrestled with: Why would that happen to me? Was it my body? Was I not a good judge of character? Had I done something wrong? Why did God allow this to happen to me?

Because of lack of evidence, there was no strong case, so the man was not prosecuted. He was hired back at the company in another position. I did have a civil case going against him, so he was not allowed in my building. They later let him go for other reasons, but it had to be documented by the human resources department closely so that nobody could say he was fired because he did this to me. He claimed that it was my fault that he had been fired twice and that I was out to get him. The human resources staff member explained that his firing had nothing to do with me and it had everything to do with his performance on the job. There was more than enough documentation to warrant his firing.

Nothing ended up happening with the civil case because he failed to show up to multiple scheduled appointments. I told him that I was upset that he had not used protection and I wanted him to take AIDS and STD tests, nothing more. His lawyer said that he showed up for the appointment and the doctor was not there. After many similar scenarios, my lawyer finally noted that there was only so much we could do. I realized I was feeling vengeful and these drawn-out dealings with this man were pulling me down, so I decided to move on and drop the civil case.

My friends and family judged me for not pressing charges, but they didn't understand that I didn't have any say in the matter. After the police gathered evidence, the prosecutors decided not to prosecute the case. It had nothing to do with me, the victim, choosing to prosecute. Since there was no evidence, the civil case was all we had.

I made many poor choices after this happened to me. To get past my pain, I went through a few counselors, many housing and job changes, and a great deal of body hatred. I became a binge eater, which I have since learned is common for people who have been sexually abused. One counselor finally asked me what exactly I was trying to accomplish by binge eating. I told her that if I were fat, nobody would rape me again. She asked if I genuinely thought I was fat, to which I replied that I was unsure because I ran often. She said I was still skinny, so I was not even accomplishing what I wanted. After discussing it at length, I realized what I was doing was trying to make myself miserable.

I constantly wondered how people felt when talking with me. The man who had raped me seemed normal but did something unexpected and out of control. The trauma dramatically impacted my work and ability to be confident in my job. If I fired someone else, was this going to happen again? Is this what happens when you are a female manager in corporate America?

I didn't attend church for a long time, and my faith wavered. When I moved out of state, I decided to try a church service. As I listened to what the pastor said, I cried. One of the men on the worship team came up to me after the service and said, "God told me to tell you something, and I don't know what it means, but God knows you are mad at him and He forgives you, loves you, and has always been there. Again, I don't understand what this means and I am really uncomfortable telling you this because I don't know you." This moment was the turning point in my life.

I had to learn who to trust and how to find my footing. I felt God assured me that it was not my fault and that I did make good choices in people and reading others' character. I had to learn how to talk about what happened with my family because we had avoided that conversation. I felt like they were ashamed of me, as if I had done something wrong. Once we discussed it, I learned that they were never ashamed; they simply didn't know what to say.

Since this time, I have been trying to figure out why it happened to me. I thought I figured it out at one point: I theorized that one day I would have daughters and would teach them to make better decisions. Then I had two sons. I realized that I was going to teach boys that "no" meant no in any capacity. They understand that even if it looked like someone was having the time of their life, if someone refused, it was over. I'm proud that I'm raising boys who understand this.

My boys, ages seven and nine, don't know the specifics of my trauma, but do know that someone was mean to me, didn't listen when I said no, and that I was not the same because of it. My husband told them that he, too, wasn't the same because of what happened, and we were raising them differently.

When I recently decided to share a hint of what happened to me on social media, a response I heard often was, "I never knew this happened to you." I found this statement humorous, as people don't wear a shirt announcing what trauma they have endured so that others will understand and be kind. We don't need to know each person's story; instead, we should merely be kind from the start. Typically, we don't want the entire world to know what suffering we have endured, to be judged, or have to explain our pain.

At the same time, I learned that it was better to acknowledge and encourage someone if they seem to be experiencing a trial. I understood how isolating it could be when others appeared to ignore my suffering. I often felt utterly alone, without support, in the darkest time of my life. It was similar to how things always appear worse at night, but they don't seem half as bad in the morning light. The pain and burden were more extensive and oppressing because no one acknowledged what I had walked through. I felt grateful for the few who listened to my story and helped me bear my agony.

It took me significant time to bounce back. There continue to be specific triggers that transport me back to that horrific night. It took much work and self-reflection to build myself back up from this awful ordeal.

Three years ago, I was out for my morning run when a guy started following me. When I saw him, I wondered where he had come from, as he seemed to appear out of nowhere. It was five in the morning, he was riding his bike exceptionally slowly, and he was not wearing a helmet. I was immediately on guard but kept running. I didn't have earbuds in, so I turned when I heard he was continuing behind me. I was approaching an intersection and decided that if I turned around at that point and he was still behind me, I was going to get as far away as possible. I turned around and adjusted my headlight to shine directly into his face to temporarily blind him, then turned off my light and sprinted away as fast as I could. I was relatively close to my parents' house, so I booked it there and let myself in through the garage door.

Somewhere along the way, after being raped, I had started to believe that God would not let it happen to me again, that surely He would only give me one colossal trial in my life. After I was followed on my run in my seemingly safe suburban neighborhood, I feared that it could have happened again.

After my dad took me home, I woke up my husband and explained what had happened. We called the police, and when they came, they encouraged me to always run with a phone. They said that this was not the first time they had heard of this guy, who frequently rode in this area, but he hadn't contacted anyone he had encountered so far. The potential for this story to have had a horrific ending left me once again frightened and trusting nobody.

Besides helping me become a better parent, another good thing that came from these experiences is that I am no longer afraid to be confrontational. I would rather overcommunicate and let someone know that their behavior makes me uncomfortable than be passive and risk terrible consequences. This experience has opened my eyes to the existence of evil people in this world. Before, I was Pollyanna-esque; I thought that if I love God and He watches over me, nothing bad could ever happen.

It took years of wrestling with my pain to figure out the silver lining in my story. I have learned much from my traumatic experiences: how to be a better parent, how to hold a difficult conversation, and how to sit in silence and be present with someone, even if I don't know what to say. I have explained to my boys that there are times when we aren't going to understand why bad things happen to us and that sometimes bad things happen to good people. I tell them that even if bad things do happen, it doesn't mean that God does not love them. These words are a good reminder for me as well as my boys. No matter how angry I grew, God still sought me out. It took a few different counselors and much time to process my experiences, but I have realized that God didn't do this to me; rather, people have free will to choose between good and evil. God remains with me no matter what comes my way, a belief that never ceases to fill me with hope.

Selina's Story
Devastatingly Perfect

Eight years ago, I started graduate school. It was something I thought I wanted and I was excited about it. I have always been an academic, so going back to school was very appealing to me. I loved it, but graduate school was very difficult. I was in a neuroscience program that was incredibly intense with classes and lab work. During my first year and a half, I was trying to decide which lab I was going to be doing my thesis work in. I rotated through a few labs in an attempt to pinpoint what I wished to do. My decision came down to choosing between a lab with an adviser who I liked and got along well with, but the research was not to my liking, or a lab where I enjoyed the research more but had more reservations about the adviser. I chose the research over the adviser.

I got through my first year and a half as a doctoral student and passed my preliminary exams. At the end of my second year, I passed my candidacy exam and I settled into my lab as a PhD candidate. That summer I finished up my previous rotation work and came up with ideas of what my final thesis should be. By October, I had to solidify what I was going to be studying. I did a lot of independent work trying to determine which direction I wanted to go with my lab. I put together a presentation for my lab group, and when I finished my presentation, the entire room was silent. In grad school, that is not a good sign. If nobody has questions, something is very wrong.

My adviser had an odd look on his face and ended the meeting. He proceeded to call me into his office and had a long conversation with me, saying that he didn't think I should continue in the program. He suggested I think about leaving early with a master's degree instead of a PhD. That was very unexpected. The rug was pulled out from under me, but at the same time, it was almost a relief. After two and a half years in the program, I was becoming more disillusioned in academia and what I would have to do as an academic. There is a lot more that goes into securing funding and doing research than I had thought, and I questioned whether this was something I wanted to do for the rest of my life.

It was during this time that I started doing more serious writing on the side. I began contemplating whether my passion wasn't as much science as I thought it was, and I considered that writing was perhaps more of what I should be doing. At this point, I can say that it was a little bit of both, but at that time, I started questioning my goals.

The conversation with my adviser ended with "take a few days to think about what you want and come back and make a decision." He told me to contact the head of education in our department to set up a time to talk through this decision. During that meeting with the department head, I was given options: I could continue in the program but not in my adviser's lab, or drop down to a master's degree without having to pay anything extra out of my pocket, or finish up a library thesis and leave.

As much as this knocked me off my feet, I was a little happy about it. There were options for me and I didn't think I could pick something wrong. I simply had to figure out what I wanted for my future. It still was a hard decision because I had it in my head that I was going to have a PhD, do great research, learn cool things, and teach. Then suddenly, this was not going to be my reality. After that meeting, I sent an email to my adviser and copied the department head, director of education, and other key people to make them aware of what was happening. My adviser "replied all" to the email, thinking I was not on the thread, saying that I was a waste of money who did not deserve to get a PhD, and many other terrible things about my ability and what he foresaw for me. It was unbelievably devastating. I had been handling the news well until that email. From my current perspective, I realize he was a bully and an abusive adviser. I presumed that the problem was not me but just that I was the last person to join the lab and that adviser was running out of funding, so he was looking for any excuse to dump me and unfortunately, made it personal.

After that happened, I called out sick to take a day off and think things through. My adviser realized what he had done and tried to apologize, but there was no coming back from that. The damage was done.

Another difficulty was dealing with my family members who had expectations that I was going to have a PhD and were disappointed because they wanted to be able to brag to their friends about me. I needed their support with whatever decision I made, not their disappointment.

I decided to stay and finish my master's degree. It was acceptable for me to stay in that lab to finish my thesis. The adviser had promised that I would be able to finish it in half a year. It was a very trying time as I worked fifteen- to sixteen-hour days to get all the work done.

Because of everything that had happened, I went into a very severe depressive episode. It was not the first time I had been depressed in my life, and I have tended to have a high-functioning depression each time. This time I worked through it but barely slept. I did go see a counselor through the university, but that was not especially helpful because my counselor and I had different agendas.

Some of the things my adviser had told me about changing to the master's degree program were not true. I lost my stipend and ended up owing the university money. What I was not told was that anyone who switched from PhD to master's for any reason would either owe a $13,000 fee or a semester's tuition. I ended up taking out a loan to pay the tuition and had to live off my savings during that time.

I defended my thesis the next summer and started job hunting. I would have left the lab if I had a job. The adviser did let me stay on as lab tech for a month as I finished up the comments for the committee on my thesis. Suddenly, a job opportunity came up. I was interviewed on a Thursday, got the job offer on Friday, and they asked me to start working the following Monday. My adviser was angry that I was leaving abruptly, but I needed the money. I was at the point where I didn't even have a month's rent anymore. Rent was due and I was unsure how I was going to pay it. Around this same time, my grandma randomly sent me a check that happened to cover my rent. The timing for that unexpected gift was incredible and, I believe, heaven-sent.

I was grateful to get the job but continued to deal with the mental and emotional trauma of what I had been through. It took me at least six months to seek out additional professional help, but I did because I couldn't get past it on my own. Even though I was out of the toxic environment, I needed to heal more. When I left grad school, most of my friends remained in school and were quite busy, so often I was quite lonely. I went on antidepressants, started piecing together all that I had learned, and leaned on my support network to finally feel I was overcoming my pain. My sister was especially helpful to me because she understood where I was coming from. She too was a scientist who had a PhD and had an abusive advisor. She expressed that I shouldn't care what others expected me to do, but to find what was going to make me happy.

My strong Christian faith changed a bit over the years, and part of that was because of my grad school experience. Being depressed and fitting in with others in the church I attended was difficult. During one study with a small group, I got angry because the thought voiced by most in the group was that it was my fault if I was depressed because I was not trusting God enough. It made me step back from that group because it was obvious to me that they had not lived with depression. I kept pushing until I found the right church that spoke to the brokenness in people. I began to see myself and the people around me the way God does, caring about a person, not about how well they adhere to what the church accepts.

About a year later, I met my husband. If I had stayed in that graduate program (which I would have done had I not been forced to change plans), I would never have met him. While in school, I was not dating or looking to date because school consumed my entire focus. Also, my husband, who is a therapist, worked close to where I lived and didn't want to take the risk of running into any of his clients, so he was not looking to date in that area. I know the silver lining of my journey is that I would not have married this wonderful person without this entire experience.

The other good thing to come from this is that I moved out of academia, which I am very happy about. I learned it was not for me and I moved into industry. Right away, I had the best boss I have ever had. He was exactly the type of person I needed to work for after having an abusive adviser. He listened to me, cared about what I had to say, and asked my opinion on things. During the first six months, I feared I would walk into a meeting and be told that I was stupid but that never happened. I loved that I was respected in this new environment. I learned to speak up for myself and be confident in my own opinions. That job was a great steppingstone for the new job I found in the past year. I am making good money, which will be beneficial for when my husband and I start a family.

The last silver lining I have discovered is that I have learned to stop pleasing other people when things do not benefit me. In the past, I would have just allowed that, but now I do what is best for me, no matter others' opinions.

Another hard truth is that if I had not had my faith during my trauma I probably would not be here right now because I would have killed myself. All I had was my faith to see me through that dark time. I came to understand what a personal relationship with God meant. While in the midst of it, I was desperate to be seen, heard, and cared for, and I got that from Him when people failed me. Now I realize that I wouldn't be able to connect with many people I have met without walking through depression. People don't understand unless they have been through it. One of the reasons I write now is so I can connect with similar people. My experience put me in a position where I can make connections with others, reassuring them that God still loves them and that their circumstances aren't their fault.

I now have the perspective to be happy about what I went through, but as I dealt with the loss of what could have been, I was devastated and depressed. If that entire horrible experience had not happened to me, I wouldn't have anything that I have now: my husband, my job, my perspective, and my faith. All of that wouldn't be as they are had I not walked through this terrible time in my life. Despite the pain, I am grateful it played out as it did.

Carmen's Story
Tomorrow Is Not Guaranteed

A few days after I graduated from high school, I headed to college for the summer semester. My mom, sister, and brother Adam helped move me into my dorm, then returned home that afternoon. In the middle of my first night there, I received horrific news: Adam had been shot and killed. I hadn't even been at college for twenty-four hours before I headed back home.

We soon learned that Adam had been out with some friends when he was murdered. As he was getting in his car, a stranger drove by and swerved, trying to hit him. A passenger in the back seat of

Adam's car, whom Adam didn't know well, had yelled at that driver. That driver quickly backed up, thinking my brother had been the one who shouted at them.

My brother was an exceedingly friendly man who never intentionally caused trouble and liked to smooth things over. I am sure Adam tried to calm the other driver when the car approached, but the passenger in that car drew his gun and shot him before the driver sped off.

The only two witnesses to the crime were my brother's girlfriend, who was in the front seat, and the man in the back seat who had yelled at the driver. The bullet that killed Adam not only went through my brother but also hit the back-seat passenger in the head. Surprisingly, he recovered well after being treated for his bullet wound. Questioning the witnesses proved fruitless.

Much gossip swirled about potential suspects and motives for the shooting. One theory was that my brother looked like a local firearms dealer known to be shady, and the shooter mistook my brother for him. There was also speculation that the guy in the back seat knew the shooter, but he didn't cooperate in the investigation, so nothing panned out from that hypothesis. One of the other suspects was in jail for a different crime and had admitted to a scenario that sounded like my brother's murder, but nothing came of that line of investigation. When that suspect got out of jail, a front-page newspaper article declared he was a changed man and now a good dad. My mom had a hard time reading the story because the paper seemed to be glorifying a man who might have been the one who murdered my brother. That suspect ended up later being murdered. There were many theories on who killed Adam, but none of them culminated in an arrest.

I returned to school directly after the funeral. I didn't know many other students since few participated in the summer session, and I had no time to make new friends before I returned home the first day. I knew I would not make friends if I did little but remain in my room and cry. Even though my brother was murdered, I had to keep all my emotions at bay. I tried to make friends at school and put on a smiling face instead of dealing with the overwhelming sadness.

It was hard to come to terms with this nonsensical death. However, pushing down my feelings only prolonged my grief. I couldn't simply sit alone and attempt to process my loss; I had to go to classes and make friends. My freshman year was challenging, my memories of it blurry. I didn't deal with my grief well and drank more than I should have during that time. Alcohol helped drown thoughts of my brother. When I reached my senior year, I realized my grades were not what they should have been, so I worked until my academics were back on track, quit drinking excessively, and began processing Adam's death.

If you had asked me at that stage in my life if there were blessings in my brother's murder, I would never have been able to come up with any. In fact, the question would have upset me. I was already angry at God because I could not understand why this happened.

I started to question everyone about the case myself; someone had murdered my brother, and there were two people in the murderer's car, along with two witnesses in my brother's car. At least one person had to know what happened that night. I tried to come up with possible suspects and nearly went crazy trying to figure it out.

The story of Adam's murder was in the newspapers and on the news for a long time after it happened. It ran on Crime Stoppers for years. Unfortunately, nobody was ever prosecuted for this crime.

With no one charged and no one imprisoned for Adam's death, I never got the closure I desperately needed. It made it more difficult to move on. Perhaps it would have been more stressful to go through a trial, but I will never know. There were no words capable of making me happy because nothing would bring Adam back. I had to forgive the murderer, having no answers and knowing I would never fully understand why it happened.

When I got married and started a family, I knew I wanted to get back to my roots in faith because I wanted my children to grow up with the same beliefs that I had. I grew up Catholic, and my faith played an important role in my life. My brother's death had hindered my beliefs for a long time, but deep down, I understood that God was good and my faith was important.

When I had my children, I was reminded how life could change in an instant. It only took one second for my brother to be murdered. He was living one moment and gone the next. Every time I leave any of my family members, even if I am simply going to the grocery store, Adam is in the back of my mind. I still visualize the moment he left me at my dorm and waved goodbye for the final time. I hate the saying "You just never know," because it feels empty and thoughtless, but feeling it and living as if every moment could be the last has made a huge impact on my life. I now see that as a blessing because I know that every time my children leave the house, they are not guaranteed to return. When I hug them goodbye, I always think of Adam and understand how things can change in a heartbeat.

Finding the good in his murder wasn't quick or easy, but it was powerful and rewarding when it came. Some may have to search long and hard for the good in a senseless death as I did, but it eventually came naturally to me when I created my own family. Adam's death gave me this daily reminder: live and love each minute, as it could be the last. Learning that lesson was hard, but I am grateful to truly understand it. Tomorrow is never guaranteed, so with Adam in mind, I love my family fiercely with every chance I have.

WHERE IS THE SILVER LINING AND WHAT DO I DO WITH IT?

Strength after Adversity

> We rejoice in our sufferings, knowing that suffering produces endurance, and endurance produces character, and character produces hope, and hope does not put us to shame, because God's love has been poured into our hearts through the Holy Spirit who has been given to us. (Romans 5:3–5 ESV)

One evening last spring, I went for a walk after dinner while my daughter took a bike ride with a friend. When I was at the farthest point from my house that I could be on that walk, I got a call from my daughter. Those of you with children know that it probably is not a good thing if you get a call from your child and not a text. She had panic in her voice as she told me that she had fallen off her bike and broken her arm. She can be dramatic and tends to exaggerate, but my mama instinct knew she was hurt badly. I learned that she was a mile from home and a mile and a half from where I currently was walking. I immediately turned around and started to run. Unfortunately, I am not a runner or in good enough shape to run that far. As I was running, I called my husband and explained the situation through my labored breathing. I had him drive to pick me up and we went to get her.

When she broke her arm, it was during the pandemic and it was scary. It was alarming that when I got to her, I could see that her arm was broken. It was awful that they couldn't set her arm and would have to do surgery. It was uncomfortable to stay in a hospital overnight while wearing masks and trying to avoid germs.

There was much to be frightened about. My girl had broken both her ulna and radius. Rods had to be inserted to fix the fractures. She was scared and so was I, but I put on my brave mama face for my girl.

Even though it was distressing that this happened to my daughter and it happened during a pandemic, it ended up being the best possible time for it to happen, if it had to happen. Since schools were closed because of COVID, she only had virtual classes. She didn't have to navigate the hallways, open her locker, or carry books with a broken arm. She could do most assignments on the computer. I had to help with a few written tasks since she had fractured her dominant arm, but for the most part, she could do her schoolwork independently. Also, soccer season was canceled so she didn't miss any practices or games, and that was a positive.

Her arm has now healed. Where each bone was broken, the bone has formed a "callus" and the rods are about ready to be surgically removed. Interestingly, the calcium concentration in the permanent scar is higher than the normal bone, making it stronger than the surrounding bone. Once it has healed, she is more likely to break the bone elsewhere than in the bone scar.

In recent years, my girl has been through several adversities. She has had to work hard each time she was told no, to get to where she wants to be. As with her fractured arm, every time she faced a disappointment or setback, she was broken but not shattered. She was able to heal and get stronger than she was before. These were lessons learned the hard way. All our wisdom, strength, and courage does not come from the smooth path before us, but from how we manage and grow from the bumps

All our wisdom, strength, and courage does not come from the smooth path before us, but from how we manage and grow from the bumps and breaks along the way.

and breaks along the way. I am convinced that we are stronger after overcoming adversity.

Your Pain Is *Not* the Blessing

I want you to understand that I am *not* saying that your trials are the blessing in your life. James 1:2–3 (NIV) says, "Consider it pure joy, my brothers and sisters, whenever you face trials of many kinds, because you know that the testing of your faith produces perseverance." God is not saying for me to be joyful that my father-in-law died or be happy that my daughter had to have surgery for her broken arm. Jesus wept at the death of his friend Lazarus. He wept for his loss and for the loss Mary and Martha were experiencing. I know I cry when my loved ones are hurting. Jesus was our example. He is not telling us not to feel sadness, hurt, frustration, or anger when going through hard things. God loves us and does not want to see us in pain, but the Compassionate One can use that pain for good. We need to find joy in what God can do with the trials we face. Our faith can be deepened if we allow it, and we will gain perseverance through our struggles. God wants us to draw near, and when we do that, we can find the silver lining and the peace that only the Almighty One can bring in the midst of our despair. That is what can make our heartache transition to hope.

When you are ready to seek the silver lining, remember how God has shown up in other trials in your life, which will help you face new difficulties with courage and faith. Trust that there is good even if it is not visible by an initial glance. You may have to delve deeper and explore further, examining many aspects of what has happened and who was affected. Has your story touched others? Did your faith get stronger or were others inspired by your faith? Did your family grow closer? Did your community come together in support? Know that you may not see the good right away; it may be months or years down the road. Perhaps there is a chance that you will not see the good on this side of heaven.

Your story may be simple, or significant and impactful, or perhaps even tragic. No matter the depth or breadth of your struggle, it plays a significant role in your life and in how it can affect others. Don't downplay your story or its impact. Our stories will look different, but it doesn't make one more significant than another. Know that God can take whatever difficulties you have experienced and use them for good.

Broken beyond Repair?

Trauma, loss, failure, catastrophe, betrayal, or hurt can be continually present in our lives long after it has passed, perhaps buried deep within. Those trials transform us, mold us, make us, and break us. Can we be broken beyond repair, just like when Humpty Dumpty had a great fall and "All the king's horses and all the king's men, couldn't put Humpty together again"?

I think the only way we are damaged beyond repair is if we don't realize that we are broken, are in denial about how broken we are, or don't put forth the effort to heal. We can't easily move on, pretending that we weren't affected by what we experienced. The pain that isn't dealt with will consume us physically and emotionally, whether we understand that is what is happening or not.

A person cannot thrive if they are living a life with neglected buried pain. You may be in denial about how broken an experience has made you. A tree with damaged roots will not have good growth without extra attention and care. If our roots are damaged by trauma and if we do not take the proper steps toward healing, our emotional, physical, and spiritual growth may be restricted. A combination of professional help, support from family and friends, and faith are vital to the healing process, so we do not linger in a state of brokenness. We don't want to remain in fragments of what our whole self could be. Psalm 147:3 (NIV) states, "He heals the broken-hearted and binds up their wounds."

If you are broken, I pray that you find the strength and courage to get help and use others for support. I pray that you will trust God and lean on the source of all peace in your times of trouble. As you put forth the effort to heal your brokenness, know that it may take time, but you can become whole. Your brokenness doesn't mean you

Your brokenness doesn't mean you are irrevocably damaged. Maybe irrevocably changed, but not irrevocably damaged.

are irrevocably damaged. Maybe irrevocably changed, but not irrevocably damaged. God can take those broken pieces, strengthen your roots, and transform them all into something beautiful.

You Will Be What You See

We do not want to continually focus on the bad and get cemented in an agonizing state of pain. If we are stuck in the muck and mire of sadness, disappointment, or loss, that is all we will be able to see. There will be gloomy days, but our mindset will shift if we seek the good all around us. Where is God at work? What are the positives of your story? We will feel more uplifted, grateful, content, and peaceful when our minds are filled with seeking goodness rather than overcome with the negative. What you seek is what you will find and who you will be.

Lessons Learned

I have learned several lessons from listening to the stories for this book. The first is that people often feel alone while dealing with their struggles because friends and family do not know what to say, so they say and do nothing. People often feel alone in their grief. Alone in their divorce. Alone in their loss. Alone in their health struggles. Alone in their worries. Why? Because people don't reach out to say, "I'm thinking of you" or "I'm praying for you." We believe we must know the "right" words to say, but in fact, people may not want you to say anything. They don't need the wisdom of saints or scholars; they want to know that someone cares and understands that they are going through a hard time. They may also want your presence. Again, they don't expect perfect words; they simply wish to have you by their side. They need someone to talk with, vent to, or a shoulder to cry on. They want to feel heard and seen. It is easier to travel a rocky road with someone by your side. People need support in their time of need and if you don't know what to say, simply being there is enough.

The second lesson I learned is that people need to feel continually loved and supported after they've experienced the death of a loved one. We often show up to give support right away, but it is important to check on those grieving weeks, months, and even years later. Tell them you are thinking of them. Send a text or card or spend time with them. It can be lonely in grief after the funeral is over and everyone else has gone back to life as usual.

The third lesson is that it is hard to reach out and ask for help when we are walking through hard times, even if someone has said, "Let me know if you need anything." The reason is that we may need a lot of different things, but we question what that person is willing to do or what they have time to do. We do not want to interrupt someone's schedule or place burdens on others. We want people to ask us specific questions, such as "I'm running to the grocery store. Can I pick up anything for you while I am there?" or "Would your child like to ride with us to baseball practice?" or "I have time during the weekdays; do you need a ride to a doctor's appointment?" It is nice to say, "How can I help?" but more helpful to give specific ideas of how you can assist.

Lean on Me

As I just said, we often resist asking for help when we are struggling with something difficult. There are many reasons for this, including feeling like we should deal with things independently, feeling too apprehensive to ask because we do not want to bother people, and feeling like others should already know what we need. We need to overcome this trepidation and ask for help. Don't carry your burdens alone. People have a desire to lend a hand when needed. The assistance blesses the receiver, but it also blesses the giver. We shouldn't deny ourselves the support of those who care or deny the giver the opportunity to provide that support. It feels so good to help, doesn't it?

When all hands are working together toward one goal, it is amazing what can get accomplished. What can appear to be an insurmountable task can be completed when all hands are on deck. We should learn from redwood trees how to work together for the common good. These trees can grow more than 300 feet tall, but their roots only go to depths of 6 to 12 feet. So what makes them so strong and durable? Their root systems spread to lengths of 50 feet or more and intertwine with the roots of other nearby redwoods. The trees are able to withstand high winds, or whatever nature throws their way, by holding onto each other and working together to create a firm foundation.

Imagine if we were more like a redwood forest: strong, solid, and hardy by holding onto and supporting one another. Imagine the multiplied blessings if we asked for assistance when our burden is too heavy to carry alone. Imagine if we would reach out to take hold of others when we are too weak to stand alone. Also, imagine if more people would heed the call to rescue others in times of need. There is strength in unity, collaboration, and cooperation.

There is strength in unity, collaboration, and cooperation.

My Challenge for You

Some trials you go through are downright horrible. People will not entirely understand what you have experienced because they are not in your shoes. They cannot understand the depth of your pain or even your daily struggles. You may have people ask you how they can help. They truly mean it. They want to bless you! How can they help? What do you need? What can your friends do to help you and bless you? Do you know what else? I promise you that *they* will be blessed by blessing you! It is a win-win situation. Do *not* fear asking, even if it seems minor or trivial.

Acknowledge and use the resources around you. Allow others to help. How would you feel if you found out a friend was struggling with something and they didn't reach out to you for help? Hurt? Disappointed? Sad?

We are taught to be independent. Asking for help is often thought of as a sign of weakness. That, my friends, is a myth we need to debunk right here, right now. There are many times when we work better together than trying to go it alone. We become stronger by using the social supports we have in place. In addition to the redwood example, consider a piece of rope. If you unwind all of the strands that make up the rope, each piece is weak and could easily break. With the individual strands twisted and woven together, the rope is stronger and more stable when tugged or contorted. When we work together, we are stronger and can do so much. When you say, "I've got this," when you are actually on the struggle bus, you deny someone an opportunity to love and care for you. Let others help! Lean on your community of friends and loved ones. You don't have to go at things alone. We are stronger together.

I feel blessed when I bless others. Isn't that the way life tends to work? My bucket is filled most by filling others' buckets. How much more beautiful the world would be if we all just put a little effort into looking around at our neighbors, friends, family, church, acquaintances, and others to see what small, kind gesture would uplift and bless those around us.

Joy breeds joy. Gratitude breeds gratitude. Feeling blessed breeds blessings. Blessing others results in being blessed.

Joy breeds joy. Gratitude breeds gratitude. Feeling blessed breeds blessings. Blessing others results in being blessed.

I hope that the stories you have read have opened your eyes to others' struggles and to the silver linings and blessings that came from anguish. I hope your stories are filled with more joy than pain. When you do have trials, I pray you always seek the silver lining. How will you use your story to help others? How will you be transformed by your story and from stories you hear? I hope you will extend kindness to everyone, remembering that we often don't understand what difficulties they face. Most importantly, it is my sincere hope that by finding fortune in your misfortune, your agonies will lessen and your joys will multiply. Keep seeking the good. It is worth the search.

> In all this you greatly rejoice, though now for a little while you may have had to suffer grief in all kinds of trials. These have come so that the proven genuineness of your faith—of greater worth than gold, which perishes even though refined by fire—may result in praise, glory and honor when Jesus Christ is revealed. Though you have not seen him, you love him; and even though you do not see him now, you believe in him and are filled with an inexpressible and glorious joy, for you are receiving the end result of your faith, the salvation of your souls. (1 Peter 1:6–9 NIV)

ACKNOWLEDGMENTS

Writing this book has been a long process, and I have many to thank for helping it come to fruition. God put this book on my heart four years ago, and I pray that the Lord uses it to draw people closer. Thank you, Father, for entrusting me for Your service.

I am incredibly grateful for all the brave souls who shared their stories with me and the world hoping that others will be able to find their own silver lining. Thank you! I pray that your stories bless many.

Thank you, Jill, for being the original inspiration (along with the divine) for this book. God used you to speak to me. I just know it! I will forever look for the blessing in anything that comes my way because of you. Thank you to the rest of my scrapbook friends Christine, Kiersten, Melanie, Karen, Kim, Lisa, Nancy, Amy, and Jodie, for being supportive in your prayers and words of encouragement. I can't wait to see you and share stories and laugh together once again!

Thank you, Charles, Brandon, and Ali, for loving me no matter what crazy ideas I have, including writing a book. I'm beyond blessed to have each of you. I love you!

I am grateful for all my friends and family who have prayed for me and encouraged me along the way. I truly appreciate your support!

Behind every writer are those that make a writer's words one thousand times better. I am thankful for my nephew, Ryan, for being my first editor. Your mastery of grammar and punctuation is quite impressive! Thanks to Mary for being another editor when Ryan was knee-deep in his college work. I appreciate all you did! Thank you, Hana and Lynne, for being professional and excellent editors and making my words, grammar, and punctuation more polished. Writing a first book comes with a huge learning curve, and I appreciate each of your expertise.

Thank you to my beta readers, Jodi, Susan, Angie, and Mary. Your feedback helped mold this book into a better version.

Thank you to my good friend, Jennifer, for listening to me talk incessantly about this book on our many walks around the neighborhood. You were a wonderful sounding board. I am blessed by your friendship and support. Thank you to my friends, Wendy and Cathy, for supporting me and encouraging me in many ways through this process. I love you all! Let's go celebrate with a bee's knees!

Thank you to Dan, Jennifer's husband and published author, for giving me information and suggestions through the writing and editing process. I know I asked a multitude of questions, and I appreciate your patience and insight. Also, thank you for leading me to my editor Lynne.

Thank you to my Friday morning Bible study group at St. Mark's UMC for praying for me and this book for quite a while. I know that God put the Priscilla Shirer's "Gideon" study in our class to use it to reinforce that I was being called to write this book and that our Holy God would equip me for the job. Thanks to Don for explaining about redwood trees in one of our study discussions. I loved that imagine of being stronger when working together. I greatly appreciate all of you!

Thank you, Rex and Morgan, for your expertise and advice. It is nice to have knowledgeable professionals in the family.

Thank you to all who helped me come up with a title for this book, especially Amy, Lisa, and Angie!

Thank you to my readers who have been with me as I've been writing my blog and creating a social media platform. I appreciate you coming alongside me and rooting for me.

About the Author

In addition to writing, Deanne Persinger is a part-time caseworker for the aged and disabled. Her job and passion are empowering clients and readers to find hope in their circumstances. Deanne lives in the Indianapolis area with her husband, two children, a cat, and the cutest dog in the world. Faith and family are of utmost importance to her. Connect with Deanne on her website at deannepersinger.com and Instagram @deannepersingerwrites.

CPSIA information can be obtained
at www.ICGtesting.com
Printed in the USA
BVHW070623151222
654214BV00004B/262